The User Is Always Right

A Practical Guide to Creating and Using Personas for the Web

The User Is Always Right:
A Practical Guide to Creating and Using Personas for the Web

New Riders
www.newriders.com
New Riders is an imprint of Peachpit, a division of Pearson Education.
To report errors, please send a note to errata@peachpit.com.

Find us on the World Wide Web at: www.peachpit.com

Acquisitions editor: Michael Nolan
Project editors: Karyn Johnson and Douglas Cruickshank
Developmental editor: Amy Standen
Production editor: Hilal Sala
Copyeditor: Rebecca Rider
Compositor: Joan Olson
Indexer: Karin Arrigoni
Cover design: Aren Howell
Interior design: Joan Olson

ISBN 0-321-43453-6
9 8 7 6 5 4
Printed and bound in the United States of America

This book is for my grandmothers, Henrietta Mulder and Irene Kaper, who both passed away during its creation.

—*Steve Mulder*

Thank you to Jennifer and Sophie for all their help and support.

—*Ziv Yaar*

Endorsements for *The User is Always Right: A Practical Guide to Creating and Using Personas for the Web*

"There's no better way to tap the power of personas for creating great designs than Steve Mulder's clear and accessible guide."

—Jesse James Garrett, author of *The Elements of User Experience: User-Centered Design for the Web*

"Steve Mulder's seminars and lectures have encouraged companies and teams to get to know their customers through personas. There has only been one thing missing in all of these years...the book. The wait is over."

—Kelly Goto, author of *Web Redesign 2.0: Workflow That Works*

"Creating and using personas is a must-do design activity in today's drive to produce innovative products and services. This book tells you how to do the research, promote the personas internally, and keep them alive throughout the development process. Steve Mulder knows his stuff, and after reading his book, you will too.

—Jared Spool, *User Interface Engineering*

"Finally, some hard numbers to support the fine art of personas. This book will help anyone bringing this powerful user-centered technique into their design process."

—Jeffrey Veen, design lead at Google and founder of Adaptive Path

In this lively and witty book, Steve Mulder shows how personas can deliver effective online business strategies and sell them to hard-boiled VPs and concept-resistant marketing directors. After reading it, you will not only create better personas, you will use them to create effective sites and sell them to your toughest clients.

—Jeffrey Zeldman, author of *Designing With Web Standards,* 2nd Edition

Acknowledgments

It takes a village to write a book. Or, rather, a community of generous colleagues, smart peers, and good friends.

First and foremost, thanks to Ziv Yaar, without whom this book would be a shadow of its current self. His words are a critical contribution to this book, but more important are his ideas and approaches, which permeate almost every chapter. I am also greatly indebted to Elan Bair and Yanling Zhang, who brilliantly live these theories about user research, segmentation, and the value of personas every day.

Many colleagues at Molecular have guided or influenced the content of this book and supported its creation. Thanks to Laura Taylor for her support and for providing the space needed to make this happen. Thanks also to the following colleagues: Alicia Arnold, Caleb Brown, Laurie Calvert, Raphael Chun, Scott Cleversey, Amara Cohen, Patrick Coyle, Tony D'angelo, Anne Fassett, Amy Field, Amanda Flohr-Egile, Darryl Gehly, Evan Gerber, Kathleen Gambale, Brian Gillespie, Grace Induni, Jeremy Kriegel, Seona McCafferty Standard, Joanne McLernon, Brian Manning, Robin Merrill, Mike Munnelly, Kevin Nichols, Manivone Phommahaxay, Drake Pusey, Amy Quigley, Theresa Regli, Stephen Weil, Kim Weller, Philip Wisniewski, Anne Wood, and Kristen Yerardi.

But wait, there's more! I'm also grateful to others who contributed to this book in a whole variety of visible and invisible ways: Lori Adams, Andy Clarke, Cathy Cormier, Melissa Crowe, Ellen Gandt, Jesse James Garrett, Kelly Goto, Jill Hammond, Michelle Heath, Jim Heid, Dave Hendry, Kim Hewson, Shawn Laymon, Jennifer Martin, Peter Merholz, Dan Saffer, Jared Spool, Jeff Veen, Dermot Waters, Laura Wattenberg, Jeffrey Zeldman, and my trusty Mac.

A special thanks to those who came before me in making personas such a useful tool. Without Alan Cooper and Robert Reimann, the godfathers of personas, this book would not exist. I'm also grateful for smart minds such as George Olsen and Harley Manning who have worked to extend personas in new directions.

My publishing team has been a delight to work with. Thanks to Michael Nolan for continuing to bug me about writing a book until I said yes, Nancy Aldrich-Ruenzel and Marjorie Baer for making this real, Amy Standen for a constant stream of fresh perspectives and editorial wisdom, Rebecca Rider for making the text better than it should be, Karyn Johnson for faithfully shepherding all the details, and Rebecca Ross, Douglas Cruickshank, Aren Howell, Hilal Sala, Charlene Will, and Kole Hicks.

Finally, thank you Becky for your love and patience throughout this crazy process.

If I left anyone out, consider me a persona non grata.

—*Steve Mulder*

Contents

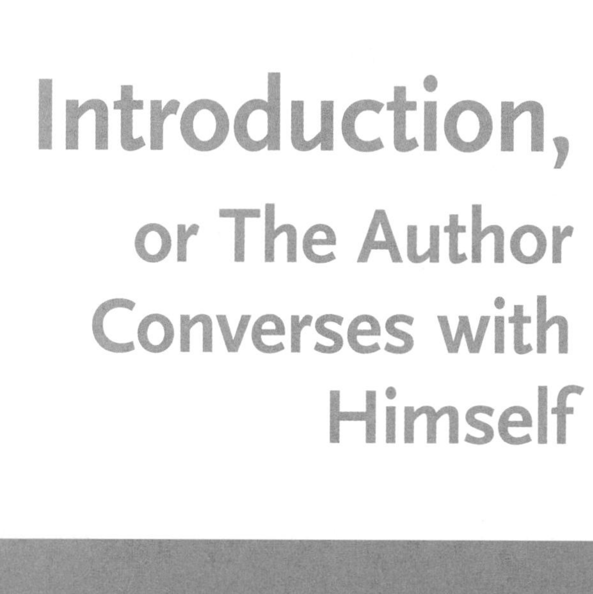

Introduction, or The Author Converses with Himself

"THE USER IS ALWAYS RIGHT"? *Isn't that a little overstated, Mr. Author?*

Well, yes and no. Certainly, you don't want every business decision about your Web site made directly by your users. This isn't a democracy, it's a business. But let's face it, the people your Web site serves are critical to your success. If you don't understand them and provide what they need the way they need it, they'll find someone who does.

So maybe the book should be called "The User Is Important to Understand and Satisfy."

Umm, I'll take that under advisement.

Yeah, right. I assume that personas help businesses focus on their users?

Exactly. You are clearly brilliant. Think of personas as a decision-making tool that brings user research to life in a way that is actionable. That's what Part I of this book is all about: why user-centered design is important, what personas are, and how they make Web sites more successful.

That all sounds fine, but what does it take to actually create these personas?

Part II is a step-by-step guide to creating personas. You have multiple approaches to choose from, depending on the time and budget you have and the type of user research you conduct. These chapters tell you how to make the most of qualitative research techniques, such as one-on-one interviews, and how to enhance persona creation with quantitative research, such as surveys and site traffic analysis. I devote one chapter to segmenting your users into groups that become personas, including new advances in using statistical cluster analysis to drive segmentation. Then, I tell you how to make your personas real: Give them a name and photo, create a background and scenarios—that kind of thing. Examples are sprinkled throughout the book to show how all of this really works.

I see, so you end up with a realistic cast of characters. Then what? How do you use the personas once you have them?

I'm so glad you asked that question! It's almost as if you're reading my mind.

I know, weird, isn't it?

Part III is filled to the brim with tips and examples for using personas for all types of decision-making, whether you're defining your overall online business strategy or designing the site's navigation. The key is to keep your personas alive within your organization, making them an explicit part of your everyday process for creating or improving the site. Chapters 8 through 12 cover how to use personas for directing business strategy, brainstorming and prioritizing features, defining site structure and design, creating content, and even measuring success along the way.

It sounds like this book tries to do everything. Who's it for?

Anybody who believes that understanding and responding to real user needs is a good idea. There's a lot here for people who manage sites and even more for practitioners who actually create personas and build stuff, whether they're called designers, marketers, information architects, user researchers, or strategists.

Golly, Mr. Author, all that sounds keen. Can I ask you more rad questions after I read this rockin' tome?

Yes, of course you can, but only if you stop talking like that. Visit PracticalPersonas.com, where I'll continue to talk about personas and cover the latest developments on this essential tool. Come join the conversation!

Thanks, this has felt like a good introduction to the book.

Er, that's why I called it that.

Oh. Yeah.

Happy reading.

PART I
INTRODUCING PERSONAS

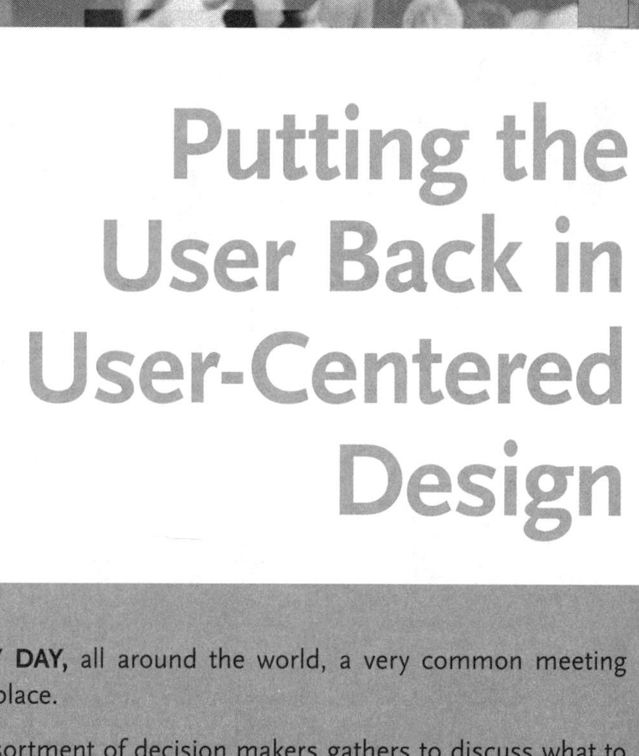

1

Putting the User Back in User-Centered Design

EVERY DAY, all around the world, a very common meeting takes place.

An assortment of decision makers gathers to discuss what to do with their company's Web site. They bring in people like you and me to present ideas and plans for taking the site to the next level. You and I, of course, talk about what users need and how to make decisions based on the real people who use the site.

Unfortunately, these meetings don't always go smoothly. Turn the page to see if this type of meeting ever happens to you....

A TYPICAL CONFERENCE ROOM IN A TYPICAL OFFICE BUILDING. THE AUTHOR AND READER STAND BEFORE THE VICE PRESIDENT, SURROUNDED BY OTHER BUSINESS STAKEHOLDERS. THE ROOM SMELLS FAINTLY OF PLEDGE AND ARROGANCE.

...AND SO THAT'S THE PLAN FOR REDESIGNING THE WEB SITE. WE BELIEVE THIS STRATEGY WILL INCREASE REVENUE ENOUGH TO PAY FOR ITSELF WITHIN SIX MONTHS. ANY QUESTIONS?

WHAT HAPPENED TO FEATURE X?

IN OUR EXPERIENCE, FEATURE X ISN'T WORTH THE INVESTMENT. OUR CUSTOMERS DON'T WANT IT.

HMM. THAT'S NOT WHAT WE DISCUSSED IN THE KICK-OFF MEETING.

UNLEASHING OUR WEAPON OF LAST RESORT: JARGON
OUR CONTEXTUAL ANALYSIS REVEALED THAT EVEN IN CRITICAL USE CASES, FEATURE X WAS NOT PART OF THE TYPICAL CUSTOMER'S MENTAL MODEL. THE PRESENCE OF FEATURE X EVEN PRODUCED COGNITIVE DISSONANCE AMONG OUR MOST LOYAL CUSTOMER BASE, WHERE THE OPPORTUNITY SCORE WAS BELOW 0.7. THE ROI SIMPLY ISN'T...
YOU KNOW...
THERE.

** WHILE THIS SCENE IS ESSENTIALLY A FICTION BASED ON AN AMALGAM OF MANY REAL MEETINGS, THIS PARTICULAR LINE IS AN ACTUAL QUOTE FROM A PARTICULARLY MEMORABLE CLIENT PRESENTATION.*

BUT INNOVATION BEGINS WITH FIRST UNDERSTANDING WHAT OUR CUSTOMERS REALLY NEED.

ARE YOU SAYING I DON'T UNDERSTAND MY CUSTOMERS?!

NO, BUT OUR ANALYSIS...
FEATURE X STAYS IN SCOPE. OKAY, ARE WE DONE?

Sound familiar? This type of experience can be a bit painful for those wise enough to believe in the principles of user-centered design. You and I know that when Web sites (or any products) are created with real people in mind (their needs, their attitudes, their crazy idiosyncrasies), the results are more successful. But sometimes people around you don't see this golden truth as clearly as you do.

What went wrong in this little scene? The VP seems to have tripped somewhere on The Great Steps of User-Centered Design:

Step 1. Recognize that business results depend on making your users happy.

Step 2. Realize that you are not your users.

Step 3. Learn about your users by interacting with them.

Step 4. Make the findings of this research understandable and actionable.

Step 5. Make decisions based on this newfound user knowledge.

Let's find out where he tripped—or rather, where the protagonist failed to persuade the VP to agree with him.

Step 1: Business Results Depend on Users

It doesn't get any more basic than this fundamental tenet of doing business online. If you picked up this book, you're already onboard with the importance of creating a successful user experience in order to achieve the business results you want, whether it's increased revenue or decreased costs.

I like to think of a person's interaction with a Web site as a conversation or negotiation. The conversation begins when users come to your company with a particular goal, such as finding the best television to buy. Through your Web site (and other channels), you respond to their requests with content and features that help them

If the user is satisfied with his or her conversation with your site, you will reap the rewards.

satisfy their goal. If the users like your response, they respond in turn with the business result that makes you happy—in this case, a purchase.

Successful businesses have known for years that this conversation begins with the user and works when the business gives users what they need in the way they need it. If the people you work with haven't yet seen the importance of satisfying user needs, may I suggest you recommend they attend an MBA program? Or perhaps something simpler: Suggest that they read *The Elements of User Experience: User-Centered Design for the Web* (New Riders Press, 2002), an excellent book by Jesse James Garrett.

(By the way, I'm using the term *user* in this book to refer generally to the people who visit your Web site. These could include existing customers, prospects, employees, the press, investors, and others. Some people object to the term, but I find it helpfully inclusive. I also like to think that we have a positive impact on the lives of our users, unlike that *other* industry that calls its customers "users.")

Step 2: You Are Not Your Users

When your colleagues (and VP) believe that satisfying users is critical, the next step in their education is convincing them that the users aren't like them.

Some time ago, I worked closely with a financial services company that was eager to create a new Web-based application for its financial advisors. The application would streamline the process of opening and maintaining consumer accounts, finally replacing the limited DOS-based system they'd been using for years. After analyzing the problem and putting myself in the shoes of the financial advisors, my team and I recommended a flexible, feature-rich solution that worked the way I thought would be best. For example, instead of being limited to a linear series of steps, financial advisors could now skip around during account setup and enter data in any order they wished. It was, of course, brilliant.

Unfortunately for my ego, there was one problem: The financial advisors weren't like me. Where I wanted more features, they wanted simplicity. Where I wanted a flexible system that allowed me to enter data in any order, they wanted a familiar, linear process with less chance of getting lost. Where I wanted to expose features to reveal how powerful the new system was, they wanted to quickly enter data and get on with their busy workday.

Web site design and development teams assume that their users think and act like they do, so they end up designing for themselves rather than for the users.

Across organizations, I've seen this countless times: Web site design and development teams assume that their users think and act like they do, so they end up designing for themselves rather than for the users. Find someone who has direct contact with users (customer service, sales, trainers, etc.), and they'll be happy to point out surprising things that team members don't know about their users.

When I need to splash some cold water on my face to snap out of designing for myself, I pause and reflect on the following truths:

- **Users have different goals than I have.** I want to improve my Web site's checkout process so that users buy more of my excellent products, my bonus check gets bigger, and my boss is impressed. These goals might prompt me to add cross-sells to the process and try to make shipping costs less prominent so that users don't abandon checkout early. Meanwhile, my users are simply trying to order that tacky calendar for Grandma and make sure it will arrive before Christmas. Pushing flower arrangements at them and hiding shipping details create obstacles to their goals, while seemingly supporting mine.

- **Users don't care as I do.** I spend every day immersed in this business and struggle to make improvements that impact the bottom line. I know my site inside and out. Meanwhile, my users are trying to interact with me as briefly as possible so that they can get on with their lives. They have no interest in how that carefully crafted navigation system works, as long as they can accomplish their goals. I'm proud of the work I do; users rarely stop to admire it.
- **Users aren't all alike.** It's too easy to think and talk about "the user" as if everyone who visits the site has the same goals, acts the same way, and thinks the same way. Intellectually, I know my users are very different, but it's tempting to create a single abstract, idealized user to design for, because it simplifies my decision-making.

All of these points are common sense. Unfortunately, common sense can easily fly away when you're in the midst of the daily chaos of managing and improving your site.

In the little comic strip earlier, the VP made decisions based on himself as a typical user, and the protagonist didn't have any argument or evidence to snap him out of it.

Step 3: You Learn About Users Through Direct Contact

If your colleagues believe users are critical and recognize that they don't know everything about the users, the next step is obvious: They need to learn more about these people. And the most efficient and productive way to do that is by interacting with them directly.

In the past, it's often been difficult to find the time or money to do a lot of user research or testing. If you were lucky, you conducted a quick usability test and that was it. You spent more time *imagining* what real users would want rather than actually talking to them.

Organizations have come a long way since then. Successful companies are now finding that direct contact with users (existing customers and non-customers) is worth the (relatively small) investment. More companies are conducting user research than ever before:

- **User interviews and field studies** tell companies what people want from their sites, what motivates these users, and where there are gaps and opportunities for serving them better.
- **Usability tests** show the obstacles on companies' current sites that are preventing users from accomplishing their goals.
- **User surveys** enable companies to validate their findings about user goals, motivators, and opportunities in statistically significant ways.
- **Site traffic/log file analyses** expose a huge amount of data on current user behavior, including common paths through the site, drop-off points, and feature usage.

I'll be talking a lot more about these research methodologies in Part II. As you'll see, it doesn't take a large investment of time or money to find out the key things you need to know about your users.

Step 4: Knowledge About Users Must Be Actionable

Compared with a few years ago, when user research was often the first thing to be scratched from a project, things are looking up. When it's available, there's more user data at your fingertips than ever before. Many of you have data points for decision-making that you could only dream about a few years ago.

The downside? You're swimming in more user data than ever before! When you're looking at the raw output from user interviews, surveys, usability tests, site traffic analyses, and customer financial data, knowing where to start can be overwhelming. You often don't have the time to sit back and *analyze* all the data to look for overall themes and connections that would be useful and actionable. Instead, you're drowning in details.

In his book *Human Options* (W. W. Norton & Company Ltd., 1994), writer and editor Norman Cousins puts it this way:

> *There is a tendency to mistake data for wisdom, just as there has always been a tendency to confuse logic with values, intelligence with insight. Unobstructed access to facts can produce unlimited good only if it is matched by the desire and ability to find out what they mean and where they lead. Facts are terrible things if left sprawling and unattended. They are too easily regarded as evaluated certainties rather than as the rawest of raw materials crying to be processed into the texture of logic.*

Data from user research is most valuable when you take the time to process it into something that is:

- **More forest than trees.** Knowing that 36 percent of users abandon registration on a certain page is not enough. You need to put this information into the context of other information on which users are abandoning the site, why they are doing so, and what improvements they might respond to. One statistic rarely tells a complete story.

- **Sharable.** If people can't quickly view the results of your research, they're less likely to agree with your conclusions. Overwhelming an audience with all available data reduces the impact of the data that matters most. Aggregating user research and paring it down into something portable and digestible is an essential step in making it useful to others.
- **Memorable.** You don't create Web sites for numbers; you create them for people. A dizzyingly large spreadsheet cannot summarize research in a way that makes the data come to life. Making data memorable is about packaging it in such a way that people will remember it when they are in a situation in which it would be useful.
- **Actionable.** In the end, user research is only as good as it is actionable. Knowing that 22 percent of your customers are 30 to 39 years old will probably have no impact on your decisions about creating the site. But knowing that 22 percent of your highest value customers leave your site because you don't offer a particular feature is something that you can act upon. You don't do research out of idle curiosity; you do it to achieve business results.

The VP in the comic strip never had a chance. The Web team conducted user research but didn't share the findings from the research in a way that the VP would find convincing, memorable, and actionable. What's the point of doing research if the output isn't usable by everyone? There must be a better way of simply *talking about users.*

This, in a nutshell, is what *personas* are good at, as you'll see in the next chapter and in Part II. They are particularly useful for making user research come to life. They put a face on user research in a way that turns data into the kind of knowledge that leads to better user experiences and better Web sites.

Personas put a face on user research in a way that turns data into the kind of knowledge that leads to better user experiences and better Web sites.

Step 5: Your Decisions Should Be Based on User Knowledge

Once you know your users and can share that knowledge in a way that is actionable, it is significantly easier to design for them instead of designing for yourself. I use "design" here in the broadest sense—*every* decision you make about the Web site should be guided by what you know about your users. This includes the following:

- **What you build.** "If you build it, they will come" is a horrible way to run an online business. Fundamental decisions about what you're creating in the first place should be driven not by internally focused business owners or technologists, but by what users need and want. Knowledge about your particular users is essential for defining and prioritizing features and content, and establishing overall scope.

- **How it works.** How your site works is just as important to tailor to your specific users as what you build. There are two major components to this. The first is *information architecture,* the craft of organizing features and content so that users can find what they need. If the site structure, navigation, and search don't work like your particular users expect, they won't stick around long enough to give your business a chance. The second component is *interaction design*—the complementary craft of helping users actually do what they need to do in order to accomplish their goals. If interactive processes such as configuring a car or checking out aren't clear to your users, the experience falls apart.

- **What you say.** In any medium, effective communication can make or break a relationship between a business and a user. The content is important, but so are the style and tone in which it is delivered, which is why it needs to be tailored to the users you're serving. And by "content," I don't just mean text, because imagery and multimedia also contribute to the messages you communicate.

- **What it looks like.** Visual design, like everything else, is effective only if it communicates what you want to the users you are targeting. Initial visual impressions can have a huge impact on the user's perception of the overall experience, and thus on how successful the conversation ultimately is between business and user. Here, too, if your visual communication fails to connect with your particular users, the conversation falters from the start.

Part III of this book explores practical techniques of how personas, in representing actual users, can be used to drive effective decision-making at every stage in the process.

Now that you've put the user back in user-centered design (and convinced your peers why that's essential for success), let's talk more about what personas are and why they work.

2 Meet the Personas

RECENTLY, A FRIEND OF MINE, Francis, started looking to buy a house, and the process reminded me once again of the importance of understanding our users.

Francis is a 33-year-old nurse living in Atlanta with her husband Michael, and for years, they have talked about buying a home. One of her favorite things to do on Sundays is to browse the real estate section of the newspaper and then convince Michael to walk through one or two open houses in the area just for fun. She loves imagining where they'd put their furniture and which house their cat Gatsby would like the best. They've lived in their apartment south of Downtown for six years but simply haven't been able to get serious about buying a home—until Michael's recent promotion, that is.

Francis and her husband Michael.

Now that they might be able to afford a house, Francis is excited. She has some idea of what they want: something fairly close to the city, not a fixer-upper, at least three bedrooms (eventually they want to start a family), and ideally a pool in the backyard. She's an ultra-organized person, so she's made sure that their finances are in order and their credit is good. She's even bookmarked a few real estate Web sites for beginning their search.

But she's also completely intimidated, because she has no idea where to start. How much can they really afford? How does the process work? When should they find a realtor, and how do they find a good one? How do they know what's a good neighborhood? She knows she has a lot to learn about real estate and is very afraid of making a mistake. Although she knows a few homeowners, she'd rather not ask them for help, because she doesn't want to appear ignorant. So her excitement is rapidly being spoiled by anxiety.

Finally, she powers up her iMac and starts looking through her bookmarked sites with the following goals in mind:

- Learn about the home-buying process, including understanding all the jargon, realtor involvement, mortgages, and house evaluation criteria.
- Find out what they can afford based on their savings, salaries, current rates, and any special programs she can find.
- Discover what areas of Atlanta are desirable, taking into account schools, transportation, parks, crime, and overall reputation.
- Find houses that match their criteria.

If you're a homeowner or soon to be one, what Francis is going through likely sounds familiar. First-time home buyers have a unique set of needs, and often a unique lack of knowledge, when they visit a real estate Web site.

Okay, I lied earlier. Francis isn't a friend of mine. She's not even real. I made her up.

Francis represents a *type* of user who comes to a real estate site. Research has revealed that a lot of people share the same goals, behaviors, and attitudes when it comes to real estate. So I created Francis to stand in for this common type of user. Francis is a *persona.*

A persona is a realistic character sketch representing one segment of a Web site's targeted audience. Each persona is an archetype serving as a surrogate for an entire group of real people. Personas summarize user research findings and bring that research to life in such a way that a company can make decisions based on these personas, not based on themselves. Instead of asking themselves how they think a feature on the Web site should work, they can ask, "What would Francis do?" Of course, it's rare that a site has just one type of user, so you typically end up with three to five personas that represent the range of all users.

Personas summarize user research findings and bring that research to life in such a way that everyone can make decisions based on these personas, not based on themselves.

First and foremost, personas are grounded in research. Creating fictional characters to represent your users would be a flaky, cute, and ultimately doomed exercise if you didn't have evidence to back up your creations. To make them credible, you need proof that:

- Each persona represents real users that you care about.
- The personas' attributes and descriptions are accurate and complete.
- The set of personas covers the full range of your users.

Your coworkers will be willing to use personas as decision-making tools only if they believe the personas were created with objectivity and at least some science. In the next chapters, you'll learn more about the qualitative and quantitative user research techniques that lead to successful personas.

PRIMARY PERSONA

Francis
the First-Time Home Buyer

"I just don't know where to start!"

- Looking for first home
- Low real estate knowledge
- Very intimidated

Personal Profile

Francis and her husband Michael have dreamed of owning their own home for years, and love to look through real estate listings together on Sunday mornings. Now that Michael's promotion has come through, they can finally get serious about it. The only problem is, Francis has no idea where to start.

She has ideas about what they want: newer home, closer to the city, 3 bedrooms, pool. But she knows she has a lot to learn about real estate, and she's intimidated by the number of factors and decisions. What can they really afford? How can they avoid buying a home in an area they won't like? Francis simply doesn't know all the steps involved in buying a house, and is reluctant to ask her home-owning acquaintances dumb questions.

What Frances wants is a site that will explain the whole process without drowning her in confusing jargon. But she also wants it to have everything she needs to actually begin the process and look for houses, so she doesn't have to go to multiple sites. She likes sites that are friendly and straightforward, especially the ones that remember who she is so she doesn't have to enter her information each time. But most of all, she wants to use a site that she can trust to give her good advice and good information.

User Goals

Francis comes to the site to…

- Learn more about the home-buying process, including jargon, realtors, mortgages, insurance, and how to evaluate houses
- Find out what they can afford based on current rates and first-time buyer programs
- Discover what areas of Atlanta are desirable, taking into account schools, taxes, mass transit, crime, etc.
- Find a house that matches their criteria
- Find the best mortgage lender
- Find the best homeowners insurance

Business Objectives

We want Francis to…

- Visit the site often (ad revenue)
- Register for email alerts and newsletters
- Subscribe to premium services
- Follow through on individual listings by contacting realtor
- Follow through on mortgage and insurance by contacting partner
- Recommend the site to others

Personal Information

Profession: Registered Nurse, Northside Hospital

Location: Atlanta, GA

Age: 33

Home life: Married to Michael (pharmaceutical sales); no children, but planning to start a family soon

Hobbies: Cooking, matchmaking among her many friends, tennis

Favorite TV shows: Oprah, The Apprentice

Personality: Outgoing, friendly, a bit meddling, detail oriented

Real Estate Information

Current home: Apartment south of downtown (for 6 years)

Household income: $70,000

Savings: $10,000

Credit: Good

Purchase timeframe: 3-6 months

Real estate knowledge: Low

Internet Usage

Internet experience: Intermediate (online 2 years)

Primary uses: Shopping, email, horoscope

Favorite sites: Coolsavings, Peapod, GAP, E Online

Hours online per week: 3

Computer: iMac, 56K modem, Internet Explorer 5

An example persona: Francis the First-Time Home Buyer.

Personas are primarily defined by the *goals* they have when they come to the site. As you saw in Chapter 1, goals are critical because they launch the conversation between your users and you. Francis, as a first-time home buyer, comes to the site with very specific goals that show what content and features she needs. Someone else coming to the same site with a different goal—such as trying to refinance a mortgage—would need different content and features to accomplish that goal. Very different goals mean different personas.

In some situations, personas are also defined by their *behaviors* and *attitudes*—that is, how users actually behave (e.g., Francis' tendency to be very organized) or how they perceive themselves or the experience (e.g., her anxiety and insecurity about her lack of knowledge). If goals reveal what features and content that persona needs, then behaviors and attitudes show how those features and that content should work.

Just as a persona has goals, the business has goals for that persona. You create personas to discover how best to serve your different types of users, but you should also agree on what *you* want them to do. Creating business objectives for each persona ensures that you don't lose sight of the overall goal: creating a conversation with users that turns into business results.

An essential part of creating a persona is making him or her real so that the team also thinks of the persona as a real person they need to satisfy. That's why I gave my real estate persona a name, a photo, and a story. And that's why it's important to document her real estate experience, her knowledge, Internet use, and key demographics. You can even create scenarios for your persona that tell the story of what you want his or her interaction with the site to be like. The result is a full-fledged persona like Francis.

You'll go through all the steps and aspects of creating personas in Part II. For now, let's look at the benefits of using personas and a few success stories along the way.

Benefits of Personas

Why are personas worth the effort? How can a one-page description of Francis the First-Time Home Buyer result in better decision-making and increased results from Web sites?

Personas Bring Focus

The first tenet of personas is that *you can't create a site for everyone.* In most cases, successful businesses target specific audiences. Creating a Web site for "everyone" often means creating for the lowest common denominator. More often than not, serving a specific audience extremely well is much smarter than partially serving a larger audience.

Personas help you define for whom you're creating the site. Creating personas forces you to spend time thinking about which types of users are critical to your business, so no one wastes precious time thinking about people who don't really matter. Instead of talking generally about "users," you can talk about precisely which people you want to target.

For example, one client I worked with (R.H. Donnelley, a yellow pages publisher) wanted to create a community-driven Web site in which consumers could provide ratings and reviews of local businesses—everything from restaurants to plumbers to florists. A site such as this can succeed only if users contribute, so my team set out to understand who was likely to contribute ratings and reviews. Many user interviews and a survey later, we created personas representing the range of targeted users of this future site, including one persona who the data showed was most likely to contribute. For this persona, we had information on where he already contributed, why he did so, and what sparked his contributions. This persona enabled the team and the larger organization to focus efforts on creating an online environment that would encourage contributions from this type of person. It was critical that we had a deep understanding of a very particular type of person in order for us to move this new business idea forward.

Personas Build Empathy

I've already discussed the second tenet of personas: *You are not your users.* People who work on Web sites know their business and know how things work, so their first instinct is usually to make decisions based on themselves. Meetings are filled with "I think it should work like this" and "I don't like sites that do things like that." But as we have seen, your users are not like you. They don't necessarily care about the things you care about.

Personas help you live in your users' shoes. As you use personas, they start to feel like real people. For instance, when you face a decision, you might imagine what Francis would want or do in this situation, not what you want. You know that personas are working when a team member refers to the persona by name: "But Francis would never use that!"

VistaPrint, a site that enables users to design and print everything from business cards to personalized gift tags, is run by a smart, sophisticated team whose members understand the importance of giving users what they want. When users want to design an item, they enter VistaStudio, a powerful Web application that enables users to customize all aspects of the design, including drag-and-drop of any element. The user research conducted by my team revealed that most users loved the customization—but not all of them. A critical segment, which became the persona Howard the Hurried, simply wanted business cards quickly that were good enough. Howard didn't want to take the time for customization, and in fact, he was more likely to abandon the site because of the Studio's complexity. Howard helped the VistaPrint team see beyond the uber-customizer they had been designing for and helped them make decisions based on a different, and very important, type of user. More on this example later.

Personas Encourage Consensus

The raw output of most user research encourages different people to come to different conclusions. One person grabs onto a particular set of data to defend his position, and another uses another data set to argue her position. As a result, each team member can have a different audience in mind when making decisions, which creates an inefficient process and a disjointed end product.

Personas bring the team together to create one shared vision of exactly whom you're designing for and what they want. Early agreement on this critical step means less miscommunication later as you make detailed decisions. This shared understanding is perhaps the most important benefit of personas, since it helps establish appropriate expectations and goal setting throughout the organization.

Personas bring the team together to create one shared vision of exactly whom you're designing for and what they want.

A few years ago I worked with a team to reinvent an existing Web search engine. Each team member brought a great deal of search expertise to the project—and a different perspective on which features and what approach would make us unique and successful. The debate was fascinating and intellectually stimulating, but unfortunately we got stuck in the debate and made little progress. So we backed up and created personas to represent our existing users and prospective new users. It took a while to agree on the set of personas, but once we did, we were amazed to find how smoothly later decisions went. Harry the High Geek (yes, that was actually the name of one of the personas) brought us together on whom we were serving and how we should do it.

Personas Create Efficiency

For every decision you make when creating or enhancing a Web site, there is a tool optimized for facilitating that decision. Page wireframes help everyone decide the content and behavior of each page.

Design mock-ups help you decide on visual composition, typography, color, and so on. Personas help you decide what you're creating in the first place.

Another way to look at it is that personas ensure that people make key decisions earlier in the process so that they don't waste time and money later. Have you ever been in a visual design review in which the conversation turns away from visual design and toward issues of whom you're designing for or what features you should have? These questions should have been answered much earlier, but since you had no deliverables earlier to facilitate this discussion, they occur now when you're looking at page designs. But of course using the design phase to decide on audience and functionality is hugely inefficient, because it means you need far more visual design review sessions, and you also need to rethink what you supposedly already decided.

When a team reviews personas early in the process, everyone is forced to think about issues of audience and features up front so that these issues are less likely to disrupt the project later. For this reason, personas seldom add to overall project cost, and they can often save time and money, because the initial time you spend on personas is more than recovered through increased efficiency.

When one retailer was creating its ecommerce site, the working assumption was that the site's structure would reflect the organization of the physical stores. At this company's stores, for instance, "Women's" referred to plus size clothing and "Misses" was for everything else. However, field studies and other user research revealed that customers respond differently to these terms online vs. offline (in the store), and the personas showed this mindset. On a Web site, customers expected that these labels would refer to ages, not sizes, and so they would have been surprised and confused when they went to the "Women's" section of the site and found only plus sizes. When the company created the site architecture and design, what would have been a long debate about brand consistency and labeling was instead a quick decision point based on research summarized through personas. The section names on the site changed to reflect what real customers understood. Whether you have big or small decisions to make, personas give you the information you need to make those decisions more efficiently.

Personas Lead to Better Decisions

Ultimately, personas work because they help everyone make better decisions. Because personas are grounded in research, all stakeholders can feel confident that these are, in fact, the right users to target, and that everyone knows exactly how to satisfy them and how that leads to business results.

Design teams were the first to embrace personas, using them as a design tool for making decisions about the user experience of a site. Teams create personas so that they can be more user centered as they work to find the best design solution for the requirements given to them. Personas are critical in the conceptual design phase as you shape the information architecture and interaction design. Deliverables such as site maps, process diagrams, and page wireframes are driven by persona scenarios and by how personas want to experience their interaction with the site. In addition, content and visual design are heavily influenced by personas, because the style or tone used to satisfy their goals can be as important as everything else. Finally, personas are useful for testing purposes, since you now know exactly who to recruit for various user-testing activities, and who the actors are for writing QA (Quality Assurance) test scripts.

Fortunately, people other than the design team are seeing the value of personas, and their use is expanding rapidly. Marketing groups aren't strangers to the idea of personas, since they've been using segmentation for years to plan and deploy targeted marketing campaigns. But unlike traditional marketing segmentation (which is often based on demographics and psychographics), persona segmentation is focused on user goals, behaviors, and attitudes. This changes the perception of users: Where they once were passive targets for whatever marketing message companies were trying to deliver, now they are proactive people with their own goals and priorities. One-way broadcasts have now become dialogues in which businesses can provide value to users in a number of ways based on the persona's needs. In addition, when marketers use the same personas as the rest of the organization, this closes the loop between *attracting* users and then *serving* them well. Companies can now talk about and plan for users in a unified way, rather than simply observe as users are tossed between internal departments.

Perhaps the most exciting development in the usage of personas is that they are increasingly being adopted to form a framework for defining business strategy. This evolution leverages the key strengths of personas (focus, empathy, consistency, and efficiency) but broadens their reach. Now personas not only help development teams align around a particular set of goals when designing a Web site, they also can help an entire organization align around the execution of a particular business strategy. Personas are expanding from a design tool you use to decide how to implement a strategy into a strategic tool you use to help define a strategy in the first place. By using personas to reveal the market opportunities, companies can better identify and evaluate the following: potential product and service offerings, channel usage, projects to implement the strategy,

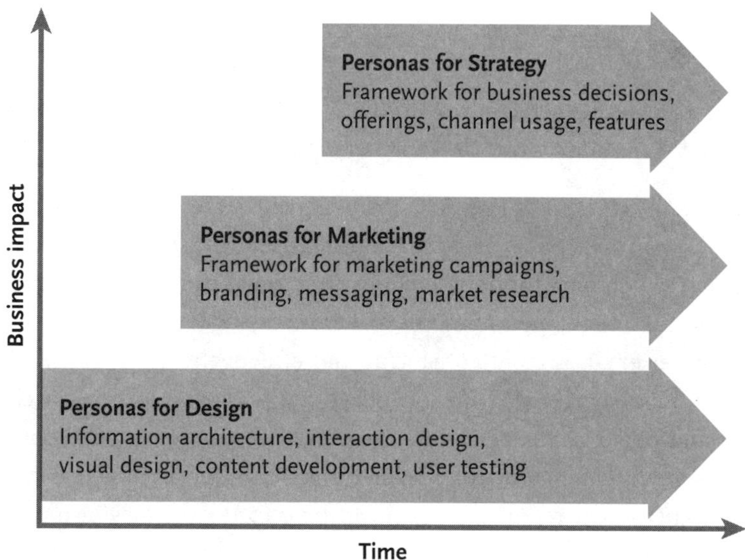

Over time, personas have made a greater and greater impact within organizations.

and even organizational needs and hiring that will increase sales or cut costs. Once personas are established, they can be disseminated throughout the organization to make sure that customer service, sales, marketing, operations, and all other units of a business are focused and aligned around the same opportunities and customers. This greatly increases the chance of the business strategy succeeding, since many good business strategies find themselves failing due to a lack of alignment, which leads to poor execution.

An example of personas driving business strategy can be found at BrownCo, a discount brokerage. BrownCo targeted the active trader market, which it defined as traders making more than 50 trades per year. In order to develop strategies for customer acquisition, the team developed segments and, later, personas of the active trader community. They did so using traditional demographics and product usage as well as customer goals, behaviors, and attitudes. In the course of developing these personas, they identified one who valued mutual fund products as well as stocks, and another who valued the advice of a traditional full-service broker. Since BrownCo did not have compelling mutual fund offerings or full-service brokers, it adjusted its business strategy to steer away from targeting these personas and instead focused on other personas where it could provide compelling differentiation. BrownCo developed a true understanding of its users, which led to a shift in overall business direction that focused team efforts and led to measurable results.

Personas work because they encourage everyone to think about actual users all the time, not just during user research and testing activities. And even for organizations that are already user centered in their approach, personas make that thinking explicit in a way that better ensures team consensus and effectiveness around what they're building and why. Personas also put a face on user research data and make it *actionable* in ways that drive design and development activities forward toward shared goals. After all, if you know which customers to make happy and how to do so, they're much more likely to make you happy by bringing you the business results that you so richly deserve. The chapters in Part III address the uses of personas in much more detail, with special focus on business strategy and design process.

Two Quick Success Stories

Speaking of business results, I've mentioned some examples so far of how personas have helped businesses, but how about some measurable results? Chapter 12 covers how to measure success, but here are a couple of quick success stories.

One quick caveat: It can be extremely difficult to measure the effectiveness of personas, because they make up one tool among many that you can use to improve Web sites. When you redesign a site based on personas, how do you know which part of the improved metrics is due to personas versus better usability, visual design, server performance, or any other improvement you make? A variety of factors influences success metrics, so most case studies on personas tend to be more qualitative in nature.

The team behind CNN.com regularly conducts user research, and in 2005 they chose to make that research more actionable by creating personas that represent its key audience segments. After interviewing a range of users and applying the findings from a survey and traffic analysis, they generated six personas and introduced them across the organization. The team has used the personas in a variety of ways that have led to site improvements. For example, making decisions based on personas resulted in increased video usage. The personas have been so well received within the company that other groups within CNN are now eager to use personas as well. These personas have successfully allowed internal teams to focus on the needs of real users to such a degree that an executive recently distributed T-shirts that proclaim "We are not the target audience."

As another example, I've worked with a specialty retailer that has the most loyal customers I've ever interacted with. This is a company that knows how to treat its customers right, and it is committed to measuring the online experience it offers in order to make sure customers are satisfied and to quantify business results from this key channel. In working with this company, my team discovered that the more channels a customer uses to purchase, the more valuable that customer is. So we created personas based on channel usage: We had a store-only persona, a Web-site–only persona, a Web site and store persona, and a Web site and store and catalog persona. We discovered that if we could convince store-only customers to also shop online, they would in fact purchase much more (rather than merely shifting their purchases between channels). Focusing on this particular store-only persona led us to a new feature idea: Customers use the site to determine which products (in which sizes and colors) are available in their local store, and even to reserve those items online for in-store pickup. The retailer soft-launched the feature and was delighted with the results: More store-only customers are now using the Web site, and many are purchasing from the site for the first time. Better yet, the company is finding that when customers reserve an item using the site, they end up spending 150 percent more on additional products when they visit the store to pick it up. Without personas and the research behind them, this idea and the business results it generated would have never become reality. You'll discover more about this retailer's story in later chapters.

Beyond the Web

This book focuses on personas in the digital realm, but the value of personas is in no way restricted to the Web. Any business that serves people (and that covers a rather huge number of businesses!) benefits from better understanding its users and creating personas to summarize, share, and act upon that knowledge.

Best Buy is using personas to reinvent the experience customers have when they walk into a store. One persona is Jill, a "soccer mom" who is the primary shopper for the family but who doesn't often visit electronics stores because she's intimidated by the complexity of these products and the jargon surrounding them. After understanding who Jill is and what she needs, Best Buy created an experience tailored for her. Sales associates are trained to spot potential

Jills and provide service as they need it. For example, on rainy days, sales associates go out with pink umbrellas and escort likely Jills into the store. Best Buy is even dedicating certain stores to this type of shopper: Kids products are displayed more prominently, there are children's play areas, and the music piped in matches Jill's typical tastes (James Taylor and Mariah Carey). Meanwhile, other services and other stores are being tailored to other personas identified by Best Buy. And it's working. One Jill-oriented store has seen its Jills increase their purchasing by 30 percent.

Another example is Philips Consumer Products USA. Philips holds three well-known brands in its arsenal: Philips Consumer Electronics, Norelco, and Sonicare. Although each brand is successful on its own, Philips has never actively pursued a strategy to cross-sell one brand's products to customers of another of its brands. In order to increase cross-selling, Philips embarked upon an effort to segment its customer database, identify customers who had purchased cross-brand, and then use information about these customers to develop strategies to target similar customers within each segment to get them to purchase cross-brand as well. These strategies became personas, stories embodying both the customer demographics for each segment, but also the customer needs within each segment. The Philips strategy could then leverage these needs to increase cross-brand purchase. For example, after these personas were developed, Philips knew which demographic and psychographic factors influenced consumer electronics customers to purchase Norelco as well. Philips then used these personas to drive the creative and marketing efforts within the organization so that they could develop marketing campaigns targeting each persona. Finally, they used propensity models for each persona to help track the success of these marketing campaigns at converting each target persona into a cross-brand purchaser.

Although this book's main focus is on the Web, many of the techniques for creating and using personas are applicable across channels. Whether you design toasters, create new retirement services, or market automated litter boxes, having a tool to enable you to focus on the needs of real people can only help bring focus to the work you do.

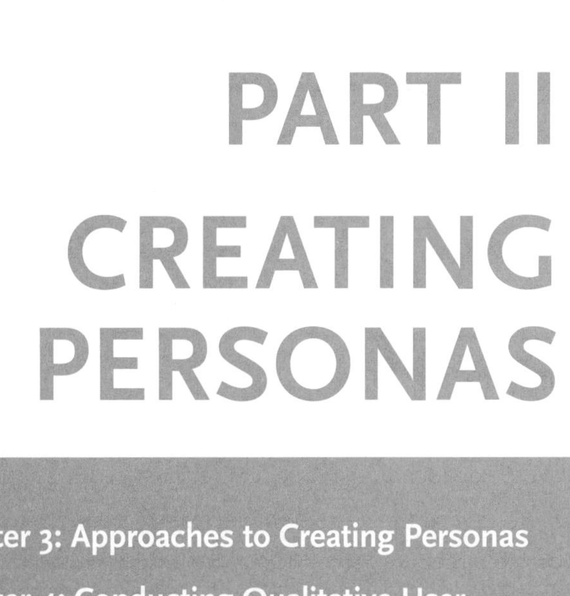

PART II
CREATING PERSONAS

3 Approaches to Creating Personas

THIS IS A PRACTICAL BOOK, focused on how to create and use personas to make Web sites more successful. It's time to get to work and create some personas.

First things first: There is no one right way to create personas. Like almost everything you do, a big "It Depends" cloud hangs over your efforts:

- It depends on who your audience for the personas is and what they need in order to agree to use personas.
- It depends on how you plan to use personas and what types of decisions you'll make using them.
- It depends on how much time and money you want to (or can) invest in this user-centered design activity.

Although the persona creation process should be tailored for each situation, there are three primary approaches explored in this book, based on the type of research and analysis performed:

- Qualitative personas
- Qualitative personas with quantitative validation
- Quantitative personas

Since the approach to creating personas largely depends on the type(s) of research you conduct, let's first explore the user research methodologies you can choose from.

The User Research Landscape

You do research to better understand your users, but exactly what is it that you want to find out about them? That's the first question you need to ask, and its answer dictates which research methods you should use, since specific methods are tailored to finding specific types of information.

One way to explore the landscape of user research methodologies is to classify them as qualitative or quantitative:

- **Qualitative research** is about discovering new things with a small sample size. User interviews and usability testing fall into this category, because they consist of interacting with a small number of users (10–20) to get new ideas or uncover previously unknown issues. Qualitative research doesn't *prove* anything, since you're talking with a limited number of people, but it's very valuable at uncovering insights that you can then test or prove. It's open-ended and often reveals things you didn't know.
- **Quantitative research** is about testing or proving something with a large sample size. Surveys and site traffic analysis (looking at your log files to see how users are moving around your site) are good examples. With hundreds or

thousands of data points to analyze, you can look for statistically significant trends and be much more certain that your findings accurately reflect reality for all users. Quantitative research can help you test a hypothesis you uncover with qualitative research.

Here's another way to look at it: Quantitative research is better at telling you *what* is happening (e.g., your log files tell you that 35 percent of site visitors never reach a product page), and qualitative research is better at telling you *why* it's happening (e.g., usability testing shows that some users don't understand the terminology used in the site's navigation).

Quantitative research is better at telling you* what *is happening, and qualitative research is better at telling you* why *it's happening.

As you can imagine, both types of research can be critical. Qualitative research is an inexpensive way to gain new insights quickly and give some direction to your site. Quantitative research helps you determine if those insights are, in fact, real—and it gives you the evidence to prove it to your boss.

If qualitative versus quantitative is one axis for exploring user research methodologies, another is what people say versus what they actually do.

- **What people say** is important because it reveals their *goals* and their *attitudes*. Goals begin the conversation between your users and you, so you need to fully understand why they come to the site and what they're trying to do. Looking at site traffic logs may reveal problem spots, but if you don't know what users' goals are in the first place, you won't know what to improve or how to improve it. Attitudes, on the other hand, reveal how people perceive themselves and these online experiences, and it's important to understand these perceptions as well. Whether Francis the First-Time Home Buyer thinks of herself as ignorant or knowledgeable is going to affect how you communicate with her on the site. Interviews and surveys are very common methods for researching what people say, and for learning about goals and attitudes.

- **What people do** is just as important, since actual *behavior* can reveal more about people than what they say. Behavior reveals not only where they might be having problems (as in a usability test), but also how they tend to use Web sites in general, which can influence how you shape your site. For example, knowing how users scan a search results page is valuable information for ensuring that your search results page is useful and usable.

The key point is this: *What people say isn't necessarily what they do.*

I've seen this again and again in usability tests. A user will clearly struggle trying to complete a task, and then claim the task was easy. Sometimes users are trying not to look stupid (guys often fall into this category), and sometimes users are trying too hard to tell me what they think I want to hear. But most often, users don't tell me the truth because they're not even aware of the truth of their behavior. It turns out that many people aren't very good at analyzing their own behavior or at paying attention to their actions. Basically, our image of ourselves doesn't always reflect reality. That's why it's important to watch what people really do, and not simply trust what they tell you they do.

My favorite story about this fundamental truth is somewhat famous in marketing circles. When Sony was introducing the boom box, the company gathered a group of potential consumers and held a focus group on what color the new product should be: black or yellow. After some discussion among the group of likely buyers, everyone agreed that consumers would better respond to yellow. After the session, the facilitator thanked the group, and then mentioned that, as a bonus, they were welcome to take a free boom box on the way out. There were two piles of boom boxes: yellow and black. (I bet you know where this is heading.) Every person took a black boom box.

What people say isn't necessarily what they do.

You need to make sure to understand both aspects, or you won't fully understand your users.

When you consider these two dimensions (qualitative versus quantitative research and what people say versus what they do), it becomes apparent how a few common user research methods support different research goals and complement one another. (I know I've spent too much time in the consulting business because I cannot resist creating a 2×2 matrix. It's like the siren's call.)

User interviews uncover qualitative insights into users' goals and attitudes, and surveys are useful for testing and validating those

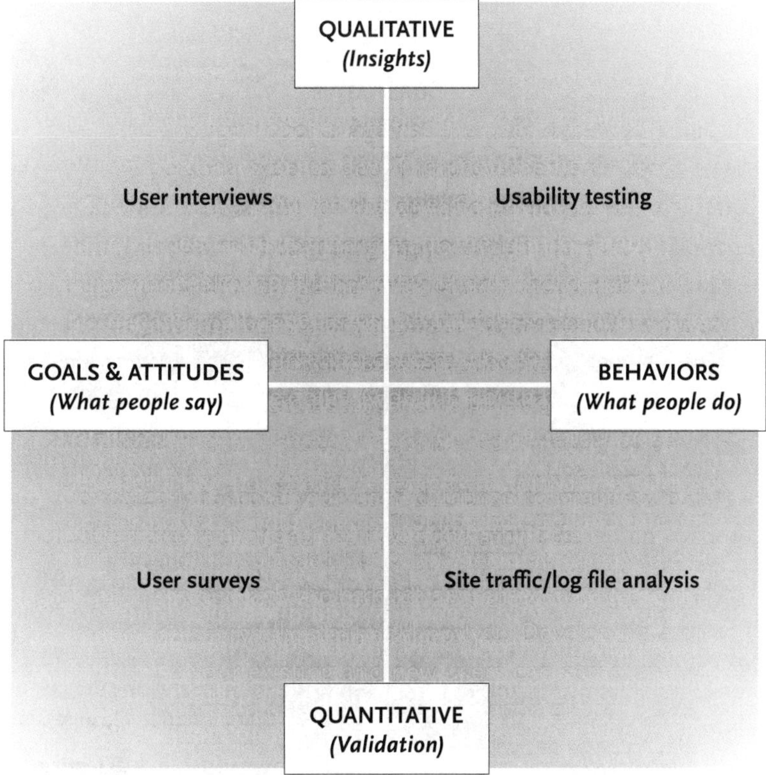

Four common research methods paint a complete portrait of users.

insights. Usability testing reveals qualitative insights on user behavior, and site traffic analysis ensures that these behavior patterns are statistically real across the broader population.

I could add many other research methods to this framework, and of course, there is much crossover in what each method can be used for. The next diagram shows how various common methods might be positioned in this matrix. The next time you're planning user research, stop for a moment and make sure you know exactly what you're trying to find out and which research method is the best match.

Now it's time to return to our regularly scheduled program: What are the three core approaches to creating personas?

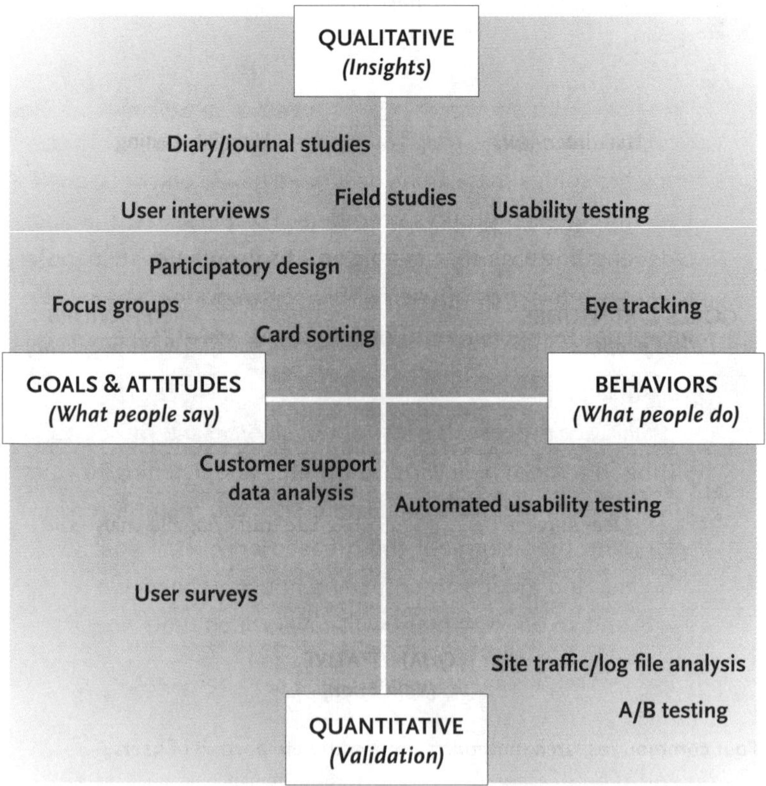

The landscape of user research and testing techniques.

Qualitative Personas

Let's start with the most traditional approach. Many organizations create personas following these simple steps:

1. **Conduct qualitative research.**

   User interviews are the most common form of qualitative research, because talking one on one to 10 to 20 users is relatively easy for most companies. Some companies conduct field studies instead, where they observe users in their native environment (their office or their home), and can thus observe behavior while also asking about goals and attitudes. In addition, you can use usability testing to observe behavior, though this is less common for generating personas. (The next chapter is devoted to how to use qualitative research to your best advantage.)

2. **Segment users based on the qualitative research.**

   Segmentation is the art of taking many data points and creating groupings that can be described based on commonalities among each group's members. For personas, the goal is to find patterns that enable you to group similar people together into types of users. This segmentation is typically based on their goals, attitudes, and/or behaviors.

   For qualitative personas, segmentation is, not surprisingly, a qualitative process. It's less about science and more about sitting in a room reviewing your notes and listening to your gut. For example, for a real estate site, you might interview users and then segment them based on overall goals: buy a house, find an apartment, sell a house, refinance a mortgage, and so on. (Chapter 6 will cover much more about the fine art of segmentation.)

3. **Create a persona for each segment.**

   Each type of user evolves into a persona as you add more detail to their goals, behaviors, and attitudes. Each one becomes realistic when you have supplied a name, a photo, demographic information, scenarios, and more. (Chapter 7 explains how to make personas real.)

These steps represent the most common approach to creating personas, and following them works successfully for a variety of organizations. It's a relatively quick process and an excellent way for companies to put their toes in the water and try out personas.

One of the first times I used personas was with a company that performed automated analyses of users' experience with a Web site. (I was and remain skeptical of the effectiveness of such a product, but maybe I'm just afraid of being replaced by a Hal 9000 computer.) As a young company testing new product ideas, this team interacted significantly with end users and already had a segmentation model in place. As part of redesigning their site and the reports they delivered, my team and I conducted interviews with existing and likely customers and found a new type of customer role that the company hadn't even considered. This new fifth segment, which soon became

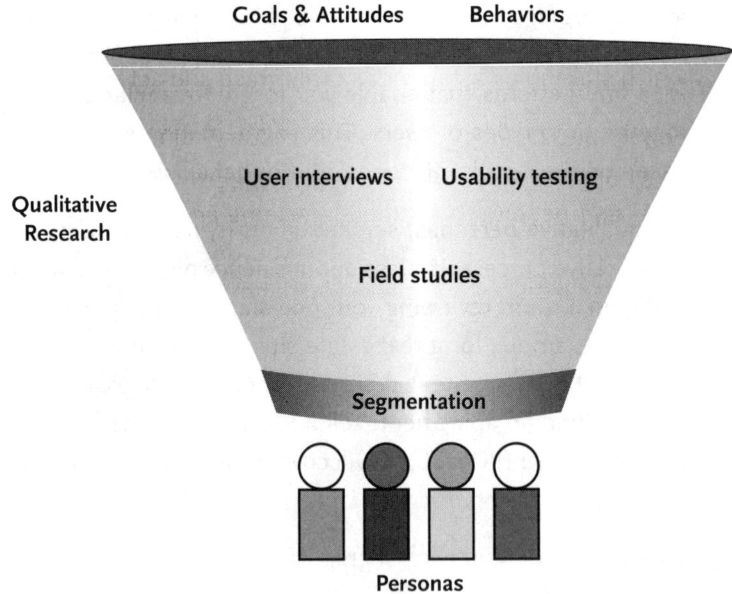

The qualitative persona process.

a fifth persona, resulted in important changes to the site and reports that increased overall customer satisfaction. Some quick qualitative research, made actionable through personas, made a difference to this business.

However, there are some drawbacks to this qualitative approach to building personas; so for each approach, let's look at the pros and cons.

Pros:

- Relatively low effort is required. A basic process with, say, 15 user interviews, segmentation, and persona creation could take just three to four weeks. If an internal team creates the personas, costs are minimal, assuming you can find users to interview.
- Simpler persona stories increase understanding and buy-in. Because you're creating personas based on interviews and the stories you've heard, chances are your personas will be defined by just one or two attributes, making them relatively easy to understand at a glance. Simplicity breeds clarity, which stakeholders can more easily grasp and act upon.
- Fewer specialized skill sets are necessary compared to the other approaches. You still need people with interviewing skills and people who can find patterns and create personas out of interview findings, but you don't need any statistical analysis skills because you're not doing quantitative research.

Cons:

- There's no quantitative evidence. The most common pitfall in persona creation occurs when someone asks, "How can you be sure all our users are like the few you talked to?" Qualitative personas are based on the idea that you can talk to a small number of users and see patterns that apply to all of your users. In other words, the risk of being wrong is higher compared to having a large sample size to back you up. If your stakeholders need quantitative evidence to buy into your process, they'll disregard your personas as a creative but ultimately unreliable tool. Some people simply need the "proof" of hard data. And who can blame them? If you're going to be making critical business decisions based on these personas, you better be as certain as possible of their accuracy—and be able to persuade others.

- Existing assumptions don't tend to be questioned. You know your business, and you have assumptions about who the users are and what they need. When any person interviews users, he or she inevitably brings those assumptions to the research. The result: People find what they're looking for. Subconsciously, people look for the things that back up their own assumptions, so that instead of discovering surprises, they simply validate an existing worldview. Too often, their segmentation will look exactly like their original assumptions instead of being affected by the research. It won't always happen this way, but it's a serious risk when doing qualitative segmentation.

Use this approach if:

- You can't invest much time and money in personas.
- Your stakeholders don't need to see quantitative data to believe and use your personas.
- The stakes aren't too high in terms of how you'll use the personas, so not having quantitative evidence is fine.
- You want to try using personas on a smaller project and see how they work before applying them to the larger business.

Qualitative Personas with Quantitative Validation

If you can invest a little more time and want to bring more quantitative objectivity to your personas, this approach is worth considering. Here are the basic steps:

1. **Conduct qualitative research.**

   Just like the first approach, you begin by conducting qualitative research that reveals insights into user goals, behaviors, and attitudes.

2. **Segment users based on the qualitative research.**

   You perform the same type of qualitative segmentation and end up with a number of segments based on particular user goals, behaviors, and/or attitudes.

3. **Test the segmentation through quantitative research.**

   Here's the new step: Through a survey or other form of quantitative research, test your segmentation model using a larger sample size to be more certain it accurately reflects reality. The goals are to confirm that these segments are in fact different, and to have evidence to back up your personas in front of stakeholders. Survey data is best for testing goals and attitudes, and site traffic analysis (less commonly used for generating personas) gives you hard data on user behaviors. The analysis you do could involve simple cross-tabs, or you could use complex statistical analysis techniques. (See Chapters 5 and 6 for more information on these quantitative research and analysis techniques.)

   For example, if you wanted to test a real estate segmentation model based on goals, you'd run a survey in which one of the questions covered the reason(s) users visit the site. You could perform a simple cross-tab analysis in Excel to examine how users' answers to this question affected their other answers (for example, did first-time home buyers rate certain features or content as more important?). If you see differences that support your plan to make these segments into separate personas, the segmentation model is successful. If you don't, you can try other ways of segmenting users and test those.

4. **Create a persona for each segment.**

When you have quantitative research for creating realistic personas, you can be more certain that decisions you make have statistical significance. Personas are no longer simply fictional creations, but amalgams of research findings with evidence to back them up. Now when you say that Francis does something or wants something, you can back up that statement with hard numbers. Quantitative data doesn't necessarily *prove* your points, but it reduces the chance that you're wrong. It's also valuable for providing evidence of the magnitude and importance of a particular issue.

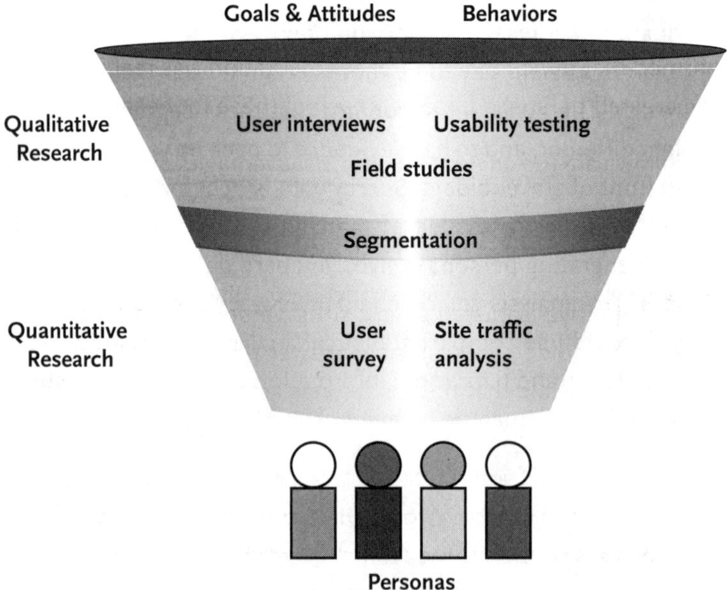

The process for qualitative personas with quantitative validation.

With this approach, you get a little more science and a little less art for your personas. The segmentation is still based on qualitative research, but you use quantitative research to obtain evidence to back up your decisions.

In the previous chapter you saw how a specialty retailer wanted to better understand how its customers were using different channels to shop and make purchases. Given that the goal was channel usage, my team and I knew from the start that this was how we would segment our users into personas. So we ended up with four segments: store-only customers, Web site–only customers, combination Web site and store customers, and combination Web and store and catalog customers. We conducted a survey and then tied in existing CRM data, so we knew which channels each survey respondent used. (See Chapter 5 for more information on Customer Relationship Management data.) Then we analyzed the survey data by looking at all the questions' answers separated by these four segments. In this way, we could see at a glance how channel usage correlated to other aspects such as how much they spent, how they perceived the company, what they liked or disliked about shopping, how important certain factors like style were to each segment, and so on. The survey data confirmed that our channel-based segmentation was real and useful, so we created personas based on each of these four segments.

What follows are the advantages and disadvantages of this approach.

Pros:

- Quantitative evidence defends the personas. To the skeptical stakeholder, you can now answer that, yes, you are reasonably certain that these personas accurately represent the user base. Furthermore, you can rattle off data that defends your case, noting for example, that first-time home buyers make up 27 percent of site visitors, and that 82 percent of this segment believes that multimedia tutorials are important or very important.

- Simpler persona stories increase understanding and buy-in. As with qualitative personas, you'll likely define them using just one or two attributes, rather than what advanced statistical analysis might reveal, which could be many factors working in combination. Simpler stories help people digest and use personas easier.
- Depending on how you analyze the data, fewer specialized skill sets are necessary. You can perform simple cross-tab analysis of the survey results on your own. You can also dig deeper to validate the statistical significance of the data, which requires statistical analysis skills.

Cons:

- Additional effort is required. Due to the extra step, the overall process could take six to eight weeks. Surveys always add time, because you need to create the survey, deploy it, leave it active long enough to get sufficient completions, and then analyze the data. In addition, if your segmentation is based on multiple factors (e.g., the goal of home buying plus the attitude of anxiety plus the behavior of being ultra-organized), a simple cross-tab analysis of survey results won't be possible, and the level of effort (and skill set) could increase rapidly.
- Existing assumptions don't tend to be questioned. A risk still exists in this approach, because you're still basing the initial segmentation on your own experiences and perspective. In other words, you could still be trying to prove what you already think you know, rather than opening up to new possibilities.
- What if the data doesn't validate your theory? If the results of the survey or site traffic analysis don't support your segmentation model, then you're looking at additional work. In the best case, you can try different segmentation models

one at a time to see if the data supports one of them. In the worst case, you have to start over and conduct a new survey or more site traffic analysis because you didn't ask all the questions that are now needed to explore other options. Either way, it adds up to more time and money.

Use this approach if:

- You have a bit more time and money to invest.
- Your stakeholders need to see quantitative data to believe and use your personas.
- You are very sure that your qualitative segmentation model is the right one.

Quantitative Personas

What if the process of creating personas could rely even a bit more on science? A third approach is emerging that I believe will become more and more common for creating personas. Instead of testing your qualitative assumption about one segmentation model, you use statistical analysis to test a variety of segmentation models at once, in order to find the model that is the most useful for creating personas.

1. **Conduct qualitative research.**

   Once again, qualitative research reveals insights into user goals, behaviors, and attitudes.

2. **Form hypotheses about segmentation options.**

   Rather than deciding on a final segmentation model right away, you use the qualitative research to come up with various potential ways you might segment the users. The goal is a list of a variety of candidates to analyze.

3. **Gather data on segmentation options through quantitative research.**

   For each potential segmentation option, there are particular questions you need to ask in a survey or particular questions you need to answer using site traffic analysis. For example, if you think users' history with the site could be a way to segment, then a survey question about how long and how often they use the site would be appropriate. The quantitative research in this approach isn't trying to prove something; instead, its goal is to assemble more data for the next step.

4. **Segment users based on statistical cluster analysis.**

   In this approach, statistical algorithms take a more active role in guiding you to a segmentation model, rather than just testing your existing assumptions. To oversimplify, you feed a set of variables into the machine, and it looks for naturally occurring clusters based on some set of commonalities. It tries many different ways of segmenting users, and through an iterative process, it finds a segmentation model that mathematically describes commonalities and differences. You could end up with any number of clusters and any number of attributes as key differentiators between the clusters. This process is a bit more complex, iterative, and still very much influenced by how you run it, as will be further explored in Chapter 6. But it's significantly different from the other approaches because the segmentation is data driven as well as human driven.

5. **Create a persona for each segment.**

   When the cluster analysis spits out the segments, you take the data and make it real through the same process as before: by adding names, photos, and stories to turn these spreadsheets into real people.

As businesses rely on personas more and more for overall strategic decisions and marketing planning, quantitative personas will grow in

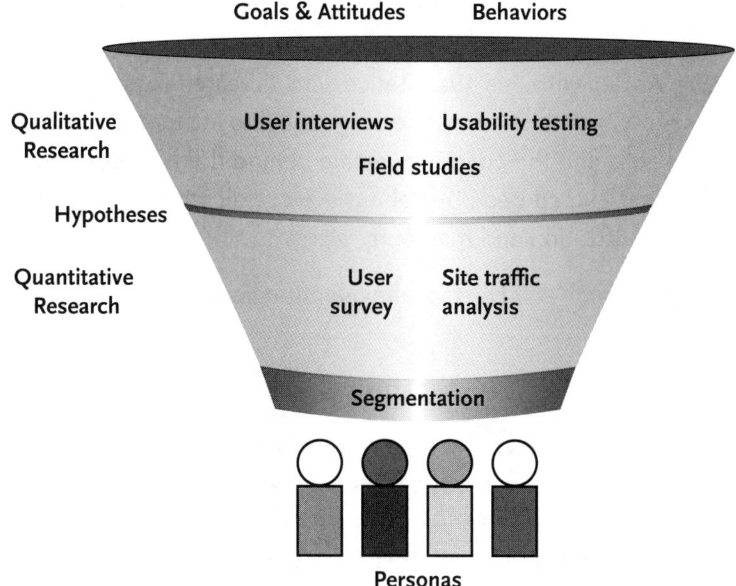

The quantitative persona process.

popularity due to the scientific rigor they bring. The increased objectivity that the quantitative approach brings to the process of creating personas aligns much more closely with the data-driven decision-making that occurs in so many organizations. Use of quantitative personas will also rise because the number of variables businesses have about users will only increase as research techniques continue to evolve. Machines are simply better than people at managing many variables at once.

When I worked with R.H. Donnelley, which I mentioned in the last chapter, I knew from the start there were many different attributes that could drive segmentation of the consumers who would visit the site to read and post reviews of local businesses. The user interviews conducted with a range of potential users led to a long list of potential segmentation options, which in turn led to an extensive survey for data gathering. An iterative process of cluster analysis on the survey results revealed that the best way to segment these consumers was based on a combination of attributes, including their usage of certain types of Web sites, their reliance on expert and consumer ratings and reviews, and their history contributing such ratings and reviews. Armed with this quantitative data, I created personas out of these segments, which made the users come to life for the company. The personas and the quantitative data behind them revealed many insights that guided decisions about the overall strategy, as well as feature prioritization and marketing plans.

Here are the pros and cons for the quantitative approach.

Pros:

- Quantitative techniques, in combination with human smarts, generate the personas. Human bias influences this approach less than the others, since you have quantitative data not only to defend the personas you've created, but to test multiple segmentation models in the first place. To a skeptical stakeholder, this sophisticated process is likely to dispel any doubts he or she might have about personas as a valid decision-making tool.
- The iterative approach finds the best solution. Where the other approaches test one segmentation option, this approach iteratively finds the one segmentation model, among a great many possibilities, that you can best use to create personas. (You're still guiding the decisions about which segmentation model to ultimately use, but you have more data and more options for doing so.) It can reveal surprising patterns in the data that no one else would otherwise have considered, and it can lead to better insights about users and better actions to satisfy those users. It helps teams think in new ways.
- More variables can be examined. Machines are better at juggling a ton of different factors at once and looking for patterns and differences that the human eye can't discover. Cluster analysis can show you things you didn't know to look for.

Cons:

- This approach requires significant effort. This type of statistical analysis takes time and is iterative, so total project length can vary from seven to ten weeks. Like all the approaches, it's mostly a serial process, since each step uses the previous step as an input (interviews to hypotheses to survey to cluster analysis).
- You need more specialized skill sets. There's a good chance you'll need to bring in a statistical analyst for this approach—someone who can apply various analysis techniques to the data. It's an advanced set of skills that you'll learn to admire deeply!
- The results could introduce new ways of thinking that could be more complicated or uncomfortable to the business stakeholders. The segmentation model revealed through cluster analysis may not be what anyone expected. It might involve a combination of many factors and be difficult to summarize. If the new segmentation goes against existing assumptions and ways of doing business, it can be a tough sell, but at least you'll have evidence to back up the major changes you'll be proposing.

Use this approach if:

- You have time and money to invest.
- Your stakeholders need to see quantitative data to believe and use your personas.
- You want to explore multiple segmentation models to find the right one.
- You believe your personas will be driven by multiple variables, but you're not sure which ones are most important.

How you read the following chapters will depend entirely on which approach to creating personas you choose. Think of this as a kind of *Choose Your Own Adventure* book. The next chapter will dive into qualitative research techniques, focusing primarily on user interviews, and it applies to all three approaches described earlier. Chapter 5, on quantitative research, focuses primarily on surveys and is relevant to the second approach (for testing your segmentation) and third approach (for generating your segmentation). Chapter 6, on segmentation, is relevant to all three approaches and will cover how to do qualitative and quantitative segmentation. The rest of the chapters are useful regardless of which method you choose for creating personas.

Here's a quick cheat sheet for choosing your own adventure for the next three chapters:

READING THE NEXT CHAPTERS

Approach	Chapters to read, in order
Qualitative personas	Chapter 4: Conducting Qualitative User Research Chapter 6: Generating Persona Segmentation (qualitative)
Qualitative personas with quantitative validation	Chapter 4: Conducting Qualitative User Research Chapter 6: Generating Persona Segmentation (qualitative) Chapter 5: Conducting Quantitative User Research
Quantitative personas	Chapter 4: Conducting Qualitative User Research Chapter 5: Conducting Quantitative User Research Chapter 6: Generating Persona Segmentation (quantitative)

4 Conducting Qualitative User Research

I WAS ASKED RECENTLY to create personas for a company without talking to any of its customers. Several years ago, this was all too common and wouldn't have even make me flinch. But now, the idea of creating personas without meeting any users is like trying to plant flowers in a bed of rocks. It just feels wrong, and I know it probably won't work.

This particular company had data on its users. There were spreadsheets on the products the users had purchased, as well as their age, gender, marital status, and number of kids. The company had the facts, but no flavor. I had no information about their users' goals, knew nothing about their attitudes, and only had a little bit of information about their behavior. Trying to create personas based on only these facts was quite painful, because without talking to these users, I had no feel for them. I was simply making things up, without any justification for the attributes I gave to them.

Personas work because they tap into a primal part of our brain: We all respond to *stories*. When we hear a story, we're able to put ourselves in the shoes of the characters, and we are drawn along by the narrative. Our instincts toward empathy kick in.

Qualitative research is all about finding stories. You meet the characters, you listen to the plot lines for their goals and behaviors, and from the way they tell their stories, you discover their attitudes. Understanding breeds empathy, and empathy enables you to generalize and retell their stories as personas.

This chapter discusses three types of qualitative research for creating personas:

- **One-on-one interviews,** the most common approach used for personas.
- **Field studies** in which you go to users' offices or homes, watch their normal routine, and also interview them.
- **Usability tests** that consist in watching people use your site to perform tasks in order to learn about real-life behaviors and obstacles.

You'll notice that focus groups are not listed here. While useful for certain activities such as concept testing, focus groups are not particularly useful for generating personas. Individual voices can be drowned out by groupthink, and since personas are all about understanding and describing individual voices, this approach is risky.

Regardless of the method, qualitative research is particularly effective at uncovering things that you *don't* know. It's open and exploratory, unlike a survey, which is best at testing what you think you already know. When you are conducting any type of qualitative research, it is vital that you are open to discovering new things that might contradict existing assumptions.

This openness is perhaps the biggest challenge when you are conducting qualitative research. Even when I'm diving into a new subject area, I find that I bring existing assumptions to interviews, field studies, or usability tests. I have theories about who these users are and what they need. Subconsciously, when I conduct the research, I look for evidence to confirm what I already believe, rather than opening myself up to new insights. For this type of research, I find it's helpful to work with a colleague, because together, we can try to catch each other's assumptions and hear what the other person might have missed.

Whether you're creating qualitative or quantitative personas, the three research techniques covered in this chapter are the primary source of your segmentation model. Through talking with and observing users, you can gather a list of goals, attitudes, and behaviors that can become potential ways of segmenting your audience and thus defining personas.

Conducting Interviews

In the qualitative research toolbox, interviews often have the best return on investment. For most organizations, it's relatively easy to find users to interview, it doesn't cost much (if anything) to talk with people in person or over the phone, and the potential for learning new things about your users is enormous.

Interviews work best when you conduct them one user at a time, so you can devote your attention fully to each individual voice. They also work best as informal, loosely structured conversations, rather than as readings of a rigid list of questions to the user. If all you do is follow an existing list of questions and you never dive deeper or deviate from the agenda, you reduce the chance of learning something new—something that perhaps you didn't even think to ask about. Serendipity and surprise lead to insights, and those are best achieved by allowing the conversation to go wherever it leads. Sometimes it is a useless tangent, but sometimes it reveals a goal, attitude, or behavior that changes how you think about the users.

Every interview should be a unique journey through that particular user's story.

VistaPrint, a company mentioned in Chapter 2, based its functionality and design on the assumption that all of its users appreciated the ability to customize their particular business cards or other printed material. When my team and I began interviewing users, our questions were geared toward understanding which features should be added to VistaStudio, the Web application that enabled users to customize their designs. But a few of the interviews led us somewhere else entirely. Instead of adding features and more design flexibility, some users wanted them removed, preferring a simpler, templated approach. These people were motivated by speed, not by perfectionism, and their wish was to avoid VistaStudio entirely. This insight, later tested in an extensive survey, evolved into a separate persona and greatly affected the redesign of the site. If we hadn't been listening in the interviews for things we didn't know, we would have missed this important discovery.

Serendipity and surprise lead to insights, and those are best achieved by allowing the conversation to go wherever it leads.

Who to Interview

The first question that arises is who do you interview? The short answer is that you need to talk with as wide a range of different types of users as possible. Qualitative research is more about breadth than depth when it comes to selecting interviewees.

But here you're faced with a chicken-and-egg problem. You want to talk with users from every segment, but you don't know the segments yet, so how can you guarantee you'll talk with equal users from each eventual segment? You can't.

But you have to start somewhere, and undoubtedly *some* knowledge about users exists in your organization, so start there. Sit down with your colleagues. Executive team members have some assumptions (and perhaps some data) about the types of users they serve. The marketing department could have an existing segmentation with which they operate. The customer service, sales, and training departments have direct contact with users and can talk about types of users off the top of their heads. In addition, you can use third-party industry research to help create initial assumptions about the types of users to find and interview. You'll come away from these conversations with some initial assumptions about what types of users to interview.

If you are working on a real estate site for people like Francis the First-Time Home Buyer, you might find users to interview by starting with goals: a few home buyers, a few home sellers, a few apartment hunters, a few refinancers, and so on. You might also go for a range of experience so that you get a couple of first-time buyers and a couple of experienced buyers.

One thing to remember about finding a range of users is that goals, attitudes, and behaviors matter most. Getting a range of ages, incomes, and other demographics is less useful (though still nice to have), because demographics aren't as helpful in determining how to segment personas. Similarly, for certain companies, it may help to talk to users in different geographies, but it isn't necessarily critical, as long as you're getting a range of goals, attitudes, and behaviors. (If your site is global, however, it's wise to interview users in various countries to see if key differences in goals, attitudes, or behaviors will impact your personas.)

Make sure to talk to at least a couple of power users. These are the loyal customers who are very active and are likely to have a great deal of feedback compared with the majority of customers who might not have strong opinions about your site. Power users are better at coming up with new ideas and insights, since they are more engaged and emotionally invested.

I mentioned previously that a specialty retailer I worked with had many loyal customers who were a joy to interview. My team and I learned a great deal from this company's power users, including things we never would have thought of on our own. For example, when the company launched a new Web site feature enabling users to see which stores carried a particular item in a particular size and color, people started using the feature in unexpected ways. Interviewees told us that they would use the tool to minimize shipping costs: They would add multiple items to their shopping cart, then see if there was a single store that carried all these items. If so, they could have all the items shipped together for a flat $5 shipping rate, which wouldn't be possible otherwise. Without interviewing power users, we never would have discovered this insight and its implications for shipping policies.

So how do you find these people? Start with existing customers. With any luck, your customer database has some information in it that will help you narrow down the list of potential victims—I mean interviewees! If you need more information, you can create a screener as part of your recruiting process. You can look for interviewees by either calling many of them and asking them the screener questions, or by emailing an invitation including these key questions to a large list of users to see who responds with answers that match your criteria.

Here's an example of an invitation email:

> **Subject: RealEstateCentral.com invitation:**
> **$100 for your feedback**
>
> Hi Rick,
>
> As a valued customer, your feedback is important to us. We would like to invite you to participate in an interview that will help guide future improvements to RealEstateCentral.com. This phone interview will take no more than an hour, and we will pay you $100 for your time.
>
> If you would like to participate, please answer the questions below and reply to this email by December 7.
>
> 1. What times would you be available on the following days for a one-hour phone interview?
>
>   Wednesday, Dec. 13
>   Thursday, Dec. 14
>   Friday, Dec. 15

2. What have you used RealEstateCentral.com for in the past? (Check all that apply.)

   __ Buying a home
   __ Selling a home
   __ Looking for an apartment
   __ Refinancing a mortgage
   __ Looking for insurance
   __ Other (please specify)

3. Approximately how many times have you visited the site in the past year?

4. How many homes have you owned in your lifetime?

5. What do you do for a living?

6. What is your phone number?

If you are selected for an interview, we will contact you by Dec. 9 with the details. Thank you!

Steve Mulder
[Include job title and full contact information]

A few quick notes:

- Make the Subject line as specific as possible to avoid spam filters (though this will be an ongoing challenge).

- For the same reason, make sure the email comes from an email address the user will recognize (@RealEstateCentral.com).

- Incentives are a great way to attract more interview candidates. I typically offer $50–100, depending on how difficult it is to find these types of users. A gift certificate or special offer can work, but cash is often better. It's a small price to pay for insights that could change your business.

- Make sure to give dates for when the users need to reply, when you'll contact them, and when the interviews are.

- Ask about their profession, so you can weed out people who work in marketing or design or are otherwise not "typical" users.
- Keep the questions to a minimum, because a long email survey is likely to keep many people from responding. Ask just enough questions to know if each person matches your criteria. The other questions you can ask during the interview itself.

Recruiting users from your existing customer database can be relatively easy, but remember that these are just your *existing* customers. Ideally you want to talk with non-customers as well, or even lapsed customers, to get the full range of potential users. For this, perhaps you have a database of registered non-customers, which is a helpful starting point. Remember that you might have more phone numbers for these users than email addresses.

You might need help finding non-customers. One inexpensive solution is to use your friends and family network. Sending an invitation to colleagues, which they can forward to anyone they know who fits a certain profile, can be very effective as long as you're clear about what type of people you're looking for. The potential for bias is a bit higher; after all, you might be talking to the husband of the VP of Strategy, who might be a little reluctant to criticize your organization in an interview. But the friends and family network can yield many great interview candidates.

Another approach is to go where your users are and recruit there. This can be a physical place like a store, or a Web site discussion board, email list, or blog. When I was working on a community-driven site, I once posted an invitation to craigslist.org and received an enormous number of qualified responses.

Finally, you can use recruiting companies to find users for you. These companies, many of which will also facilitate the research if you wish, excel at finding users that match a specific set of criteria. As the list of criteria gets longer, the price goes up, as does the amount of time it takes to work with the recruiter to find the right people. If you have very specific needs, try finding a recruiter with previous experience in that industry. In addition, beware of recruiters who reuse the same people over and over again; these "serial testers" often seem to make a living getting paid for this type of research, and as a result, you may not get real-life data.

There's one more key question about who to interview: How many interviews should you conduct? A rule of thumb is to interview five users per segment. I realize the same chicken-and-egg problem arises, but start with your existing assumptions. For our real estate site, this means five home buyers, five sellers, five apartment hunters, and so on. If you're a bank and have two completely different sites for consumers and for businesses, think about how you might segment the consumers and segment the businesses. If your users are more homogenous, five per segment is usually enough. If you see a great deal of variety in goals, attitudes, and behaviors, you may want to increase it to ten per segment. I don't recommend more than that, because the law of diminishing returns kicks in. As you interview users, the rate at which you learn new things decreases over time. Sure, you may gain a new insight in the thirtieth interview, but possibly at the price of sitting through six utterly useless interviews beforehand.

Be flexible about who you interview. If after interviewing 10 people you realize you're missing an entire type of user, add a few more into the mix. If you've reached 18 and haven't learned anything new since number 13, cancel the remaining interviews.

Interview Logistics

While you're planning who to interview, you also need to figure out the logistics of where, when, and how.

You can conduct these one-on-one interviews in person or over the phone. In-person interviews have the advantages of encouraging a better personal connection (often resulting in more insights) and allowing you to read body language. The downside is the travel time (for the user or for you) and expense. I typically do user interviews over the phone and find that an informally facilitated phone interview can reveal just as many insights as an in-person conversation.

For phone interviews, find a quiet room and a quality conference phone. Trust me, you won't want to conduct a lot of interviews with a phone handset cradled on your shoulder.

If users are traveling to you, set up a quiet room without a lot of distractions. Users are less likely to be honest inside a company's headquarters, so consider a neutral third-party location.

When scheduling interviews, keep in mind that many people in your targeted audience work during the day, and thus they will prefer to do interviews first thing in the morning, over lunch, or after work. Try to be flexible. Also, don't create a schedule that's cruel to yourself: Allow for breaks between interviews, don't forget to eat, and try not to conduct more than five or six interviews in one day. You want time to absorb what you're hearing.

Each interview should be an hour or less. There are exceptions to this rule of thumb, but in general, you'll start to lose users' attention after an hour. You'll find that interviews vary in length as you're conducting them, with particularly talkative or insightful users easily filling an hour, and less helpful interviews ending after 20 or 30 minutes.

Finally, don't conduct interviews alone and try to take notes yourself. It's extremely difficult to be engaged in a conversation with someone and at the same time attempt to document everything you're hearing. Recording the audio is a good solution, but I find it's more efficient to have a dedicated note-taker (who is generally quiet the entire time) in the room. Four ears are better than two. However, if the interviews are in person, don't make the interviewees feel like you're ganging up on them by including even more observers.

Interview Topics

Because interviews leading into personas are more useful when they're more informal, create a checklist of topics to cover, rather than a verbatim questionnaire to follow. You may use a default order when running through the topics, but this will vary depending on where each conversation takes you. Also, don't feel obligated to cover every topic in every interview. Moments of insight more commonly occur outside of the prepared questions.

Here are topics I typically cover in interviews for persona creation:

- **History with the company**

  When and how they first heard about the company
  Why they first interacted with the company
  What their first interactions with the company were like (any channel: store, Web, phone, catalog, etc.)
  When, how, and why they first visited the Web site
  If they accomplished that initial goal on the site and why or why not
  What their first impressions were
  What made them come back
  How often they visit the site
  Whether they've registered, made a purchase, and so on, and if so, what they purchased, why, and how much

- **Domain experience and knowledge**

  How they'd describe their knowledge about the domain
  How often they've accomplished tasks related to this domain
  What other Web sites they've used for doing these things
  When and how often they use them

  What they like/dislike about the other sites
  How this site compares

- **Goals and behaviors**

  What they did on their most recent visit to the site—step by step
  What their typical process is when visiting the site
  Which features or content they use most/least and why
  Things they'd like to do on the site but can't

Things they wish were easier or different
How, when, and why they use a different channel instead of the site (email, phone, physical location, etc.)

Attitudes and motivators

How they'd describe the site to a friend
How they'd describe the process of using the site
What they like most/least about the site
What would influence them to use the site more

Opportunities

How they respond to new ideas/features/content that the site is considering
How often they would use the new features, and why
Of all the things discussed, what the most important improvement is

The checklist of questions used for VistaPrint user interviews is shown below as a more detailed example.

History with VistaPrint

How long have you used VistaPrint?
How did you first hear about VistaPrint?
Why did you first choose VistaPrint?
What were your impressions of VistaPrint before making that first purchase?
How about after your first purchase?
Why did you choose VistaPrint the next time?
How often do you visit the VistaPrint Web site?
How often do you order through VistaPrint? How much do you spend with VistaPrint?

Domain experience and knowledge

Tell me a bit about what you do: industry, business size, role, and so on
Do you use [product-type]? How do you go about getting those? What source do you use and why? How much do

you spend? (Product list: business cards, letterhead, flyers, postcards, brochures, folders, folded cards, return address labels, invitations, printed magnets)

How do you find out about new things like this?

How do you think VistaPrint compares with [competitors]?

▶ Goals and behaviors

What types of projects have you used VistaPrint for?

What's your typical process for a project like this? (content, design, graphics, approval, payment, delivery)

What brings you to the site?

How do you usually get the design you want? Have you used the site to create your own designs? What did you think of that experience?

Have you ever called or emailed VistaPrint? For what? How did that go?

▶ Attitudes and motivators

Overall, how would you describe what it's like doing business with VistaPrint? (adjectives)

What do you like best about VistaPrint?

What do you like least about VistaPrint?

When you print something, how important to you is price (from 1, not at all important to 5, extremely important)? Why? How would you rate VistaPrint on price (from 1, terrible to 5, excellent)? Why?

Same question for design template choices

Same question on having an easy-to-use Web site

Same question for print quality

Same question for timeliness

Is there anything else that's important to you?

Do you get emails from VistaPrint? How often? Are they useful?

Do you feel like you have a good sense of everything that VistaPrint offers?

- **Opportunities**

  Are there things you can't do with VistaPrint that you would like to do?
  Is there anything else that would make your life easier?
  How likely would you be to use the following things if they were available? (List of features to test)

Finally, here are some tips for conducting the actual interviews:

- One of the best ways to discover insights is to have users walk you through their typical process. Give them an open-ended question and let them talk for as long as possible. Slow them down and have them cover every step.
- Part of that deserves repeating: Let them talk for as long as possible. The more you do the talking, the less you learn from what they have to say. One trick is to pause fairly often. People don't like silences, and often fill them by speaking more.
- Avoid asking questions that have yes or no answers. Get them talking.
- Beware of using jargon. Tailor your language to what is familiar to the user. For instance, they might not know what "channels" are.
- Put some distance between yourself and the Web site so that the user is more likely to be honest. Talk about what "they" (the Web site team) might do to improve the site, not what "we" might do.

Output of Interviews

What do you get out of the interviews when you're done, besides a feeling of being overwhelmed with raw notes? The main outputs are candidates for segmentation and opportunities for testing.

First, when you sum up all the interviews, you'll have a master list of user goals, behaviors, and attitudes you're heard from users. You may sense which of these candidates will be most useful for segmentation, but you'll find that it is worth considering the entire list when you're ready for that step. (We'll tackle this in Chapter 6.)

Second, if you plan to conduct quantitative research, you'll have a list of ideas that you want to test. These can be new feature requests or ideas for improvement. You may have also heard other themes that need validation, such as a few people mentioning that they often get no results when they conduct a search (time to check the log files), or the tendency for wealthier users to like the site more (make sure to check for that in the survey).

A final note about interviews: Drawing conclusions from several interviews can be risky, especially if you don't take the time to analyze the output and find the nuggets of insight that could be useful. Distributing the raw interview notes can be dangerous and can encourage business stakeholders to draw their own conclusions, rather than reacting to a well-thought-out summary and a framework for viewing the interview findings. The interpretation of the data is at least as important as the data itself.

Running Field Studies

In interviews, you learn what users *tell* you about their goals, behavior, and attitudes. In field studies, you can actually see for yourself. Observing natural behavior can be an eye-opening experience, because as mentioned earlier, people aren't always conscious of (or willing to share) the truth about how they use or what they want from Web sites. Sometimes this type of research is called *contextual inquiry*, because you gain more context about where, when, how, and why these people use your site.

Field studies do double duty—they enable you to observe natural behavior and typical goals, but at the same time, they help you ascertain the user's attitudes and perceptions having to do with their goals and behavior. Like interviews, field studies occur one user at a time, but this time the data comes from the user's native environment—whether that's an office, a home, or even an "in the field" location, such as a retail store in which you observe real-world shopping behavior.

There are two basic types of field studies: appointments and intercepts. Appointments are made in advance, like interviews. Users agree that you can observe them, essentially tailing them as they follow their everyday routine using your site and other sites and channels to perform their common tasks. You ask questions along the way to better understand what they're doing and why. These sessions are often two or three hours long, but they can go longer if you really wish to immerse yourself in their world.

Intercepts are a bit different, because you don't recruit users beforehand. Instead, you go to where multiple users are (such as a retail store or a trading floor), and you observe them without their knowledge. After watching them for a while, you approach a particular user you want to understand better, and ask if he or she is willing to participate in an interview based on what you've seen so far. The user can continue to perform daily tasks with you watching, or you can turn the encounter into a one-on-one interview, depending on what you're trying to discover. The advantage of intercepts is that you can be more certain you're watching normal behavior, because unlike appointments, the users don't know you're watching. The potential downside is that you don't know how many users will agree to a follow-up interview, or how much time they'll have.

Another variant of the field study occurs when no direct contact with users ever occurs. You simply observe their behavior from a distance without interviewing them. However, I find that if you're going to do a field study, it's worth combining observation with interviewing in order to get the complete picture. You want to understand *what* they do as well as *why* they do it.

As you may have guessed, field studies are more of an investment than interviews. They take at least twice as long to conduct, and that doesn't include travel to and from the different locations. In addition, recruiting users for field studies can be more difficult, because they're committing to a longer session, and they might be reluctant to have you tail them.

But frankly, there's nothing better than going to where your users are, watching them for a while, and then asking them questions in order to gain new insights into who they are and how you can better serve them. If it's important to your site's success to understand the environment in which your users work, try to make a field study happen.

There's nothing better than going to where your users are, watching them for a while, and then asking them questions in order to gain new insights.

When you're conducting a field study, the most important thing to remember is that you're there to observe natural behavior. We know from Heisenberg's Uncertainty Principle that it's impossible to observe something without affecting it, but your goal is to not disturb users' normal routines. To accomplish this, talk as little as possible, especially early on. Set the stage by explaining why you're there, and then encourage the users to do what they would normally do (in the relevant domain, of course; you don't want to watch them taking out the trash—this isn't a silly reality TV show). Then shut up.

Users may take a while to get comfortable with being watched, or they may never get used to it. For instance, they may become chatterbox tour guides as they walk you through their normal process, and never really fall back into their normal, quiet routines. Your job is to be quiet and take notes. If you see something you want to ask about, write it down and ask later so that you don't disturb their normal flow. If you do have to disturb them, try to confine yourself to asking simple questions about what they're doing, rather then evaluative questions about why, because making users reflect on their actions pulls them farther away from normal behavior.

The second part of the field study session closely resembles the interviews described earlier. Make sure to come with a list of topics to ask about (see the list of interview topics earlier in this chapter), but also make sure to spend time asking questions about what you see. How do they use the site? When do they go to a competitor or a different channel? What shortcuts or tricks do they use along the way? What other applications do they use? What features do they not use? This is the time to encourage the user to self-reflect. Many times these follow-up questions spark insightful discussions about why users do certain things. Sometimes it is useful to have them walk you through what they did earlier in order to trigger memories. Your overall goal is to put what you see into the larger context of what they're thinking.

As with interviews, it's wise to conduct field studies in pairs, so you ensure thorough note taking (and so that you have another pair of eyes and ears to validate what you see and hear). Again, don't overwhelm users by bringing more than one person with you. I also recommend bringing along a camera to record the environment in which users operate.

The output of field studies is similar to that of interviews, though the quality and quantity can be richer because of the direct observation. You'll have a master list of goals, behaviors, and attitudes as segmentation options, as well as many ideas and opportunities you may wish to test.

A couple of years ago, when some of my colleagues worked with a retailer to create a new ecommerce site, the assumption was that the online experience would mirror the in-store experience as closely as possible. To understand the in-store experience, my colleagues conducted a field study in a few different stores, followed by one-on-one phone interviews to ensure that they had talked to the full breadth of customers. They discovered that although there were some elements of the in-store experience that users demanded to be preserved on the site (e.g., easy checkout), there were also key differences. For example, although shoppers loved spending time in the stores browsing and looking for the perfect item, they disliked doing this on Web sites. When shopping online, they wanted to find clothing much more quickly and by very specific attributes such as size, color, and price range. Shoppers wanted the interaction to feel different from the store. Insights such as this one were discovered only because my colleagues took the time to observe natural shopping behavior in addition to talking to users.

Performing Usability Tests

Usability testing is a classic qualitative technique for observing user behavior. You sit users down in front of your site one at a time, give them tasks to perform, and watch to see where they encounter obstacles. Users often supply their perceptions as well, so you get both behaviors and attitudes as output.

However, traditional usability testing often isn't as helpful for creating personas. I rarely use it because I learn more about the site's problems than I learn about its users. When you give specific tasks to users, the test becomes about the user goals you have chosen instead of the users' unique goals. Because goals are so critical to understanding what users need and how to best serve them, usability testing may bias the persona creation process.

If you can't run a full field study but still want to observe some user behavior, consider conducting usability testing that's more open-ended. Rather than supplying users with tasks, ask them what their typical uses are and if they'll show you how they use the site for these purposes. The usability test transforms into more of a field study, since you're observing and not directing the users' actions.

If you're running a usability test to inform the creation of personas, try running it remotely. Use screen-sharing software (e.g., Macromedia Breeze Live or WebEx) to see users' actions and a conference phone to talk. When people are using their own computers in their own environment, more natural behavior can emerge than in a traditional lab setting.

You saw earlier that some VistaPrint customers surprised my team in the interviews by requesting *fewer* customization features for designing their business cards or other print material. A few of them complained that parts of the process felt too time-consuming or difficult. But, as often happens in interviews, they couldn't necessarily remember where in the process they felt this way, so we didn't know which features were creating obstacles for them. To figure this out, we conducted a usability test (with specific tasks as well as open-ended time) to learn more about this issue. Although many users had few problems with the site, there was a segment of users that corresponded to the segment we interviewed who didn't want full customization. We could now observe exactly which features slowed them down or affected their perceptions, and make sure that we treated these features as optional and outside of the normal flow in the redesigned site. Without observing first-hand what we heard in the interviews, we would not have been able to target improvements so specifically.

Other Resources

As you're pulling together a plan for qualitative research, don't forget to look around your organization for any existing research on your users. Each group (Sales, Marketing, Customer Service, Training, etc.) will have its own slant on the information, but those unique perspectives can reveal insights that will influence how you conduct interviews, field studies, or usability tests.

It's worth asking around for the findings or raw notes on any of the following:

- Previously conducted user interviews
- Focus groups
- Usability tests
- Surveys
- Customer service/support reports
- Financial analysis of user purchases
- And so on

In addition, find out if any third-party research was conducted for the company in any of these areas. When consultants come in, they always leave behind a report or two (or ten).

Speaking of third-party research, there's a decent chance an organization is writing about your users somewhere. Organizations such as Forrester Research and JupiterResearch publish a huge amount of data spanning all manner of industries, and often they have a wealth of information about users for those industries. In addition, look for organizations that focus specifically on your industry vertical. For example, Corporate Insight publishes highly regarded, in-depth reports on the financial services industry.

As with any research, some parts of it will be more helpful than others. Once, while working on a site redesign, I was given the findings of a previous user survey and was most amused to find a slide showing the results of the question, "What colors do users prefer?" Needless to say, I did not feel obligated to take the bar charts literally and use "cool tones" in the new design, as 44 percent of users seemed to desire. A critical part of conducting any research is knowing which data is important and which is, well, not so much.

Congratulations on reaching the end of a very long chapter. Qualitative research is a critical step to creating personas, so it's worth spending the time to get it right. If you're creating qualitative personas, skip to Chapter 6 on segmentation. If you can add quantitative research into the mix, Chapter 5 awaits you.

5 Conducting Quantitative User Research

BECAUSE USER-CENTERED design works, I apply it not only to creating Web sites for end users, but to internal processes as well. If I know the decision makers I'm working with and understand their goals, behaviors, and attitudes, I'm much more likely to succeed as I propose directions for the site. I remember a particular project kick-off meeting with a new client during which my team was describing our proposed process for the redesign. We would create three different visual design directions, then narrow them down to one chosen direction. Usually, companies we work with love this step, because most clients have a strong opinion about what good design is. But not this crowd. Instead, they wanted to know what data they would use to decide between the three designs. This was such a metrics-driven organization that they were unwilling to make such critical decisions based on their instincts alone. It was an eye-opening moment in the project and, frankly, wonderful because it provided immediate insight on how to work with them effectively.

As a result, we added concept testing to our process, conducting a survey to test each visual design direction against the targeted brand attributes. The quantitative data made the decision-making process easy for the group, and we knew immediately that we would have to apply quantitative research techniques throughout the project to be successful. So we used them for personas as well, utilizing a survey, site traffic analysis, and CRM (Customer Relationship Management) data analysis to generate quantitative personas.

The Value of Quantitative Research and Analysis

For some people, proof for any decision resides in numerical data, and this is where quantitative research fits the bill. Surprisingly, few companies use quantitative analysis and traditional market research tools in developing personas. This is despite the fact that quantitative research can provide a great deal of value and insight to most persona projects. This can be attributed to a few factors. First, the persona movement did not originate with the market research community but with the information architecture and user experience communities, which are more interested in art and craft than in the science of market research groups. Second, because the level of interaction between user and company on a Web site is far more complex than most other non-store channels (think about the level of interaction a user has with a company's Web site compared to the level of interaction he or she has with the same company's catalog or direct mail), Web site teams needed more complex insight into user interactions than most market research groups can provide. Third, for most of its short history, the Web has been relegated, in most companies, to second-string status as a marketing channel (quite wrongly, but that is a whole other book). As a result, market researchers have rarely been interested in addressing that channel.

Instead, they've often left the Web group to its own devices when divining users' intentions.

On the whole, this benign neglect has not been such a bad thing. Without the constraints of the traditional market research focus on demographics, customer value, and share of wallet, Web groups have developed two key insights that market researchers can stand to learn from. The first is that focusing on and segmenting users based on their goals, behaviors, and attitudes (rather than demographics) is often far more effective at identifying key differences that the company can use effectively. Second, by taking a lot of user information and packaging it in the easy-to-access interface of a character's story, companies can make their user research information much more accessible to everyone within the organization than the standard slide after slide of tables and numbers. This, in turn, drives stronger company alignment around user needs, leading to more effective strategy and execution.

But this benign neglect may be coming to an end. Recently, we've begun to see a shift in how companies treat their Web sites. Increasingly, companies are realizing that their Web site needs to be a cornerstone of their marketing, sales, and servicing efforts. As a result, market research groups are increasingly getting involved in the decision-making process around the Web site and are challenging Web groups to apply the same rigor to user research as has been traditionally applied to the company's other user research efforts. I've heard many sad stories of persona creators being vigorously challenged on the statistical relevance and accuracy of the recommendations they've made to a multibillion-dollar company based on the findings of 15 interviews. As this trend continues, both user experience and Web groups are going to have to get comfortable applying the quantitative analysis needed to convince traditional market research groups as well as senior management. The good news is that in addition to satisfying market research groups, these tools and techniques can benefit the Web site and the user tremendously by helping to resolve weaknesses in the current user experience research and methodologies, resulting in a better experience for the customer.

So, why is quantitative research increasingly useful? The first obvious reason is that you can look at a larger number of users than you can with qualitative research. In qualitative research, you always wonder if you have talked to enough people. If you interview 10 people, you wonder if you should have interviewed 15. If you interview 15, you wonder if it should have been 20. Since many mid-to-large-size companies have thousands, if not millions of customers, finding a relatively cheap and fast way to understand the goals, behaviors, and attitudes of a large number of users is essential. Quantitative research provides tools for evaluating very large populations of users—in some cases, *all* the users—in a matter of weeks.

The second benefit of quantitative research is that it enables you to better judge the magnitude and priority of an effect, which is difficult to do with qualitative research. Take, for example, the case of a team of my colleagues who worked with BrownCo (a discount brokerage) to learn about their customers' online trading experiences. The team had conducted a dozen interviews and had developed quite a list of features, functionality, and user interface changes that BrownCo needed to make to the Web site in order to facilitate a better and more competitive user experience. However, BrownCo had limited development resources and needed the team to prioritize these changes. Based only on the qualitative interviews, this task was impossible. After all, how could they compare one customer's emphatic statement with another customer's equally emphatic statement? The team members could speculate and use their best judgment, but it was their carefully prepared quantitative research that provided specific answers. These quantitative answers were critical for determining the Web site's priorities from among a group of competing goals.

Finally, but perhaps most significantly, quantitative research enables more flexibility with what you can do with the data. Because quantitative data is numeric instead of textual in nature, it is more pliable and can be linked and compared to other pieces of numeric information, giving you a more complete view of the user than you'd get with qualitative data. One common technique is to tie the quantitative information from a survey to financial information from a customer record. This lets you estimate the financial value for each persona, which is a useful way to prioritize which personas to serve more effectively.

Quantitative data is more pliable and can be linked and compared to other pieces of numeric information, giving you a more complete view of the user than you'd get with qualitative data.

At a high level, quantitative research is particularly good at three things:

- **Testing hypotheses.** If you want to validate something you think you know, quantitative research is a perfect tool, because it gives you statistically significant evidence to prove or disprove your hypotheses. For example, if you suspect that first-time home buyers are more likely to use video tutorials than more experienced home buyers, you can test that hypothesis in a survey, while also looking at current usage in your log files. Also, if you've done qualitative segmentation based on interviews and want to validate it, a survey can provide supporting data.
- **Looking for patterns.** Quantitative research can also be effective at *refining* hypotheses, because it provides a large enough sample size of data for you to look for patterns using techniques such as cluster analysis. As you'll see in the next chapter, you can generate persona segmentation out of the quantitative data itself, even if you only have the most basic understanding of what could drive the segmentation.
- **Gaining new insight.** Finally, because quantitative information is numeric, it enables you to build upon your validated hypothesis to gain new insight into your users' behaviors. Once you understand how your users segment out, you can identify all the other differences between the segments—even differences you may not have thought about in the first place.

As discussed in Chapter 3, your decision to use quantitative research comes back to your audience, who will use the personas. Do they need statistically significant evidence before jumping onboard your personas bandwagon? If so, quantitative data is your ticket to stakeholder buy-in.

This chapter discusses the three types of quantitative research used for creating personas:

- **Surveys** are excellent for obtaining a large sample of responses on self-reported goals, behaviors, and attitudes. Surveys are typically the most useful quantitative method for creating personas because you can quickly cover a large number of users, easily gather data on almost any topic, and convert user goals, behaviors, and attitudes into numbers in order to segment, prioritize, and link user information to other sources of data.
- **Site traffic analysis** of log files helps you understand the actual behaviors of users on your site. By analyzing all the visits to your site, you're able to deal with the entire user base rather than just a small sample. This translates into extremely detailed information on actual Web usage—more detailed than you can obtain about any other channel to date.
- **CRM (Customer Relationship Management) data analysis** can enhance your understanding of users by allowing you to examine the data you already have in customer records: their transactions (purchases, dates, channels, etc.), financial data (overall worth over time), and demographic data.

Your goal is to have a complete portrait of every user on whom you have data:

- What users say: survey data
- What users do: site traffic analysis, CRM data, and self-reported survey data
- What users are worth: CRM data and self-reported survey data

The more complete your record is for each survey respondent, the more attributes you have to work with when validating or generating your segmentation and making your personas real. One of the biggest strengths of quantitative data comes from leveraging multiple sources of information in order to more fully understand users. In my experience, some of the greatest insights I have uncovered in personas have come from linking user information from two or more data sources.

Quantitative research requires more careful planning than open-ended qualitative research, because you only get out of it what you put in. Once your survey is deployed, you can't add more questions that might have been helpful. Quantitative research brings a bit more science into the art of creating personas, so preparation is worth the time you spend on it. Therefore, before you dive into the research techniques, the first step is to determine what type of research you need, given your objectives.

Planning Quantitative Research

The field of quantitative research and analysis is broad and deep. It is very easy to be either so overwhelmed that you find it difficult to get started, or to plunge in too quickly and spend the next six months uncovering a wide variety of insights that don't advance your understanding of users in any meaningful or actionable way.

To avoid these pitfalls, plan ahead. If you're conducting quantitative research, follow these steps:

1. **Identify what you want to learn.**

   The most common mistake in conducting quantitative research is to dive in and start writing survey questions or looking at log file data before you stop to figure out exactly what you're trying to learn. Look before you leap. Measure twice, cut once. A stitch in time saves nine. You get the idea. Because quantitative research and analysis take time, you should have a reason for every survey question you ask, every log file query you create, and every CRM report you run. Don't waste time on things that won't affect your personas, such as survey questions about users' favorite colors. On the other hand, you don't want to forget to ask something that you might need later. Thorough planning helps to ensure efficiency and comprehensiveness.

2. **Choose the right source of data.**

   Once you know what information you are looking for, the next step is to identify the best source of data for that information. In quantitative analysis, as in qualitative analysis, different sources of data are better suited to answer different questions. In addition, different sources of data have different strengths and weaknesses. Choosing the right source, or the right mix of sources, will help you save a lot of time in analysis as you search for the answers.

3. **Clean and prep the data.**

   Once you have all the data you need, don't jump right into analysis. To ensure valid results, you can't skip what is probably the most time-intensive step: evaluating the data for accuracy and completeness and filling in any gaps. In 100 percent of my experiences with these kinds of projects, I discovered problems with the data that I had to uncover, understand, and address. If I didn't spend the time to do this, these problems would have completely skewed the results of my analysis. Skipping over this step is the second biggest mistake people make when performing quantitative analysis.

4. **Choose the right analysis.**

   Finally, once you have all the data cleaned, you need to know which quantitative analysis technique to use in order to process the data into the insights you are looking for. Chapter 6 will explore this further.

Qualitative Personas with Quantitative Validation

If you're creating qualitative personas and using quantitative research to validate your qualitative segmentation (discussed in Chapter 6), you want to be very specific about exactly which attribute(s) you believe define your segmentation. For example, let's say that after interviewing 15 users for your real estate site, you believe the personas will be primarily defined by a combination of the following attributes:

- Goal for visiting the site (e.g., buying home, finding apartment, selling home)
- Knowledge of real estate

With your segmentation narrowed down, you can brainstorm ways to gather data on these attributes in order to test whether they define differences between users that you can develop into personas. In other words, you want to make sure that users who have different goals and different levels of knowledge are actually different enough in terms of what they need from the site. If they have the same needs, there's no point creating different personas for them.

Here are potential methods for gathering data on each attribute:

- Goal for visiting the site (e.g., buying home, finding apartment, selling home)
    - Survey question on the frequency of site visits for each possible user goal
    - Survey question on the importance of each possible goal to the user
    - Site traffic analysis on how clicks to various sections of the site (on buying, renting, etc.) might correlate to other behaviors, such as registration, purchases, email response, customer service usage, and so on.
- Knowledge of real estate
    - Survey question on previous real estate experiences
    - Survey question on the user's self-perception of real estate expertise

Typically, there are multiple ways to gather data around a particular attribute, and it's worth spending time up front evaluating all the ways that might be useful. By the end of this exercise, you'll end up with a list of exactly what you need to ask in a survey or what you need to analyze in log files or CRM data, in order to test your segmentation.

One thing to keep in mind is that information about actual behavior is the most valuable, because it's the most accurate. You'll get more accurate results about site visits from log files than by asking users about site visits in a survey, because users often don't remember such details correctly, and their memories can be biased by their perceptions of your site or of themselves. Actions speak louder than words.

Now that you know precisely what information you need in order to test your qualitative segmentation, you can create a list of additional information you'd like to gather on users' goals, behaviors, attitudes, and demographics. For example, it might be interesting to discover whether your segments differ in other ways, such as use of the Internet, frequency of site visits, technology savvy, need for handholding, age, gender, and so on. Go back to your notes from the qualitative research to see what attributes you might pursue. Then explore those attributes through the same process just described, devising the best way to gather data on each attribute.

Quantitative Personas

If you're relying on quantitative research to generate your segmentation, then the first step is creating a list of all the potential segmentation options you've heard or considered thus far. I've found that the best way to walk through this is to use the following familiar categories:

- Goals
- Behaviors
- Attitudes
- Demographics

Go through the notes from the qualitative research and write down everything that could possibly define differences between people you talked to, including attributes that might only be secondary but are still worth gathering data on, such as age or income. You might need to prioritize this list later if there are too many items to research, but at this stage, comprehensiveness is the goal.

What follows is an example of this process played out for R.H. Donnelley, who wanted to create a site where consumers could read and contribute ratings and reviews of local businesses.

- Goals
  - Usage of different business categories (e.g., restaurants, retail stores, lawyers)
  - Importance of different business categories (e.g., restaurants, retail stores, lawyers)
  - Importance of being perceived as a community leader
  - Importance of being perceived as an expert
  - Importance of social networking
- Behaviors
  - Weekly usage of the Internet
  - Usage of the Internet to research each business category
  - Usage of offline resources to research each business category (yellow pages, newspaper, etc.)
  - Usage of Internet resources (mailing lists, blogs, portals, rating/review sites, etc.)
  - Usage of local search sites (Yahoo! Local, Yelp, yellow pages sites, etc.)
  - Usage of social networking sites (Friendster, LinkedIn, etc.)
  - Usage of expert ratings/reviews
  - Usage of consumer ratings/reviews
  - Contributions of ratings/reviews
- Attitudes
  - Degree of familiarity with each business category

  - Satisfaction with local search sites (Yahoo! Local, Yelp, yellow pages sites, etc.)
  - Importance of word of mouth for selecting products
  - Reliance on friends and family for selecting local businesses
  - Reliance on expert advice for selecting local businesses
  - Reasons for contributing ratings/reviews
  - Factors that make a review useful
  - Technology affinity, savvy
  - Degree of organization and planning ahead when searching

- Demographics

  - Age
  - Gender
  - Education
  - Income
  - Marital status
  - Kids
  - Years living in current town, neighborhood

The next step, as discussed in the previous section, is to explore all the ways you can gather data on each of these attributes. Below is an example from the same company:

- Usage of consumer ratings/reviews

  - Survey question on how often they read ratings/reviews when researching products
  - Survey question on how often they read ratings/reviews when researching local businesses
  - Site traffic analysis on the number of log-ins per month
  - Site traffic analysis on how many review pages users visit per session and per month
  - Site traffic analysis on any correlation between number of reviews read and click-through to the business Web site
  - CRM reporting on the number and dates of purchases reported back by business customers

Here's a paragraph worth repeating: One thing to keep in mind is that information about actual behavior is most valuable, because it's the most accurate. You'll get more accurate results about site visits from log files than by asking users about site visits in a survey, because users often don't remember such details correctly, and their memories can be biased by their perceptions of your site or of themselves. Actions speak louder than words.

Information about actual behavior is most valuable, because it's the most accurate. Actions speak louder than words.

As you might expect, this process takes time. I find that the most efficient way to tackle it is to lock myself in a room with my colleagues and plenty of whiteboard space and/or sticky notes. After a couple of hours, we're left with a list of exactly which survey questions we need to ask, which log file queries to create, and which CRM reports to run. This planning process saves an enormous amount of time later, and it ensures that you'll get all the information you need and avoid discovering too late that you forgot to ask one critical survey question.

Testing Other Hypotheses and Opportunities

No matter which approach you're using to create personas, the qualitative research inevitably leads to some hypotheses that aren't related to segmentation. For example, for VistaPrint, my team and I had a sense from our user interviews that some existing customers simply weren't aware of the breadth of products VistaPrint offered. If we could validate this hypothesis, it would inform the upcoming redesign. So we explored different ways to gather data on this hypothesis:

- Site traffic analysis would tell us how many people navigate to each product page.
- A survey question would tell us how many people had previously purchased each type of product, either at VistaPrint or elsewhere.

- If our analysis of these two data points showed that different product pages weren't getting the amount of traffic that they should based on what we knew about purchase behavior, we'd have evidence of a lack of product awareness.
- In addition, we could ask a survey question testing users' knowledge of what VistaPrint offered, or another question on how much they felt they were aware of the range of VistaPrint's products.

There's no master list of hypotheses you might test in this way, because they vary tremendously by domain, company, and users. Ziv Yaar, contributing author of this book, covers his wall with hypotheses he'd like to test. For each hypothesis, he adds sticky notes detailing the data he'll need to test the hypothesis, with different colors representing the source of that data. This unique wallpaper sets the framework for the quantitative research, and often the framework for the overall business strategy as well.

Here are some of the types of hypotheses you might encounter:

- Brand perception and design issues that could be affecting business results
- Marketing reach issues that might prevent users from knowing about or receiving your message
- Product awareness, quality, or messaging issues
- Service and support issues
- Web site usability issues that could be affecting business results
- Channel usage behaviors or preferences that might influence overall business strategy
- Particular improvements, new products, features, or content that might better satisfy users

This last item is particularly important, because conducting quantitative research is an effective way to gather data for prioritizing

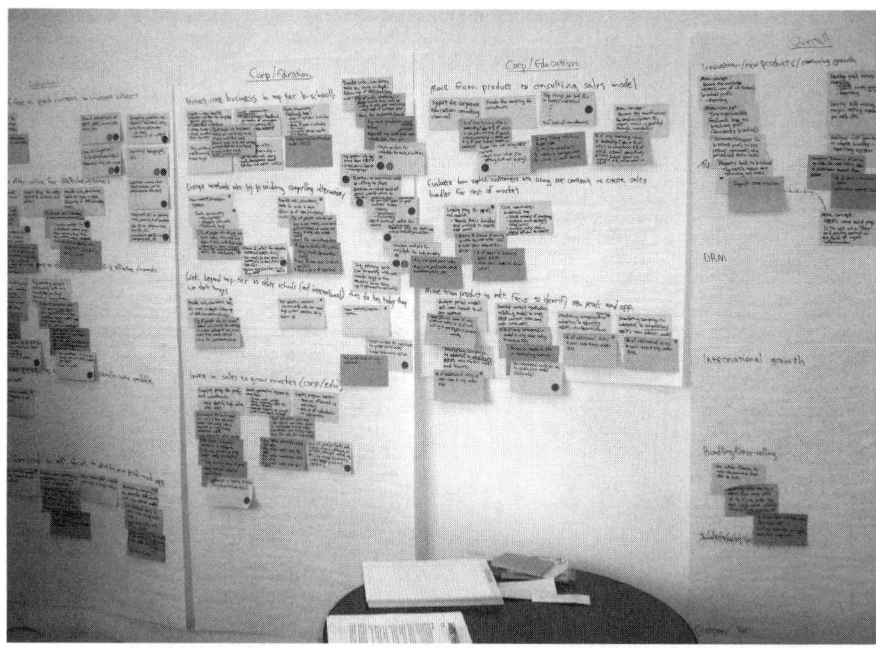

Ziv's wall of sticky notes, with hypotheses and data to gather for each one.

opportunities, especially which areas of the site to invest in and which new features or content are worth developing. This requires, of course, that you create a comprehensive list of improvements, features, and content to test. Sources for this list include the following:

- **Stakeholder interviews** often cover wish lists of improvements or features that decision makers believe would be successful, or existing features about which they are skeptical.
- **User interviews** and **usability tests** can reveal existing problems and requests for new features or content.
- **Third-party industry research** often includes an assessment of best-in-breed features or future trends.
- **Competitive analysis** of direct competitors and related players can lead to a full inventory of existing features and content for testing.

	SuperPages	YellowPages.com	Switchboard	Citysearch	AOL CityGuide	Yahoo Local	Google Local	Evite
URL	superpages.com	yellowpages.com	switchboard.com	citysearch.com	digitalcity.com	yahoo.com	google.com	evite.com
Search Interface								
Keyword/category	Yes	Yes	Yes	Yes	Yes	Yes	Yes	Yes
Business name	Yes	Yes	Yes	Yes	Yes	Yes	Yes	Yes
Location	Yes	Yes	Yes	Yes	Yes	Yes	Yes	Yes
Neighborhood list				Yes				
Advanced search:								
Street	Yes							
Phone	Yes							
Results per page	Yes							
AND vs. OR matching		Yes						
Search for all businesses on a particular street	Yes							
Reverse phone number lookup	Yes	Yes	Yes					
Reverse address lookup		Yes						
Search by distance (near an address)	Yes	Yes	Yes					
Search within a map	Yes							
Search by area code		Yes						
Zip code lookup	Yes	Yes	Yes					
Area code lookup		Yes	Yes					
Search help/tips	Yes	Yes	Yes					
List of recent searches			Yes					
List of recently viewed businesses								Yes
Browser toolbar available			Yes					
Browse Interface								
Browse by category	Yes	Yes	Yes	Yes	Yes	Yes		
Categories on home page				Subset	YP home page	YP home page		
Alphabetical index	Yes		Yes					
Browse locations								
Results List								
Category matches	Yes	Yes	Yes	Yes	Yes	Yes	Yes	Yes
With numbers	Yes	Yes	Yes	Yes	Yes	Yes		Yes
Popular categories first	Yes		Yes			Yes		
Hierarchical display	Yes	Yes						
Narrow results by:								
Types of products	Yes		Yes					
Brands offered	Yes		Yes					
Services offered	Yes		Yes					Yes
Commercial, industrial, residential	Yes							
Payment types accepted	Yes							
License types	Yes							
Emergency service types	Yes							
Certification types	Yes							
Rating						Yes		
Location/city/neighborhood								
Category-specific attributes			Yes			Yes		Yes
Narrow to exact location entered	Yes							
Narrow by price								Yes
Narrow by distance	Yes			Yes	Yes	Yes		Yes
Narrow by zip code		Yes			Yes			
Narrow by neighborhood					Yes			
Show results on a map	Yes			Yes	Yes		Yes (by default)	
Show only reviewed businesses								
Standard business information:								
Name	Yes	Yes	Yes	Yes	Yes	Yes	Yes	Yes
Address	Yes	Yes	Yes	Yes	Yes	Yes	Yes	Yes
Neighborhood								
Distance				Yes	Yes	Yes	Yes	Yes
Phone	Yes (requires click)	Yes	Yes		Yes	Yes	Yes	
URL	Yes					Yes	Yes	
Email address	Yes							
Categories			Yes	Yes	Yes	Yes		
Average rating				Yes	Yes	Yes		Yes
Date of recent rating								
# ratings/reviews								Yes
Review excerpt						Yes		
Web search			Yes					
Payment methods			Yes					
Products			Yes					
Services			Yes					
Featured business information:								
Color	Yes		Yes					
Image	Yes	Yes	Yes					
Background	Yes							
Description	Yes	Yes	Yes			Yes		
Click to call	Yes							
Graphical ads		Yes						
URL	Yes	Yes	Yes					
Email address	Yes	Yes		Yes				
Phone				Yes				
Sort order	Featured first, then alpha	Featured first, then alpha	Featured first, then alpha	Featured first, then distance	Rating	Unknown	Unknown	Distance
Sort options	Alpha	Alpha	Alpha, distance	Alpha, distance, rating	Alpha, distance	Alpha, distance, rating		Alpha, rating
Ads on results page	Yes	Yes	Yes	Yes	Yes	Yes	Yes	Yes
Business Page								
Name	Yes	Yes	Yes	Yes	Yes	Yes	Yes	Yes
Address	Yes	Yes	Yes	Yes	Yes	Yes	Yes	Yes
Neighborhood								
Map	Yes	Yes	Yes	Yes	Yes	Yes	Yes	Yes
Businesses nearby								
Driving directions	Yes	Yes	Yes	Yes	Yes	Yes	Yes	Yes
Directions to nearest subway stop					Yes			
Parking info					Yes			
Phone	Yes	Yes		Yes	Yes	Yes	Yes	Yes
Categories	Yes		Yes		Yes	Yes		
URL	Yes			Yes		Yes	Yes	Yes
Email address						Yes		
Description	Yes			Yes		Yes		
Hours			Yes		Yes	Yes	Yes	Yes
Products & services	Yes		Yes	Yes			Yes	Yes
Brands	Yes						Yes	
Price range					Yes			Yes
Specialties	Yes						Yes	Yes
Payment options	Yes				Yes	Yes	Yes	Yes
Commercial, industrial, residential	Yes							
Certifications, licenses	Yes		Yes					
Years in business	Yes			Yes				
Images						Yes		Yes
Ads for competitors			Yes	Yes	Yes	Yes		
Email to a friend				Yes	Yes	Yes		Yes
Ratings/reviews				Yes	Yes	Yes	Yes	Yes
Editorial profile				Yes	Yes			Yes
Web search for business						Yes	Yes	
Send info to mobile phone			Yes			Yes		
Plan an event here								Yes
Other info sources					Switchboard, infoUSA		SuperPages, Citysearch, Yahoo, DigitalCity, more	Citysearch
Ability to add/suggest information					Yes			
Add photos								
Personalization	**Free registration**			**Free registration**		**Free registration**		**Free registration**
Favorites list	Yes			Yes		Yes		Yes
Saved locations	Yes			Yes (cookied)		Yes		

A competitive analysis lists many features down the left and competitors across the top.

Surveys are particularly effective for testing features and content, as the next section discusses. But as with everything else, gathering data on which features are worth investing in requires careful planning up front so that you know exactly what you want to test.

Finally, take advantage of the fact that you're doing this research by asking around in the organization about other hypotheses people would like to test or other data people would like to gather. For example, the marketing department might like to use this opportunity to gather information on how many people find the latest email campaign useful. The customer service department might want to benchmark customer satisfaction with their services.

Be careful what you ask for, because the amount of research you'll need to do could skyrocket quickly with everyone's requests. But since you'll be reaching out to users in a survey anyway, it's worth asking.

Now that you've decided what to research, you can dive into the individual quantitative methodologies: surveys, site traffic analysis, and CRM data analysis.

Conducting Surveys

Surveys were once an expensive proposition, involving time-consuming phone calls or expensive mail-in questionnaires. Thanks to online tools such as Zoomerang and SurveyMonkey, conducting a survey is now faster and much less expensive. If you're not already running regular surveys to get to know your users better, you should be.

Because surveys are a relatively easy way to gather quantitative data on users' goals, behaviors, attitudes, and demographics, this tool is the first choice if you want to conduct quantitative research. But it's important to remember that what you're getting is self-reported data—that is, what users tell you about themselves, not necessarily what they actually do. For this reason, complementing survey data with site traffic analysis and CRM data analysis is wise when you are able to do so.

Who to Survey

First things first: Who should you survey? Like one-on-one interviews, the goal is to gather data on the full breadth of users. Cast the net wide, including as many types of users as possible: existing online customers, existing offline customers, former customers, visitors who are not yet customers, and prospects who have never visited the site. If it's relevant, you might want to add audiences such as internal users (employees), job seekers, the press, analysts, partners, and so on.

Surveying existing customers is the easiest, because you probably already have their email addresses, and, as current customers, they are more likely to respond to a survey invitation. Just make sure that they have opted in to being contacted by you for this type of activity. You'll also want some sense of how up to date the email addresses are; hundreds of bounced email invitations can ruin an otherwise lovely day.

Aim for a good sampling of each of your user-types to ensure that you have enough data on each segment to draw accurate conclusions. This requires making sure, to the greatest extent possible, that you send out invitations to the different groups in a manner that is proportional to their distribution among the overall user base. In our ongoing real estate example, if you have twice as many home buyers as home sellers and apartment hunters, make sure that you send twice as many invitations to home buyers as home sellers and apartment hunters. The intent is to start with a list that is similar to your users. Then when you go to define a new segmentation, you know that it is based on the actual user base. Sometimes this can be a difficult goal, and it doesn't guarantee that you'll get equal responses from each segment, but it should get you going in the right direction.

Here's an example invitation email:

> **Subject: RealEstateCentral.com survey: Chance to win $1,000**
>
> Hi Rick,
>
> As a valued customer, your feedback is important to us. Please take 10 minutes to complete a quick survey that will help guide future improvements to RealEstateCentral.com. By completing the survey, you will be entered in a drawing for $1,000 (read contest rules).
>
> Please click the link below to begin. The survey must be completed by Friday, December 15.
>
> Begin survey
>
> Steve Mulder
>
> [Include job title and full contact information]
>
> [Include any disclaimers or legalese here if necessary]

A few quick notes:

- Make the Subject line as specific as possible to avoid spam filters.
- For the same reason, make sure the email comes from an email address the user will recognize (@RealEstateCentral.com).
- Keep the email short and sweet. Your job is to get them to click to the survey as quickly as possible.
- Tell them approximately how long the survey will take to complete, so they know what to expect.
- Tell them how long the survey will be open.
- Give users a way to opt out if they no longer wish to receive emails such as this invitation.

- Incentives are a great way to improve the completion rate of your survey. This could be cash or some other prize. When possible, try not to make it something related to your product or service (i.e., do not offer free products or a discount on services). The reason is that this will skew your answers by attracting more people who like your product than those who do not. After all, if you swore you would never shop at a particular store again, how motivated are you going to be by a 10-percent discount as an incentive? If you offer a prize that has no relationship to your products, well, some people might like it more and some people might like it less, but these folks should be evenly distributed across your user base rather than skewed in one way or another. A drawing works well, but make sure you clear everything with your legal department and publish any rules or disclaimers for your raffle.

If you have users' email addresses, that's all you need to get started. But if you don't, there are other options. To reach other people who visit your site, you can deploy the survey from your site, with a prominent message on key pages or, better yet, a pop-up window. (It's rare that I recommend using pop-ups, but in this case, they work well at getting users' attention.) Don't just put this on your home page, since many visitors to your site may enter from another page.

Keep the Web-based invitation concise:

> **RealEstateCentral.com survey:**
> **Chance to win $1,000!**
>
> Please take 10 minutes to complete a quick survey that will help guide future improvements to RealEstateCentral.com. By completing the survey, you will be entered in a drawing for $1,000 (read contest rules).
>
> Begin survey
>
> [Include any disclaimers or legalese here if necessary]

Invitations via email or the Web site will result in getting current customers or site visitors, but if you want non-visitors, you'll likely need some outside help. Companies such as Greenfield Online excel at finding users who match specific criteria. They have an existing panel of people from all walks of life who regularly fill out surveys.

Here's how it works: After telling them what types of people you want and how many, they analyze their existing panel of users to determine how difficult it will be to find those types of people. They then give you a price quote and talk through your options. You can write the survey, or they can help you with the details. Then they deploy the survey, keeping it live long enough to get you the number of responses they promised. They then send you the raw results for analysis.

The cost of using a third-party panel varies depending on the criteria you want and the number of responses you want. But this is a very effective way of reaching prospective users.

And now we come to the often-asked question: How many survey results is enough?

Rather than hiding behind the tempting answer of "It depends," I'll offer this rule of thumb: a minimum of 100 survey completions *per segment*. If you're doing qualitative segmentation, you already know your segments before the survey and can watch as the results come in to see if you have enough. But if you're doing quantitative segmentation, you don't know the segments beforehand. In this case, think about how many segments you suspect you'll end up with, and if those segments will be evenly distributed among all the users. Your answers will help guide the total number of responses you want, which could range from 400 to 1,000.

So, let's say you wanted 500 survey completions. How many email invitations should you send out? I've found that the completion rate of surveys varies primarily based on the strength of the relationship between the business and the user. Incentives can boost this a bit, but not as much as you might assume. A good starting assumption is that 2 to 3 percent of people who receive the email invitation will complete the survey. I've seen as low as 1 percent and as high as 14 percent (for a retailer with the most loyal customers I have ever seen). In this example, to get 500 completions, you'd have to send out around 17,000 email invitations, assuming a 3-percent completion rate.

Of course, these numbers may not be possible. You may simply not have anywhere near this many email addresses, or you may not get up to 100 completions per segment. In that case, use what you have. Your findings can still be directionally valid even if you have only 50 completions per segment. A "quant" (quantitative analyst) might object that you don't have statistical significance, but some evidence is better than no evidence. To really understand what kinds of numbers you need for statistical significance based on your specific situation, it's best to find an expert, since these rules of thumb aren't written in stone.

Designing the Survey

An entire book could be written on writing effective surveys. But since that's not how I want to spend this book, I'll devote a few pages to the most important things you need to know to get the most out of surveys for persona creation.

Think of the survey as a conversation, with one question flowing naturally to the next.

Keep your survey as short as you can. When a survey is longer than 15 minutes or so, completion rates drop off. As you develop your survey, test it on some unsuspecting peers to see how long it takes them to complete it. Revise accordingly.

Think of the survey as a conversation, with one question flowing naturally to the next. The more comfortable users are while taking it, the more likely they are to complete the survey and answer truthfully. This means that the order of the questions is important, not only because you want to make users feel comfortable, but also because the sequence of questions can create bias. For example, if you begin your survey by asking users to prioritize new features, and then you ask them a question about overall site satisfaction, their response to the second question will be influenced by the list of features you just presented to them.

When I write a survey, I use the following list as a starting point for the order in which I ask questions:

- Current goals, usage, and behavior, including channel usage
- History with the site and company
- Use of or importance of existing features and content
- Satisfaction with existing features and content
- Overall reaction to new concept(s)
- Importance of new features and content
- Psychographic questions
- Demographic questions

I begin with questions about goals and behavior because I've found that self-perception of goals and behavior is most likely to be influenced by later questions. After that, it's on to questions about past experiences and the existing site, before I dive into questions about new ideas. Finally, I leave the more boring questions (age, income, blah, blah, blah) for the end, since by then, users might be weary of the survey and don't want any questions that force them to think. Also, beginning a survey with boring questions can lower completion rates.

Another general rule, as mentioned before, is that asking about behavior is often better than asking about importance, because the answers are typically more accurate. When asked if a feature is important, users often swing to the more positive side, because the feature sounds like a good idea, or they imagine other people would like that feature, or they're just trying to please. When you ask people how often they would actually *use* such a feature, they get more realistic.

Use clear, familiar language in surveys. Jargon or unexplained acronyms result in more drop-offs and potentially less accurate data.

Know the language of your users and stick to it. Your users are likely to be much less familiar with your site's vocabulary than you think. Instead of asking them about the "wish list" feature, ask them about "the ability to save a list of favorite products." Clarity is more important than succinctness (though, of course, you're striving for both).

For any of these topics, avoid yes/no questions. You want to gauge their goals, behaviors, and attitudes on a scale as much as you can. You can do so much more with this type of data (referred to as a Likert scale) than you can with the binary yes/no data you get from checkboxes.

I tend to use a 1–5 scale for most questions. A 1–10 scale presents too many choices to users, who can seldom answer questions with such finely tuned distinction. If you use any fewer than five answers, you don't get enough data points.

This 1–5 scale can be applied to a range of question types:

- **"How often do you..."**

  Never — About once a year — A few times a year — About once a month — Several times a month (These values vary depending on the goal or behavior you're asking about.)

- **"How important is..."**

  Not at all important — — — — Very important

- **"How likely would you be to..."**

  Not at all likely — — — — Very likely

- **"How would you rate..."**

  Poor — — — — Excellent

- **"How much do you agree that..."**

  Strongly disagree — — — — Strongly agree

By the way, you don't have to label each of the five answer values. I often label just the extremes, as shown here.

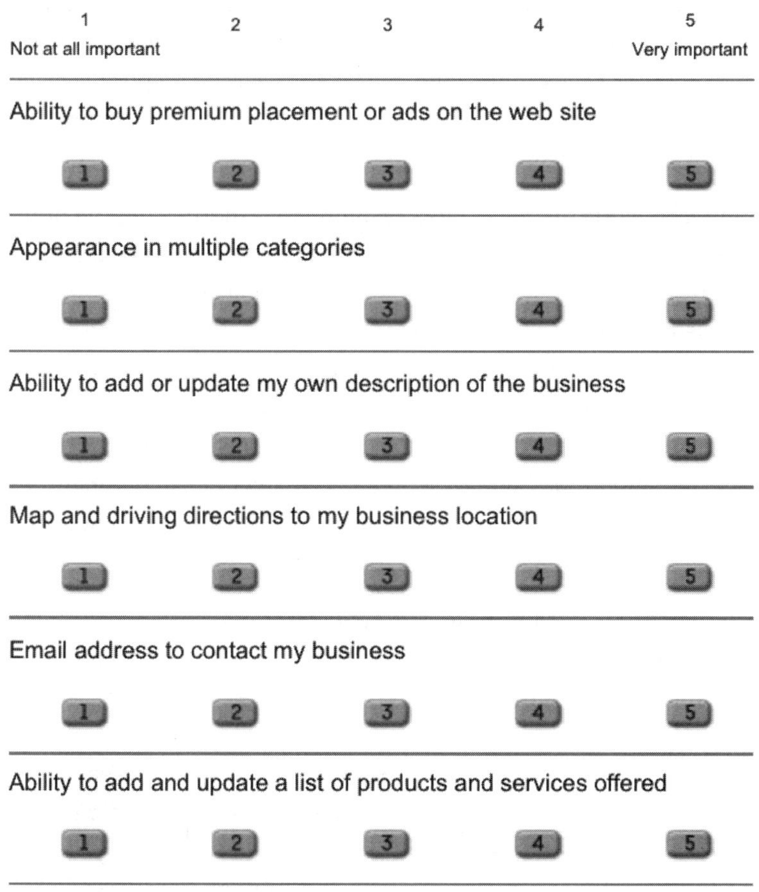

An example of a scaled survey question.

When using a scale, use it consistently. One should always mean less (in amount, frequency, importance, and so forth), and 5 should always mean more.

For some questions you might be forced to add a "Not applicable" option, but avoid doing so unless absolutely necessary, because it makes analysis of the results more difficult.

Most questions will end up being these types of scaled questions, often referred to as matrix questions because each one consists of individual items down the left (goals, features, statements, etc.) and the rating scale across the top. It may seem overwhelming to have so many of these scaled questions, but users are very adept at clicking radio buttons and making their way through the survey. Again, test the length to make sure.

In order to eliminate bias, I also recommend randomizing the order of the items within each question. For example, if you're testing a long list of features, randomizing that list can ensure that an item's score isn't being affected by the fact that it was always at the end of the list, by which point users could have become tired of clicking. Most online survey tools make this type of randomization easy. You don't want to randomize when the options need to be presented in a specific order that users expect, such as a list of salary ranges, or when you have a factual question that shouldn't be affected by order, such as an alphabetical list of job industries.

In some cases, you'll want to use open text fields instead of having the user select from a predetermined list of answers. When you have a question with a numerical answer and you're not sure of the best way to break the answers down into groupings, consider letting the user type a number instead. For example, if you want to ask about how many hours users are online per week, you could create predetermined answers such as "1–5 hours," "6–10 hours," "11–15 hours," and so on. But if 95 percent of your users are online just 1–5 hours per week, you won't end up with helpful data for this question. In such a case, it is better to let users simply type in the number of hours and see how the distribution ends up. You'll also get more accurate data this way, because users are entering an exact number and not a range. (This approach requires more data cleanup later, as you'll see, but it can be worth the effort.) Other good candidates for open text fields are age, spending habits, years spent doing something, and salary.

Beyond this particular use of open text fields, avoid them, because, trust me, you won't have the time it takes to manually read through hundreds or thousands of free-for-all responses. Sometimes I include one general comments field near the end of the survey so that users feel like they can have their say, and so that if I do happen to find time, I can read through comments and see if there are any new insights I haven't tested. This field can also inspire persona quotes, which will be covered in Chapter 7.

Here are a few final tips for maximizing completion rates for your survey:

- Break up a long survey into multiple pages to make it seem faster. Make sure to show a progress indicator ("Page 2 of 4") so your users can see their progress and understand how much of the survey remains.
- Make all questions optional unless absolutely necessary. You don't want one objectionable question to stop someone from giving you good data.
- Keep the visual design of the survey simple and clean. The focus should be on the questions. This isn't the time for brand-immersive experiences.
- Use any skip logic (showing different questions depending on a previous answer) carefully, since it will add to analysis time.

To show what a survey might look like when it all comes together, listed below are some of the questions from the survey my team and I deployed on behalf of VistaPrint. Compare these questions to the interview topics in Chapter 4, and you can see how the quantitative research extends and tests the themes explored in the qualitative research.

- How did you first hear about VistaPrint? [Single select from options.]
- When did you first visit VistaPrint? [Multiple select from goals such as "When I was starting a business."]

- Which of the following have you purchased from VistaPrint? [Multiple select from product categories.]
- Approximately how much have you spent at VistaPrint in the last two years? [Text entry field.]
- When ordering these types of products, how important are each of the following factors to you? [From 1–5 importance scale for items such as price, professional designs, print quality, customer service by phone, fast delivery, etc.]
- How would you rate VistaPrint in the following areas? [From 1–5 satisfaction scale for the same items.]
- How much do you agree with the following statements about VistaPrint? [From 1–5 level of agreement scale on brand attributes such as reliability, value, speed, etc.]
- What other items have you printed in the last two years not using VistaPrint (Either because you've made them yourself or you've purchased them from someone else)? [Multiple select from product categories.]
- Where else have you done this type of printing in the last two years? [Multiple select from list of competitors.]
- Why do you use the places above instead of VistaPrint for these items? Please rate the importance of each reason below. [From 1–5 importance scale for items such as price, quality, speed, personal interaction, etc.]
- Approximately how much have you spent on these items in the last two years (not including VistaPrint)? [Text entry field.]
- VistaPrint is in the process of developing new features. How important is it to you that VistaPrint provide each of the following? [From 1–5 importance scale for short feature descriptions.]

- If you could change one other thing about VistaPrint, what would it be? [Text entry field.]
- What industry is your business in? [Single select from industry categories.]
- How many people are there in your business, including you? [Text entry field.]
- How effective is your company at marketing and promoting your business? [From 1–5 scale.]
- How long has your company been in business? [Single select from options.]
- When you create something on VistaPrint, which of the following best describes your typical process? [Single select from options.]
- How many times do you typically visit the site to create one item? [Text entry field.]
- [There were also various demographic questions that I won't bother to list here.]

The time my team and I spent carefully planning and writing these survey questions (and considering the order in which they appear) was well worth it.

Deploying the Survey

Online survey tools such as Zoomerang make the logistics of launching surveys fairly simple. You enter the questions into the tool, preview the survey to test it, and then launch it, either by importing all your email addresses or by generating a survey URL that you can send out.

Test, test, test. Make sure the URL in your email invitation is correct, make sure users will get the right thank you page after the survey, and make sure there's nothing wrong with the formatting in different

Web browsers. Once the survey is live, you can't go back and change much without affecting the validity of the data.

Consider your audience when deciding which day to launch the survey. For many business users, launching on a Friday can be risky, because your email invitation could get lost in their inbox over the weekend and could more easily be disregarded as spam. On the other hand, a consumer audience might be more likely to take the survey if the invitation arrives on a weekend.

Once you have launched your survey, the key metrics to monitor are the click-through rate and the completion rate. The click-through rate measures what percentage of the people who received your invitation click through to take the survey. This often indicates how compelling your invitation and incentives are. If you are not seeing good numbers here, you might need to adjust one or both. The completion rate measures what percentage of people who start the survey end up finishing it. The mean for this on most 15-minute surveys is 80 percent, but this is greatly affected by your users' loyalty, the incentive you offer, and the questions you ask. If you start seeing completion rates south of 65 percent, you might need to address the total number of questions in the survey or increase the incentive substantially.

You'll find that most survey completions occur within the first 48 hours after launch, as people immediately follow the link from the email invitation. Completions gradually drop off from there. Leaving the survey open for five to seven business days is usually enough to guarantee sufficient responses.

As the days go by, keep a close eye on the number of survey completions you're getting. You might want to send out a reminder email halfway through, because these reminders almost always result in another spike of completions.

Cleaning and Preparing Survey Data

The next chapter thoroughly covers how to use the survey results, whether they serve to validate your qualitative segmentation or to generate quantitative segmentation. But before you dive into the analysis, it's time to clean and prep the data. Data cleansing is one of the most overlooked and misunderstood topics in quantitative analysis. As mentioned earlier, if the data going into your analysis is garbage, the results will be garbage as well.

There are three primary reasons why people do not do a good job of cleaning data: They don't understand how involved it can be, they don't understand their data well enough to know what needs to be done, and they don't understand the tools and methodologies well enough to know how to do it. A good rule of thumb is that 75 percent of the time used in quantitative analysis should be spent in data validating and cleansing, and 25 percent in everything else from planning to analysis.

This is a great time to bring in a *quant* (quantitative statistical analyst), someone with experience cleaning medium-sized to large sets of data. If you're conducting statistical analysis, you could certainly muddle through on your own if you have the skills, but bringing in an expert makes the entire process more successful and more efficient.

The first and most important step is understanding the data you have. Do you clearly understand each column or variable of the data? You should know what the variable represents, what the acceptable range of values is, and how the data was collected (if you do not already know). Do you know which variables define a unique user, or do you need to interpolate this for yourself? Also, is the data categorical or continuous? For example, "What is your favorite color?" is categorical, meaning that the different answers cannot be related on a common scale, whereas "What is your age?" is continuous, because different answers can be related on a common scale. If it is continuous, is the data on an unbounded scale (e.g., "What is your age?") or a bounded scale (e.g., "On a scale of 1–5 how important is the following?")? If there is missing data, how is that denoted, with a blank in the data, or with a number (for instance, –1 is often used to denote missing data)? If the data lies in more than one table or spreadsheet, how do you relate a line of data in one table to a line of data in another (in database terms, this is the join relationship)?

Clearly understanding the data, especially if this is not data you have collected, is essential before you decide how to clean it. Now you can see why I recommend finding a quant.

One thing you'll want to do is clean up the freeform numerical data. Remember how I recommended using open text fields for some numeric answers? It's time to make sure this data is usable. If you asked people to enter their current salary, for example, you'll find that some people probably entered the "$" and others used commas within the number. Strip out everything but the number so that your data will be squeaky clean for the analysis step.

Next, remove the outliers. Some people will have entered junk data in the open text fields, such as "2" or "too low" for salary. You may also come across surveys in which people answered every question the same way, simply to get the incentive. Look for these outliers or response patterns and remove those survey completions from your data set entirely, so they don't affect your conclusions.

You may also want to *normalize* the data—that is, put all the values of all the questions onto a consistent scale for easier analysis. I often use a 0–1 scale for all questions. Typical questions on a 1–5 scale map to the 0–1 scale, with an answer of 1 being mapped to 0, 2 being mapped to 0.25, 3 being mapped to 0.50, and so on. Normalization is not something you necessarily need to do in order to look at the data, but it becomes important if you wish to perform quantitative segmentation, because the algorithms employed require that all variables be on the same scale to prevent the segmentation from skewing. This makes sense when you think about it: How do you compare an answer on a 1–5 scale with an answer on a 1–10 scale? Without normalization, the 1–10 scale appears greater than the 1–5 scale.

The overall message is this: Don't use the survey data until you're sure you can trust the output.

Performing Site Traffic Analysis

Now that your survey data is ready to be analyzed, you can explore whether you're able to add more quantitative data to the process. The first possibility comes from looking at your log files to capture behavioral information on how people currently use your site. The beauty of this data is that you have at your fingertips every single click all your users have made on your site, so the data is, to say the least, robust. But this can also be a downside because you get so much data that you may find it difficult to know what to do with it. For example, one of the chief Web analysis vendors, Coremetrics, offers more than 300 different site usage reports. Such a staggering number is more information than any one individual or company needs. The challenge is to find the one or two right reports out of those 300. Another weakness is that while log files tell you a lot about *what* users do on the site, they are useless when it comes to telling you *why* they do what they do. This is why combining site traffic analysis with a survey can be so useful.

Here are the two ways to use site traffic analysis data for creating personas:

- Look for overarching behavior patterns that you can associate with each segment based on your analysis of the findings so far.
- Tie a particular individual's clickstreams to his or her survey responses, thus enhancing each user's record for more quantitative analysis.

Let's start with an example of the first method. Working with a retailer recently, my team uncovered a great many insights while analyzing the log files, one of which was that the vast majority of site visits began on a category page, rather than on the home page. Because most of these visits did not have a referring URL that had directed the user to the site (for example, from Google or some other source), they had to be results of either situations where the user directly typed the URL into his or her browser or where the user had followed a link in an email message. Meanwhile, we also had survey data that pointed to something else that was interesting: Many users said they relied on emails from the retailer to stay up to date with the latest trends and offerings. We knew that these emails primarily featured product categories and linked to category pages. Thus, we made the association that many users were probably opening emails and clicking to category pages as their way of entering the site, thus explaining the log file data. This behavioral detail informed the personas, and shifted the strategy for better communicating with and serving this type of user.

This approach requires making a leap of faith—that you're making correct associations of log file data with segment behavior. My team couldn't prove that the users who entered the site on category pages were the same users who relied on the emails, but we felt the inferences were solid, based on the qualitative research, and thus we felt comfortable using them for the personas.

You can tie an individual user's log file data to that same person's survey responses, and by doing so, you can know with certainty that specific behaviors correlate with specific attitudes.

The second way of using site traffic analysis is more promising and defendable because you tie an individual user's log file data to that same person's survey responses, and by doing so, you can know with certainty that specific behaviors correlate with specific attitudes. Of course, this assumes you are in fact able to grab log file data for a particular user and to identify that same user in the survey results.

Recently, my team worked with a retailer on a multichannel feature that enabled users to visit the Web site and see if an online product was also available in their local store. The business was extremely interested in just how effective such a feature would be in driving users to the store to make the purchase. The challenge was that in our survey, users were unwilling to guarantee that just seeing that the item was available in the local store would mean that they would go and purchase the item. However, by looking at the log files and tying that information to the actual store purchases, it was possible to infer that 38 percent of all customers who went to the site and looked up the local stores carrying a particular item ended up purchasing that item within two weeks.

Whatever your approach to using site traffic analysis data, there is a wealth of information you can explore about various user behaviors, including the following:

- **Entry pages:** Where do users enter your site?
- **Referrers:** Where do they come from? If it's a search engine, what search terms did they use to find you?
- **Exit pages:** Where do they leave?
- **Common paths:** What pages do they visit in what order?
- **Feature usage:** What content and features get the most traffic?
- **Search terms:** What do they search for?
- **Conversion rate:** What percentage of site visitors make a purchase, register, become a lead, or satisfy another such business goal?
- **Duration:** How long did they spend on your site?
- **Frequency:** How often do they visit?

It's easy to get lost in a sea of data. Make sure to stay focused on the things you need to learn. You'll have access to varying data, depending on your analytics package. For the richest data set, I recommend finding someone who can run custom reports against the raw log files so that you can find exactly what you need rather than relying on out-of-the-box reports.

When combined with survey results, your record on each individual now contains a richer set of data, because you have responses for every survey question, as well as this additional data on that person's site behavior. More factors translate into a more complete picture of users and thus more realistic raw material for segmentation and persona creation.

Analyzing CRM Data

The final piece of quantitative data you can add into the mix is data you already have in your customer records: transactions, financial data, and demographics. By tying an individual's history and worth to his or her survey responses, you can look for correlations that could better define or describe your personas. One particularly useful technique is to determine the financial value to the business of each persona so that you know which personas are most valuable to the business and therefore which deserve more attention. Prioritizing site improvements or new features becomes a lot easier when you can associate a dollar value with each persona who might use them.

Transactional data reveals which customers have purchased which products or services—something that many organizations track. Typically, a database exists in which a customer's unique ID is associated with a product or service purchased, as well as the date of purchase and any miscellaneous information collected at the time of the purchase (such as the channel in which the purchase occurred or any contact information for the customer such as mailing address, email, phone number, etc.). For retail companies, this information often comes directly from their transaction systems. For indirect vendors such as consumer packaged goods companies, this information might come from warranty cards the consumers fill in and mail to the company. In traditional customer research, this transactional data is often the cornerstone of customer segmentation, using such tools as RFM (Recency-Frequency-Monetary) analysis. These tools can be valuable in developing personas, as the products that users purchase and the frequency at which they do so are driven by their needs and can strongly affect their Web site goals and behaviors. For example, a customer buying a thousand-dollar microscope once every five years for a medical lab has very different behavior than a customer buying a two-dollar test tube every month for the same lab. Understanding which customers are buying what and how often is a first step toward understanding their different needs and behaviors. As with Web site log files, the most outstanding weakness of this data is that it does not tell you anything about *why* a customer did or did not purchase an item.

Even organizations that don't track customer data at the transaction level usually track overall financial data for each customer. Again, this usually entails having a database in which a customer's ID is associated with some aggregate spend number (total dollars this customer has spent) over some time period (usually the last one to five years), and in some cases their spending is broken out by channel (how much he or she ordered in the retail store, via the Web, via telephone, etc.). As with the customer transaction data discussed earlier, this information is often used in traditional market research to segment the customer base into quartiles or deciles from the most valuable customer to the least valuable, as a way of driving marketing strategy. For persona development, this information, by itself, is not very useful. However, when linked with other information such as surveys, it can be very important in helping you quantify the relative monetary value of different personas to a business, and thus it can be useful in helping you prioritize among the various personas.

For example, when my colleague Ziv was working with the discount brokerage BrownCo, he generated five different personas. Two of them were remarkable in that they were both frequent users of BrownCo's Web site and both were critical of some of its trading support tools, although they had very different needs. However, when Ziv calculated the average revenue per trade of each persona, by linking the financial data of each customer with their persona segment, a very interesting thing emerged: One group, named the Speed Demons, who complained about features and functionality, had an average revenue per trade that was near the lowest possible. In other words, they were only making the types of trades that got them the lowest rates that BrownCo offered. And since BrownCo was, at the time, offering the lowest rates in the industry, this data and some further probing of the customers made it clear that despite their feature and functionality desires, these customers were in fact only loyal to the lowest price vendor and would remain so without any new features or functionality. In other words, focusing on them wouldn't affect the revenue they brought in, because they were solely price driven. By contrast, the other group, the Heavy Traders, had extremely high revenue per trade, indicating that they were interested in more than just the lowest price. So when it came time to prioritize among which features and functionality would be built, the Heavy Traders' needs were prioritized much higher than the Speed Demons' needs.

The third type of CRM data is demographic information, which comes in standard flavors: age, income, marital status, occupation, geography, race, and so on. It is often used in market research as the basis of segmenting the customer base, or as the starting point for trying to identify the differences between segments. It can prove to be very valuable in developing marketing plans, which often involve mapping a target segments' demographic information to the venues that cater to those demographics. However, their track record in persona development isn't as successful, as the next chapter discusses. While this information may be valuable in providing richness around a particular persona (especially if a particular persona maps closely to some demographic variable), it is rarely a driving factor when you're creating personas, because personas are driven by goals, behaviors, and attitudes.

There is one other way to add CRM data to your customer records if you don't already have the data. It's called third-party append data, and it covers a broad range of customer data that can be acquired (for the right price) from third-party aggregators of information such as Experian in B2C and Dun and Bradstreet in B2B. These third-party aggregators are in the business of collecting as much data about individual customers as possible and then making a catalog of this data available for companies to append to their own customer records. This data includes wide-ranging attributes such as purchasing patterns, activities, hobbies, donations, pets, car ownership, home purchase price, and much more. (Yes, Big Brother is watching us all.) This data is usually priced in terms of dollars per thousand customers appended. Some of these third-party aggregators have even done their own segmentations of the broad consumer market with detailed descriptions of each consumer segment, including its motivations and drivers, and they make this segmentation available for append on an individual customer basis. Both the strong and weak point of this data is the same: relevance. If you are building a Web site for car owners, appending the types and number of cars they own might be extremely useful for helping you understand the drivers (excuse the pun) behind goals, behaviors, and attitudes. If you are building a Web site for women's apparel, it might not be. The biggest drivers in determining relevance are time and money. It costs time and money to append this information to your customer data and it costs time and money to then analyze all the appended data to see if it has any value in enhancing your understanding of the personas. In any case, it is not the sort of thing I usually recommend you get into unless you have quite a bit of expertise in the data itself.

Congratulations! At the very least, you now have all the raw survey data you need to either validate your qualitative segmentation or generate your quantitative segmentation. In the best case, you have enhanced those user records with data from site traffic analysis and/or CRM data, so you can look at even more factors to build your personas. So let's get on with segmenting your audience into groupings that will become your personas.

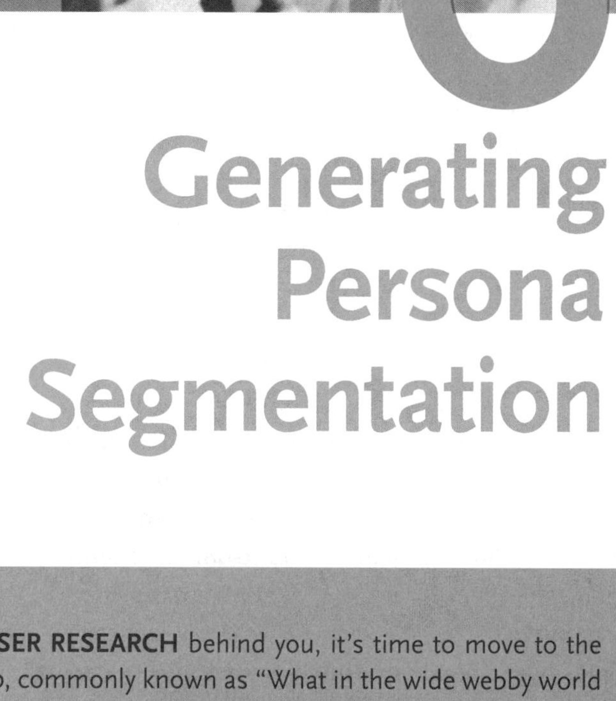

6 Generating Persona Segmentation

WITH USER RESEARCH behind you, it's time to move to the next step, commonly known as "What in the wide webby world do I *do* with all of this information?"

Imagine, if you will, a pile of rocks. It's your mission to describe the different types of rocks in this pile. You can do this in many ways, of course. You could organize the rocks by size and then describe each group. You could group them by color or texture. Or you could dust off that geology degree and group them by type (sedimentary, igneous, and so on). Organizing all of these individual rocks into clusters is what *segmentation* is all about.

Every user of your Web site is unique. But in order to be able to talk about who your users are and to act upon that knowledge, you have to group them into segments, which then become personas. How you create these groupings is absolutely critical and is perhaps the most difficult part of creating personas, because if the core way you define your personas isn't clear or useful, the personas won't be either.

There isn't one right way to do segmentation. Even with quantitative research and analysis, segmentation is not a science. Think of segmentation as the art of finding patterns and stories in the data, whether your data comprises qualitative user interviews or quantitative survey results.

The refrain of this book so far has been "goals, behaviors, and attitudes," so it won't surprise you that I recommend starting your segmentation exploration with these attributes. What you *won't* want to do is start with demographics and psychographics, the way traditional marketing segmentation is often done. When marketing groups segment users, they do so in order to *sell* to people, and so traditional demographics (age, income, gender, and so on) make sense, because these attributes often correlate to market acceptance or likelihood of purchase. But in creating a Web site, we're not just selling something to people—we're building something that they will actually *use*. Thus, we want to focus on attributes that reveal how people will actually use the site: goals (what users want to do), behaviors (how they do it), and attitudes (how they perceive the experience or themselves).

Think of segmentation as the art of finding patterns and stories in the data.

And now for the often-asked question: How many segments should you end up with? I'll try to resist the ever-present temptation of saying, "It depends" and instead give this rule of thumb: Aim for three to six segments per site. If you have only two segments, chances are you're missing some key differences between users. If you have more than six (which is the more common problem), you can probably combine segments. The challenge with having more than six segments is that they develop into too many personas for your team to keep straight.

I once heard a story about an organization in which one department created a set of personas for its own use, and the personas were so successful that the news spread throughout the organization. As a result, other departments started creating their own personas. Soon, the organization had over 100 personas representing its users. You can probably imagine the result: There were so many personas to think about, with so much overlap among them, that people stopped using them.

You'll notice that I recommend three to six personas *per site*. If you're a bank and you have two separate lines of business—one for consumers and one for business banking, each with its own Web site—you'll probably want to create two sets of personas. The alternative is to create one consumer banking persona and one business banking persona, which would probably fail to capture the rich differences within each group.

The entire segmentation process is collaborative and iterative. Regardless of your approach, you'll want to involve key stakeholders throughout the organization. Include product owners, marketing, design, customer service, sales, and so on—everyone who interacts with or serves customers and has a take on the types of users who are out there. If you don't involve these stakeholders in the process of segmenting users, it's far less likely they'll buy into your recommendations. In addition, revisit your segmentation on a regular basis. You might want to gather all the key stakeholders together once a year to make sure your segmentation approach still feels right and is useful. Every few years, conduct additional research to check in with real users and validate your segmentation. Users change, businesses change, environments change, so step back once in a while to check that your personas are still valid. Of course, if the focus of the business changes significantly, don't wait for your yearly checkup to revisit the segmentation.

As outlined in Chapter 3, there are three approaches to creating personas. The sections in this chapter correspond to each of these methods:

- Use qualitative segmentation to create personas based on interviews, field studies, and/or usability tests.
- Conduct quantitative validation of qualitative segmentation if you're using a survey to test whether your qualitative segmentation makes sense.
- Use quantitative segmentation to test various possible segmentation options using statistical analysis of survey results, site traffic analysis data, and/or CRM (Customer Relationship Management) data.

Testing Segmentation Options

Before diving into the three approaches, it's worth exploring how to evaluate different segmentation options. Whether you're taking the qualitative or quantitative route, at some point, you have to decide whether a particular segmentation approach is useful and valid. Segmentation is an art, but there are a few criteria you can use when considering each option.

When you're trying out a particular segmentation option, ask yourself these questions:

- **Do the segments explain key differences you've observed?** In talking with users, you notice differences between individuals—what they do, how they do it, what they think, and/or who they are. The first thing to ask when you're testing a segmentation option is whether this segmentation approach adequately explains those key differences. For example, if I'm considering segmenting users of my real estate site based on how often they use the site, I might ask myself whether this segmentation approach explains why some people use the house search features while others use apartment search. Finding that this approach doesn't answer that question, I might consider a different approach. If I segment by user goals instead, suddenly this difference makes sense, because one segment is house hunting and another segment is apartment hunting. This is an obvious example, but you get the idea.

- **Are the segments different enough from each other?** Personas are defined by what makes them unique. If you have two segments who use the site the same way, need the same things, and think the same way, and the only difference between the two is their age, then you probably have one segment, not two.
- **Do the segments feel like real people?** This test is somewhat vague, but it's critical because personas work best when people think of them as real users. Ideally, each of your segments should immediately remind you of one or more people you interviewed. When you describe them, your colleagues should be nodding their heads, because the segments remind them of other people as well. These segments represent your users, so they should be very familiar at first glance.
- **Can the segments be described quickly?** Personas walk a fine line between realism and abstraction, or between complexity and simplicity. On one hand, each segment should feel like a complicated and multifaceted real person, with a rich array of goals, behaviors, and attitudes. On the other hand, if it takes you a half-hour to describe the complexity of one segment, no one is going to remember all that detail or be able to act upon it. It's better to find the one, two, or three factors that best define each segment and oversimplify slightly in order to increase comprehension.
- **Do the segments cover all users?** Make sure that every user you interviewed (and other users you know about) fits into one of the segments you're exploring. If users fall between the cracks, you might want to try another option. Don't forget about offline customers, non-customers, internal users, press/analysts, job seekers, and other types of users. You

might not end up creating personas for all of these segments, but you should at least consider them in this process.

- **Is it clear how the segments will affect decision-making?** Ask yourself how you'll use the personas if you go ahead with this segmentation option. If you segment based on the user's salary range, will that inform decisions about features, interaction design, copy, and so on? Or would another approach, such as segmenting based on users' knowledge about your topic area, be more useful?

It comes down to this fundamental question: *Can you tell stories with the segments?* If you can turn the segments into stories about real people in real situations that resonate with your teammates—stories that the team can act upon when they're making decisions about the site—then you know you're on the right track.

Creating Qualitative Segmentation

So you've interviewed users, reviewed your notes, and assembled a list of all the goals, behaviors, and attitudes you heard from users. These are all possible ways you could group users into segments. But where do you begin?

I typically try the following approaches, in this order, to seek out the best way to segment users:

1. Segment by goals.
2. Segment by usage lifecycle.
3. Segment based on a combination of behaviors and attitudes.

With all of these approaches, keep in mind that this is an iterative, exploratory process. You can segment your audience in many perfectly valid ways; your goal is to find the way that is the most useful for those who will use the personas and what they'll use them for.

My biggest piece of advice, as I said earlier, is to make segmentation a collaborative process. Get people from across the organization into a room with plenty of whiteboards. Position this process to others as a brainstorming workshop. You'll bring the results from the research and they'll bring their experiences and existing knowledge. Spend the first part of the workshop brainstorming various segmentation approaches, then go back and evaluate the leading contenders. This is a great opportunity to educate your colleagues on the value of personas and the process of creating them.

Segmenting by Goals

When exploring segmentation options, start with user goals. Grouping users by what they're trying to *do* is often the most effective way to define personas. This makes sense, because as you remember from Chapter 1, all Web interactions begin with goals. Each user visits a site in order to do something—even "just browsing" has user goals behind it.

In many situations, goals also connect most closely with decisions you need to make about your site. Let's resurrect our real estate example. The primary goal of Francis the First-Time Home Buyer is to buy the right house. Wrapped up in this goal are many needs that must be met for Francis to achieve her goal. She needs to understand the home-buying process, for instance. She needs to be able to search for houses by criteria that are important to her. She needs to be able to follow up on houses that look interesting. And so on. There are features and content that can help meet each of these needs. To help Francis understand the home-buying process, the site might contain tutorial articles, how-to videos, expert Q&As, and so on. In addition, the way these features work must meet Francis's needs. If the expert Q&As are filled with real estate jargon or are condescending in tone, Francis's needs will not be met. By starting with Francis's goals and breaking them down into needs, you can draw direct connections to the features and content she needs and how they should work.

It's worth spending time thinking through goals and needs so that you find the right level of specificity as you list the segments' various goals. I like to imagine what a user might say if I suddenly interrupt her while she's on the site and ask her what she's doing at that particular moment.

> *Me:* What are you doing right now?
>
> *The User:* I'm trying to figure out what "points" are.
>
> *Me:* Why are you trying to do that?
>
> *The User:* I'm trying to learn how the whole home-buying process works.
>
> *Me:* And why is that?
>
> *The User:* Because I want to buy a house.
>
> *Me:* Why?
>
> *The User:* Mainly I'd love to be more independent.
>
> *Me:* Why?
>
> *The User:* I just think I'd be happier.

The conversation begins with the discrete task this user is trying to perform, a task that meets one of her needs, which in turn meets one of her goals. As I keep annoying her with "Why?" we go higher

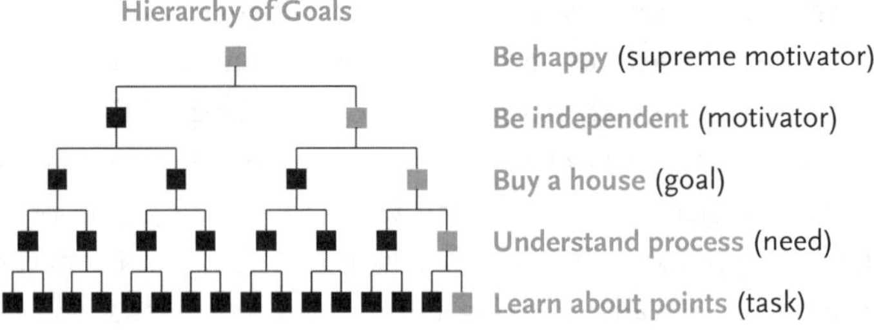

In exploring different approaches to segmentation, it's helpful to establish a hierarchy of your users' goals.

and higher up the hierarchical tree of goals, until we end up with the mother of all supreme motivators: to be happy.

Your challenge is to establish the right level of goals to talk about as you work through segmentation. At the bottom of the tree are tons of small tasks that aren't worth listing. At the top of the tree are a few overarching motivators that are too broad to be useful for differentiating segments. Somewhere in the middle is the right level of specificity for describing the goals of your users.

For goals, think in verbs. Even something as cerebral as "Understand the home-buying process" is an activity that requires action. When you're listing goals, make sure they all begin with a verb.

For example, after interviewing users of the hypothetical real estate site, you might have a list of goals such as the following:

- Buy a house
- Buy commercial property
- Find an apartment
- Sell a house
- Get a mortgage loan
- Get insurance
- Find a moving company

These actions are about halfway up the hierarchy of goals, and they immediately feel like a useful way to segment all the users of the site based on the tests discussed earlier. You can imagine that each of these goals represents a type of user with unique needs, and that their different goals explain key differences between the segments. You can describe these segments quickly and, collectively, they cover all users. You can also turn them into realistic people, and as personas, they can affect decisions you make about site content, features, information architecture, design, and so on.

Segmenting by Usage Lifecycle

Sometimes segmenting by user goals isn't as obvious as the examples just discussed, or the resulting segmentation doesn't pass the tests and you want to try another approach. In that situation, try analyzing the usage lifecycle of the site.

Think about how one person could use your site over time, and how those uses might change as the person moves through the entire lifecycle of your site, product, or service. For example, in the real estate domain, one person might start out as an apartment hunter, then a few years later he or she might come back to the site looking to buy a house, and then 10 years later, he or she might come back to sell that house. Three different points of usage along the lifecycle could become three different personas.

An important point here is that the same person could use the site at different times as different personas. A persona isn't a specific person, but more like a hat that a person wears when he or she come to the site in a particular situation, time, or mode of use. As that person (or situation) changes over time, he or she plays the role of different personas.

This approach to segmentation is still fundamentally based on goals, because you're looking at *why* people are coming to the site and what they're trying to do at different points in the lifecycle. But this approach is a different framework for thinking about users, and sometimes you may find it useful when you're considering segmentation options.

I once worked with a company that sold software that analyzed Web sites and delivered reports on their usability. During interviews with their customers, my team gathered a lot of information on exactly how and when the reports were used. We documented everything we heard about the usage lifecycle of the reports, and we sketched out the various journeys reports took within different organizations.

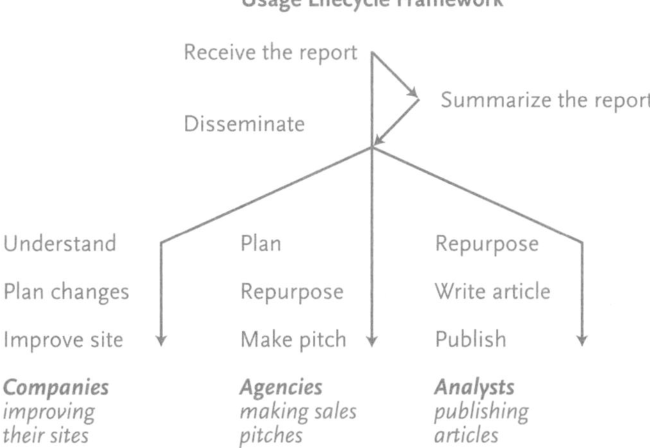

There are three primary ways that the reports are used in different companies.

Then we mapped each interview respondent to this framework so that we could see the trends and patterns in usage. In this diagram, each line shows an individual user (only a subset of users is shown here).

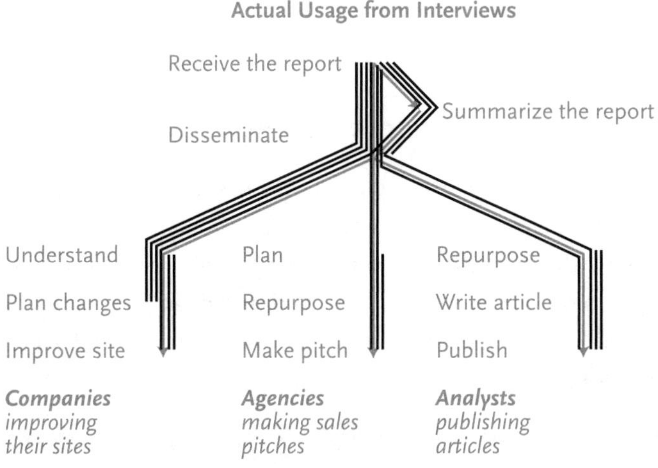

We mapped actual behavior to the framework; each line shows the real usage of each person we interviewed.

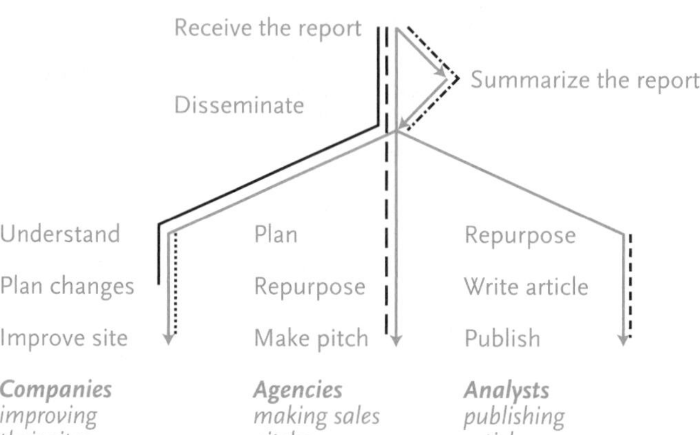

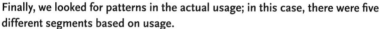

Finally, we looked for patterns in the actual usage; in this case, there were five different segments based on usage.

We then grouped these patterns together into segments (final diagram); the resulting personas were incredibly helpful for redesigning the reports. We learned, for example, that there was a persona, represented by the dotted line in the lower left, who was responsible only for using the report to plan changes and improve the site, nothing more.

Segmenting by Behaviors and Attitudes

The segmentation options explored so far have been one-dimensional, based solely on one variable (user goals). But sometimes goals aren't the best way of segmenting users. Sometimes what users are doing doesn't reveal critical differences as much as *how* they're doing it. This is the time to pull out behaviors and attitudes from your long list of segmentation attributes.

Take the real estate site, for example: If you felt goals or the usage lifecycle wasn't passing the tests as the right way to segment users, you might narrow down the list of behaviors and attitudes and test them. Options could include the following:

Behaviors:

- Frequency of real estate activity
- Frequency of visits to the site
- Channel usage for various needs
- Use of competitors

Attitudes:

- Knowledge about real estate
- Motivators affecting users' likelihood to buy or sell
- Perception of the company/brand
- And so on

I've found that looking at a combination of behaviors and attitudes can ultimately result in better segmentation. If you're evaluating a long list of segmentation options and you've narrowed the list down to the most promising candidates, a very useful strategy is to plot them against each other. Put one attribute on the vertical axis and one on the horizontal axis. Let's try two from our real estate list: frequency of real estate activity and knowledge about real estate.

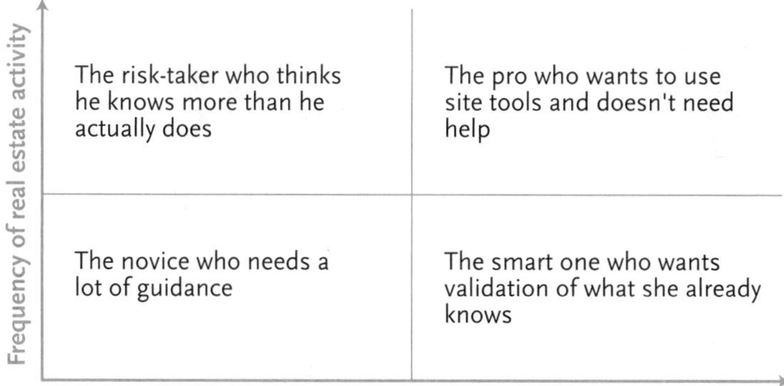

Exploring one segmentation option for a real estate site.

If you divide the graph into four quadrants, you get a 2×2 matrix that enables you to evaluate whether each quadrant could be a persona. In this example, someone who doesn't know much about real estate and who doesn't participate in real estate transactions feels very much like a novice who would need a lot of guidance. On the other hand, a less active person who knows more about real estate probably isn't looking for basic instructions, but validation of what she already knows. In this way, you can try to describe the segment created by each quadrant, then see if the segments pass the segmentation tests at the beginning of this chapter. If not, you can try a different combination of attributes on a new matrix to see what might result in a useful segmentation model.

I once used this approach when I was exploring segmentation for an ecommerce site that covered a huge variety of product categories. I found it difficult to segment based on user goals, so I started plotting behaviors and attitudes and trying various combinations. One combination—the amount of time users spent on the site vs. how much knowledge they had about the products they were seeking—proved to be very useful, and I ultimately used this segmentation to create personas.

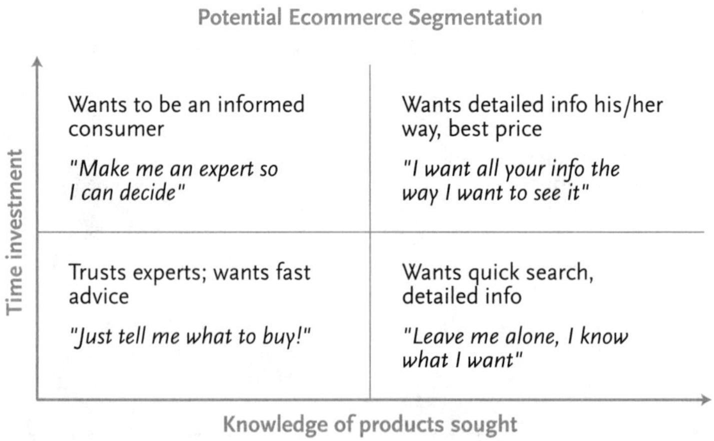

Potential Ecommerce Segmentation

Time investment ↑ / Knowledge of products sought →		
	Wants to be an informed consumer *"Make me an expert so I can decide"*	Wants detailed info his/her way, best price *"I want all your info the way I want to see it"*
	Trusts experts; wants fast advice *"Just tell me what to buy!"*	Wants quick search, detailed info *"Leave me alone, I know what I want"*

Knowledge of products sought

The segmentation approach for an ecommerce site.

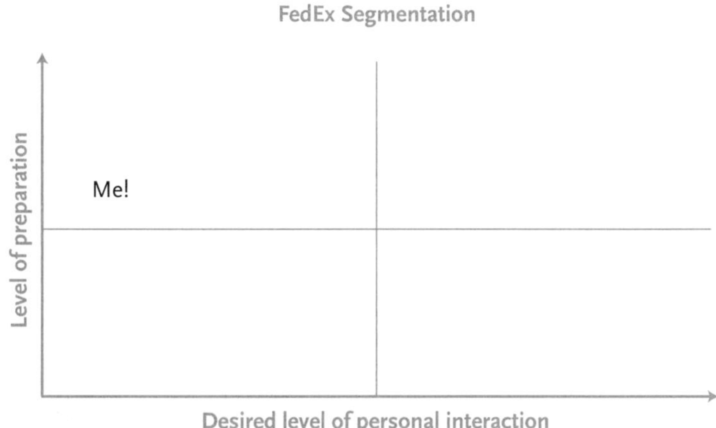

I love how FedEx defines its segmentation.

FedEx also uses this matrix approach for its segmentation, which is based on the combination of how prepared the user is for using the FedEx Web site and how much personal interaction he or she wants. When you're exploring and testing these segmentation options, sometimes you come across one such as this that simply feels right. I can't resist plotting where I fall as a user on this 2×2 matrix!

Technically, you don't need to restrict yourself to two-variable combinations. Once, when working on a Web search engine, I explored combining three variables to establish the segmentation. I plotted segments in a three-dimensional space, which worked conceptually but was, I admit, more difficult to quickly scan and understand. The more variables you use, the more complex and difficult it becomes to remember your story.

Remember, you aren't likely to discover only one magically correct segmentation model. Your mission is to explore all potential segmentation approaches and, by evaluating each one, determine which will be the most useful for your specific situation.

When you have a segmentation approach you're happy with, breathe a sigh of relief, because you've made it through one of the tricky parts. If you're conducting a survey to test your segmentation, go back to the previous chapter to learn more, then come back here and

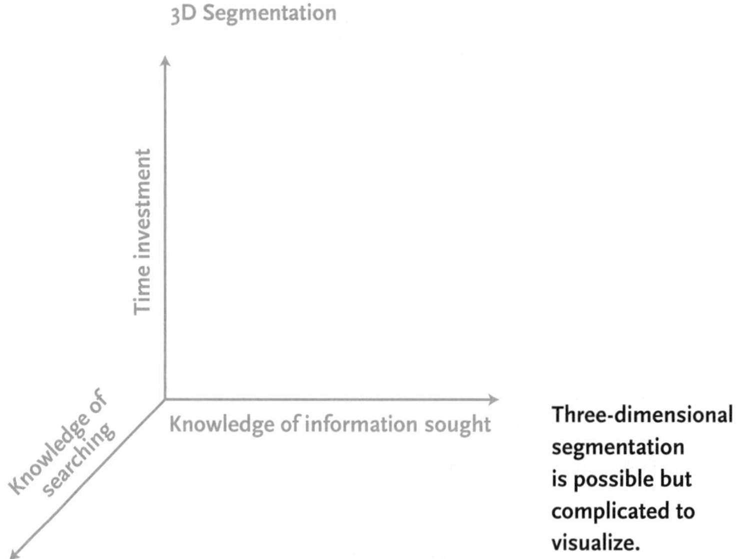

Three-dimensional segmentation is possible but complicated to visualize.

keep reading. If you're not running a survey, skip to the next chapter. (See, I told you this was like a *Choose Your Own Adventure* book.)

Conducting Quantitative Validation of Qualitative Segmentation

And now for a quick refresher: You can use quantitative research to test an existing theory about segmentation, or you can use it to generate data about a number of different segmentation options. Think of the first type as explicit segmentation and of the second type as emergent segmentation. This section covers the first usage, in which you have a good idea of how you'll segment users, and you want to gather quantitative data to validate whether your theory is sound.

As mentioned in Chapter 3, there are two things you can do to accomplish this quantitative validation, depending on the level of rigor you want to bring to the process and the skill sets you have available:

- **Cross-tab analysis of the data.** First, slice the data based on the variable you're using for segmentation. For example, if you're segmenting based on goals and have a survey question that asks people why they come to the site, you can view the data to see how users' answer to this question affected their answers to all the other questions. If people answer questions differently based on what their goals are, you have evidence that goal-based segmentation is real. This analysis is fairly easy to do in Microsoft Excel through pivot tables (which I'll cover shortly), and it provides you with a fast way of analyzing the effects of one or two variables.

- **Statistical analysis to validate the differences.** Cross-tabs are valuable for seeing key differences, but they don't necessarily show whether the differences you're seeing are statistically real. In other words, they don't show how significant the differences are. If you want to go the extra step and calculate ANOVAs (analysis of variance) for the segmentation data, find a statistician and skip to the next section for an overview.

This section focuses on cross-tab analysis, which, in Excel, works through pivot tables. A pivot table is a way to slice data by a particular attribute so that you can explore different ways of segmenting users. Fortunately, you don't have to be an Excel expert to work with pivot tables. (Otherwise, I'd be in trouble.) First, let's start with some raw data—in this case, you have a small amount of fake real estate information to work with. (If your data comes from an online survey, the online survey tool should enable you to download the raw results and open the file in Excel.) In this example, you know the following about 15 users: their main goal, their real estate knowledge (on a scale of 1 to 5, with 5 being high), whether they've used three competitor sites, their marital status, and their age.

Let's say you want to test whether segmenting by goal would be a useful segmentation option. (With pivot tables, it's easiest to select only one data point to use for segmentation.) In Excel, begin by selecting all the rows and columns that have data (as well as the column headers), then select Data > PivotTable. The PivotTable Wizard appears with the following steps.

User	Goal	Real estate knowledge	Used Realtor.com	Used ZipRealty.com	Used Yahoo.com	Marital status	Age
1	Buy house	4	X		X	Single	41
2	Refinance	5	X	X		Divorced	43
3	Find apartment	2			X	Single	24
4	Sell house	5	X	X		Married	52
5	Buy house	3			X	Married	37
6	Find apartment	2			X	Single	28
7	Refinance	5	X	X		Married	44
8	Sell house	4			X	Divorced	57
9	Buy house	3	X		X	Single	34
10	Buy house	4	X	X	X	Married	36
11	Refinance	4				Married	48
12	Sell house	5	X		X	Divorced	43
13	Find apartment	1			X	Married	30
14	Sell house	4		X	X	Married	41
15	Find apartment	2				Single	22

Here's how each of the 15 users responded to the survey.

Step 1: For finding the data you want to analyze, select Microsoft Office Excel list or database, and click Next.

Step 2: The range of cells should already be selected, so simply click Next.

Step 3: To position the pivot table, place it on the same worksheet as your raw data. Click Existing worksheet, then click a cell in the main window that's off to the right of your raw data in an empty area.

Click the Layout button to specify which variable you'll use for segmentation. In the Layout dialog box, drag Goal into the Column area. Then drag the other variables (except the user ID field and any single-select data, such as marital status) into the Data area. When you're finished, click OK, then, back in the Wizard, click Finish.

The result is a pivot table in your spreadsheet in which the values of each data point are broken out by segment (each goal in this example).

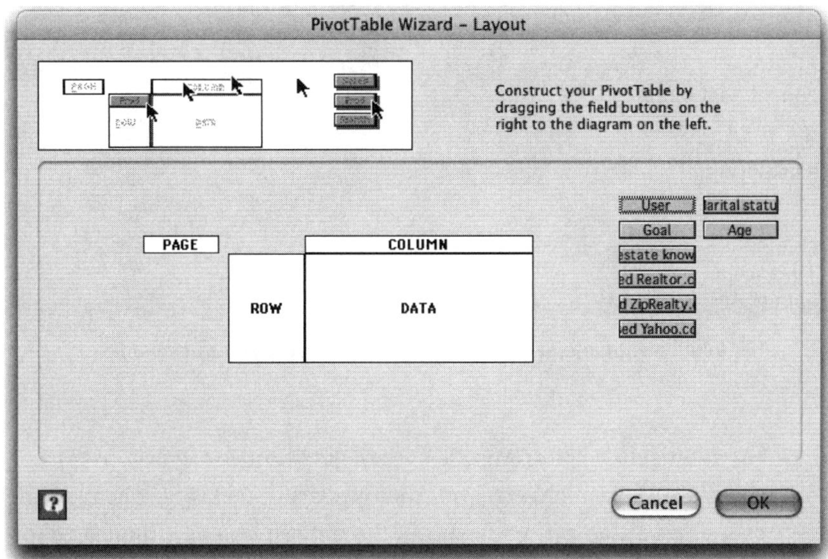

The Layout window of Excel's PivotTable Wizard.

For instance, in the following example, four house buyers used Yahoo.com, compared with three apartment hunters, zero refinancers, and three house sellers.

Before analyzing the data, however, you need to change the values for some data points so that they are more useful. Let's take the first one: real estate knowledge. In the default pivot table, scaled questions like this one are initially presented as sums of the values. But you want means (mathematical averages) instead so that you can compare the average response of each of the segments. Select that row of cells, then right-click (or control-click) and select Field Settings. In the dialog box, select Average. To round the values, click the Number button, and in the next dialog box, select Number from the list. The value should default to two decimal places. Click OK to close both dialogs. Now you're back at the pivot table, with mean values shown for real estate knowledge.

Age is another data point where you want to see means, so follow these same steps.

	Goal				
Data	Buy house	Find apartment	Refinance	Sell house	Grand Total
Sum of Real estate knowledge	14	7	14	18	53
Count of Used Realtor.com	3		2	2	7
Count of Used ZipRealty.com	1		2	2	5
Count of Used Yahoo.com	4	3		3	10
Sum of Age	148	104	135	193	580

The initial pivot table, with the survey data broken down by segment.

For multiselect data (e.g., a survey question for which users can check multiple answers), no changes are necessary, because the default pivot table already shows the data in an easy-to-analyze format. In the example, you can use the simple counts of which segments used which competitor sites to compare the segments.

Marital status is an example of single-select data, where the user can choose only one value (i.e., radio button questions). The process for slicing single-select data by segment is a little different. First select all the raw data again, just like when you started. Then select Data > PivotTable to create a separate pivot table for marital status. Go through the PivotTable Wizard as before, and position this new pivot table directly below your existing pivot table. When you get to the Layout dialog box, drag Goal into the Column area, like before. Then drag Marital status into the Row area, and finally drag User into the Data area. You'll need to create separate pivot tables like this for every single-select piece of data.

This process creates separate pivot tables below your main pivot table, but the columns line up so that you can easily scan all the data by user goal. As a final step, you want to change the values for your new pivot table. Select just the data fields, then right-click (or control-click) and select Field Settings. In the dialog box, select Count, then click OK. Now you can see how many of each segment are single, married, or divorced.

	Goal				
Data	Buy house	Find apartment	Refinance	Sell house	Grand Total
Average of Real estate knowledge	3.50	1.75	4.67	4.50	3.53
Count of Used Realtor.com	3		2	2	7
Count of Used ZipRealty.com	1		2	2	5
Count of Used Yahoo.com	4	3		3	10
Average of Age	37.00	26.00	45.00	48.25	38.67

Count of User	Goal				
Marital status	Buy house	Find apartment	Refinance	Sell house	Grand Total
Divorced			1	2	3
Married	2	1	2	2	7
Single	2	3			5
Grand Total	4	4	3	4	15

The final pivot tables, with data for each segment ready for analysis.

Now your pivot table is actually useful, and you can start evaluating whether this segmentation option will work. In this example of silly data, the segments appear to have clear differences between them. Apartment hunters know less about real estate, are younger, don't use competitor sites except Yahoo!, and tend to be single. House sellers, on the other hand, know a lot more about real estate, are older, are more likely to use multiple competitor sites, and are more likely to be married or divorced. You get the idea. You can now examine four segments to see if they pass the tests described at the beginning of this chapter. Now you have data supporting your analysis, rather than just hunches based on a few user interviews.

Excel can be a bit of a pain to work with, but if you want to test a segmentation option with quantitative data, pivot tables are a reasonably straightforward solution. If your initial theory about segmentation doesn't pass the tests, you can always try segmenting by another variable instead. This trial-and-error approach might be time-consuming, but it usually results in a segmentation option that works.

Applying Quantitative Segmentation

A few years ago, my colleague Ziv was working with the discount brokerage division of a major bank, developing personas for its customer base. After talking to customers, he made a list of all the attributes that he felt might significantly influence their Web behavior. First, was their level of experience as traders. The more experienced traders typically wanted more sophisticated features and tools. Second, was the type of products that they traded (stocks, mutual funds, options, foreign exchanges, etc.). Different products had different trading strategies; some required more frequent visits to the Web site, others, less frequent visits. To trade some products, a user had to view a lot more information at once to make a trading decision. The age of the customer influenced his or her behavior as well, as younger customers tended to be more open to performing their trades and getting their information across a wider range of devices (IVR [Interactive Voice Response], Web site, mobile, IM, etc.) than older customers. In addition, he felt that three or four additional variables (use of margin, number of brokerage firms they used, and whether they were trading for retirement or not) were also of some consequence.

At this point, Ziv had a few options. First, he could have chosen one or two variables and tried to segment based on that. However, this was not viable, because the entire team agreed that no *single* issue could explain all the customers' behaviors—the relationships were more complicated than that. Second, he could try to create segments that addressed every combination of all the variables. But that option wouldn't work, because there are millions or billions of combinations of all the variables. It would be impossible to explore every combination manually. His third option was to choose a small number of combinations that he felt were most prevalent among the customers. However, the number of customer interviews he would have had to perform just to adequately explore all the options would have been daunting (hundreds at a minimum).

This is a common situation: You have a list of attributes you think might be good candidates for segmenting users, but you're not altogether sure which few will be the most useful. You feel that there are multiple drivers for segmentation and that their relationships and interrelationships are not easily expressed in one or two variables. You could try them one at a time and use quantitative data to test each attribute, but that would take too much time, and wouldn't test combinations of multiple attributes. What you need, my friend, is statistical analysis.

As previously mentioned, adding more science into the segmentation process isn't a panacea. Statistical analysis is as much art as science, since it's guided by human assumptions and interpreted through human experiences and biases. Applying statistical analysis of quantitative data doesn't make you 100 percent accurate; rather, it means the chances of being wrong go down (without ever hitting zero). Just as flint points helped the cave man, statistical analysis provides you with a set of tools for exploring a set of options that you can't explore by hand. But as you know, statistically significant data can also go a long way toward convincing others that you know what you're doing.

Statistical analysis is as much art as science, since it's guided by human assumptions and interpreted through human experiences and biases.

In a nutshell, quantitative (or emergent) segmentation involves feeding potential segmentation attributes into The Machine, letting statistical analysis techniques have their way with them, and seeing what clusters come out the other side. Typically the result is a few different segmentation options for you to evaluate. The process is highly iterative, as you try different combinations of attributes to explore various options and ultimately select the segmentation option that looks the most useful according to the tests at the beginning of this chapter.

The metaphor I have unwisely chosen to describe this process is sausage making. (My apologies in advance.) The basic steps are as follows:

1. Select the attributes you want to feed into the process.
2. Decide how many segments (i.e., personas, or sausage links) you want.
3. Turn the crank on the statistical analysis and watch as the various segmentation options emerge.
4. Evaluate each segmentation option.
5. If you're happy with the results, profile the segments by running all the data points through the chosen segmentation. Otherwise go back to step 1 and try again.

It's a complex process, and you'll want to partner with a statistical analyst to do it right, but you'll be rewarded with a rich set of segmentation options that often go beyond anything the human mind can typically figure out on its own.

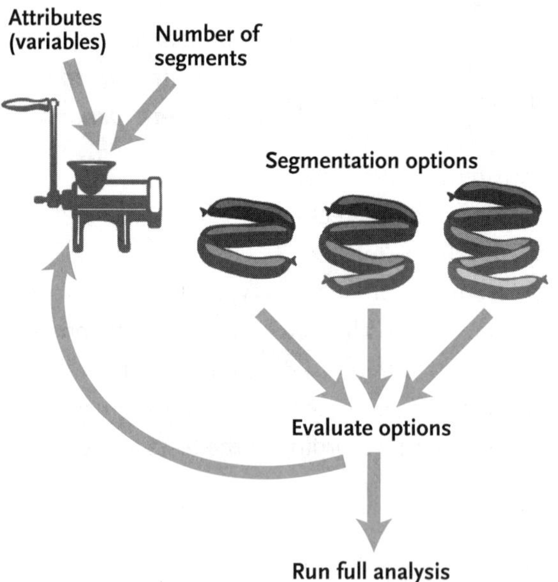

The quantitative segmentation process, told through the fine art of sausage making.

In some ways, this process is not all that different from qualitative segmentation with quantitative validation (see the previous section), where you first define the variables of interest, then segment based on each one of them, look at the results, and choose the one or two that work the best. The key difference is the introduction of the sausage factory—this black box statistical algorithm that analyzes thousands of lines of data to extract the segments for you. In both cases, you are fishing for the segments that best describe the users as you understand them based on your research and knowledge of the business. Quantitative segmentation simply enables you to identify potential segments when there is no single "smoking gun" variable with which you can segment.

1. Select the Attributes

The first things to feed into the process are the dependent variables you want to use as potential candidates for driving the segmentation. Basically, you pour in a subset of goals, behaviors, and attitudes (and maybe a few demographics) and let the cluster analysis determine which of those attributes best describe differences between the clusters it generates. Some of them emerge as key drivers, some of them as partial drivers, and some of them won't drive the segmentation at all.

Note that I said to use a *subset* of your total list of segmentation candidates. Technically, you can pour in every single attribute on your list to see what comes out the other side, but there are a few problems with this approach. First, the sausage grinder treats all attributes equally. It doesn't know that certain attributes (such as goals) are much more useful for defining personas and telling a story than other attributes (such as number of kids). Creating a subset of more meaningful attributes helps guide the analysis in a useful way. Second, the more attributes you throw into the mix, the longer it takes you to evaluate the segmentation options (step 4), because there's so much to examine. Third, more attributes also means that your segments are that much more complex, making the resulting personas more difficult for others to quickly understand, remember, and act upon.

So, begin with a subset of attributes. Through the process of conducting qualitative research and analyzing the master list of goals, behaviors, attitudes, and demographics, you'll gain some sense of which attributes are likely to be the most useful for driving key differences between users. Get the team together and prioritize your list of attributes into primary candidates, secondary candidates, and non-candidates.

Remember the example list of segmentation candidates from the last chapter? Here is how we initially prioritized them for cluster analysis.

Primary candidates:

- Usage of offline resources to research each business category (yellow pages, newspaper, etc.)
- Usage of the Internet to research each business category
- Usage of local search sites (Yahoo! Local, Yelp, yellow pages sites, etc.)
- Usage of expert ratings/reviews
- Usage of consumer ratings/reviews
- Contributions of ratings/reviews
- Importance of word of mouth for selecting products

Secondary candidates:

- Importance of being perceived as a community leader
- Importance of being perceived as an expert
- Weekly usage of the Internet
- Usage of Internet resources (mailing lists, blogs, portals, rating/review sites, etc.)

- Usage of social networking sites (Friendster, LinkedIn, etc.)
- Reliance on friends and family for selecting local businesses
- Reliance on expert advice for selecting local businesses
- Reasons for contributing ratings/reviews
- Technology affinity, savvy

For the first round, we poured in just the primary candidates. As we explored various segmentation options later on, we added the secondary candidates as well.

I recommend not including any attributes that deal with users' reactions to new ideas, improvements, features, or content. Think of these as the effects that you want to measure. They're the independent variables that will be directed by the segmentation generated by the dependent variables.

How many attributes should you use initially? Once again, I'll resist retreating into "It depends" and put a stake in the ground: A good starting point 5 to 10. Keep in mind that each attribute could have multiple data points. For example, for the attribute "Usage of Internet resources," you'll have a unique value for each resource you ask about (mailing lists, blogs, portals, etc.). Any 5 to 10 attributes could actually include a great many more data points.

The point is to start relatively small and work your way toward including more attributes if you need to. Your goal is to figure out which attributes are most effective at describing key differences, not to tell a story about every single attribute in your list.

2. Choose the Number of Segments

The second thing to feed into the cluster analysis is the number of segments or clusters you want (which is also the number of personas). How many sausage links do you want out of the meat grinder? When I work with a statistical analyst on this process, I typically have him or her run the analysis using a range of segments so that I end up with a few segmentation options to evaluate.

As mentioned earlier, you should aim for three to six segments per site. Sometimes you might start with asking for four and five clusters, and if you want more, you can always go back and run three and six clusters as well to compare the results.

3. Turn the Crank for Segmentation Options

This isn't a statistics book, but let's review cluster analysis to help you work through these steps. A number of different clustering algorithms are available, and one of the most commonly used is K-means clustering. At the simplest level, what this algorithm does is this: Given a series of records (survey results or other data) each with the same N variables (e.g., questions from the survey) and a goal for the number of segments it needs to find (typically called K), K-means attempts to return K centroids, where each centroid represents the minimum distance between itself and all the points within the segment. (A *centroid* is the collection of means for each variable.)

The simplest way to think about this algorithm is to take the case of four records in which a survey asked two questions: How much do you like the color red (on a scale of 1 to 5 where 1 is not at all and 5 is very much) and how much do you like the color green (same scale). The survey responses are shown in the table below.

You could easily plot these records on a chart, as shown in the figure to the right (top).

Record	How much do you like the color red?	How much do you like the color green?
1	1	1
2	2	2
3	1	4
4	2	5

Four example responses for the world's simplest survey.

If asked to group this data set into segments, you might say that two segments appear obvious candidates: people who do not like either red or green and people who like green. Visually represented, it might look something like what you see in the second chart below.

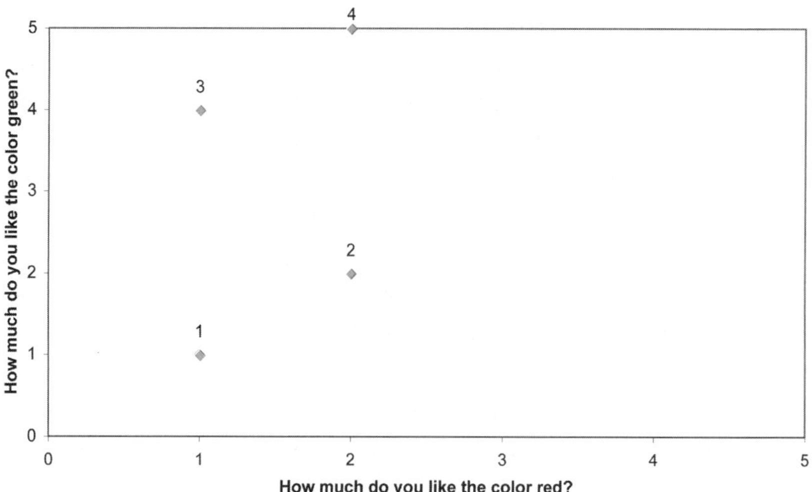

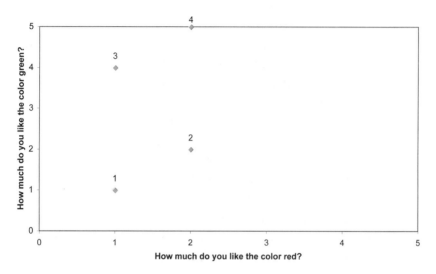

The survey responses plotted on a chart.

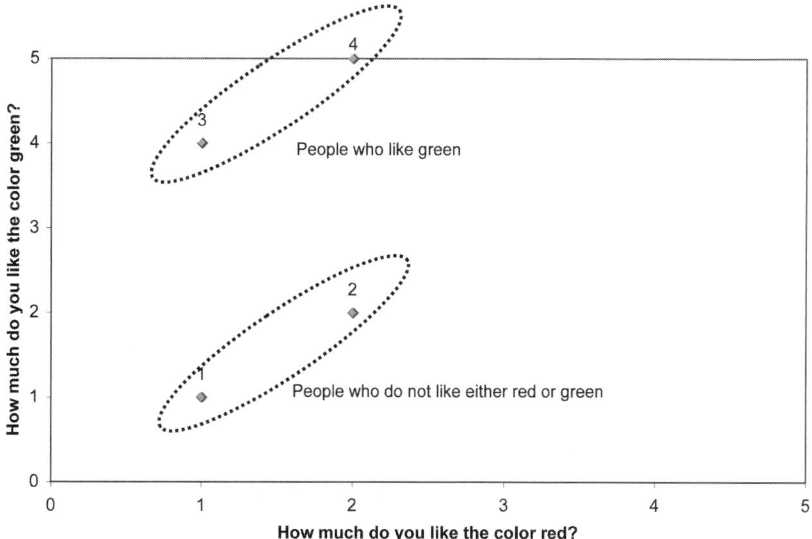

The data points clustered into two segments.

To talk about these segments, you need to look at the values of the centroids, the centers of each segment, which in this case might be the average of the two points of each segment (see the figure below).

Although this example is pretty easy to do by visual inspection, you can make it more complex in two ways. First, you can add more records to the problem. Imagine if you had to do a visual inspection of two thousand records instead of four. Second and perhaps more challenging, you can add more variables to the problem. Let's say you have another variable: How much do you like the color blue? To represent the four records you already have, you need a three-dimensional diagram (with the new question occupying the Z-axis). How about if you add another question: How much do you like the color orange? Now you need a four-dimensional diagram to represent your four records. Add another question and you need a five-dimensional diagram, another and you need a six-dimensional diagram. Now let's say that for each of these six questions, you have two thousand records instead of four, and you can start to see why

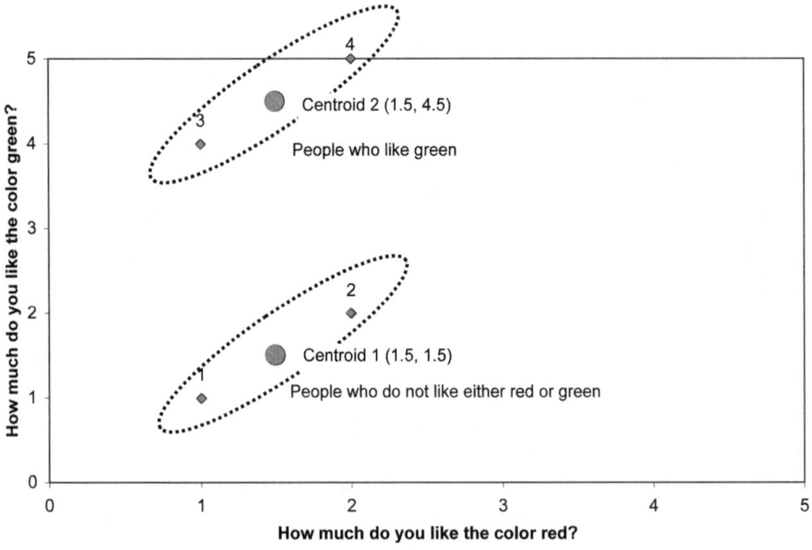

A centroid added for each segment.

you need a mathematical algorithm to figure out the segments and the centroids.

The actual K-means algorithm works something like this:

1. Assign every record to one of K sets. This is usually done randomly, but you can also follow a specific algorithm.
2. Plot the K centroids by calculating, for each centroid, the means of all the records in that set.
3. Reassign all the records into new K sets by figuring out, for each record, which is the closest centroid (calculated in the previous step) to that record.
4. Repeat steps 2 and 3 until the centroid locations stop changing from iteration to iteration.

Using our previous four-record example, the process of identifying the two centroids using K-means might look something like what you see in the following figure.

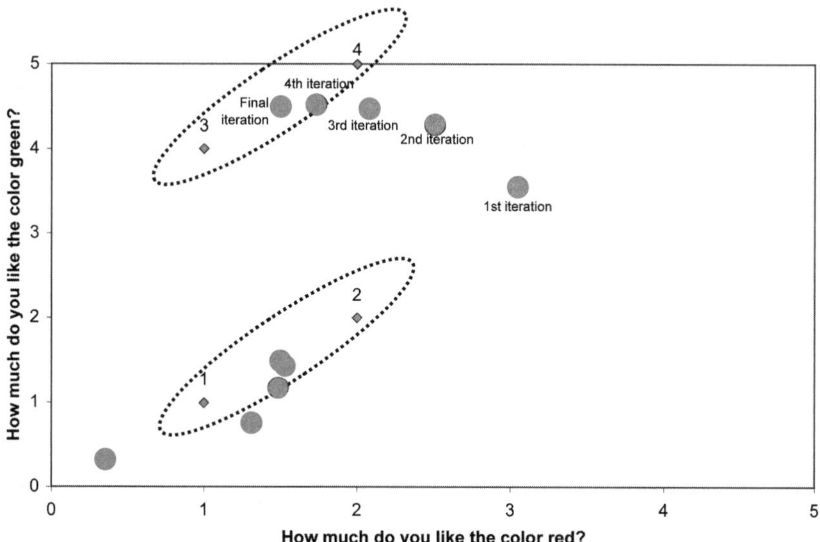

Iterative steps for trying out different centroids.

There are two big drawbacks with K-means. First, it does not find the optimal number of segments. You need to provide the number of segments you want it to find (the K). Second, because K-means has no understanding of the concepts behind the records and the variables it is being asked to crunch, it does not guarantee that it will find the optimal segmentation solution, just *a* solution. In the context of our previous four-record example, K-means could come back with a solution that looks like the figure below.

Although this solution might be statistically correct, it may make no sense when you understand the context behind the variables. Once again, it is up to you to take the output of K-means and evaluate whether it makes sense or not (see the next section). This is why this sort of statistical analysis is an iterative process, meaning that you have to try a number of different K's and a number of different variables, look at the results, and go with the one that makes the most sense from the business context.

Okay, enough background on how cluster analysis works.

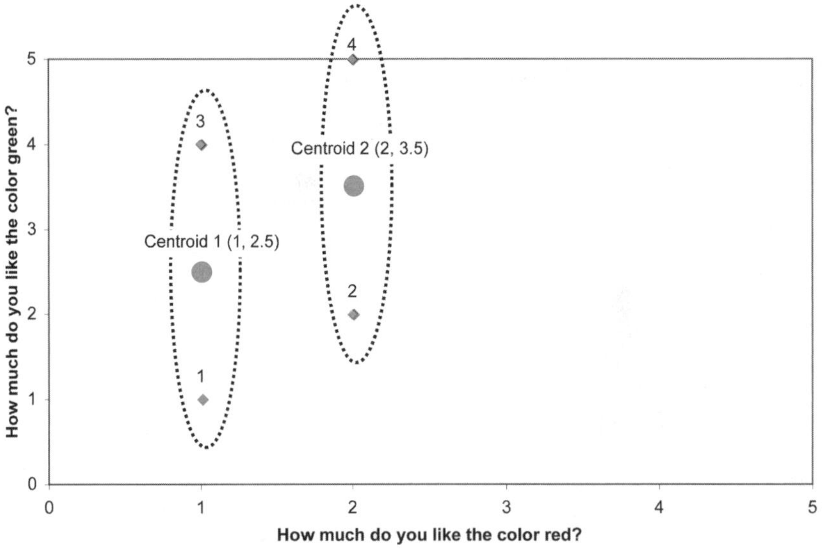

Another segmentation option K-means could find using the same data.

When you run cluster analysis, what comes out the other side are segmentation options. Maybe you get an option with three clusters (i.e., personas), an option with four, and an option with five. For each option, you get a ton of data so you can evaluate it.

Okay, actually, it's not quite this clean (nothing ever is). Each option you get looks more like the following diagram, which shows how example data breaks down into seven segments, with the numbers showing how many users fall into each segment. Three of these segments include very few users (18, 4, and 13); you can discard these outlier clusters as part of the noise. Then you have a four-segment option. A general rule of thumb is that an acceptable segmentation scheme is one that describes 75 percent or more of the data, with a typical scheme describing 85 to 95 percent of the data. So, when you work with your statistical analyst and tell him or her the number of segments you want, let him or her know that this is the number *after* eliminating the outliers.

For each segmentation option, you get a spreadsheet of data like the next example (only the first several rows of this are shown on page 151). For each variable down the left, the mean values are shown for each cluster, as is the overall mean.

If you are working with a statistical analyst, you should always ask him or her to provide you with three things, depending on the type of question in the survey: the mean, the median, or the frequency distribution for each survey answer or other data point.

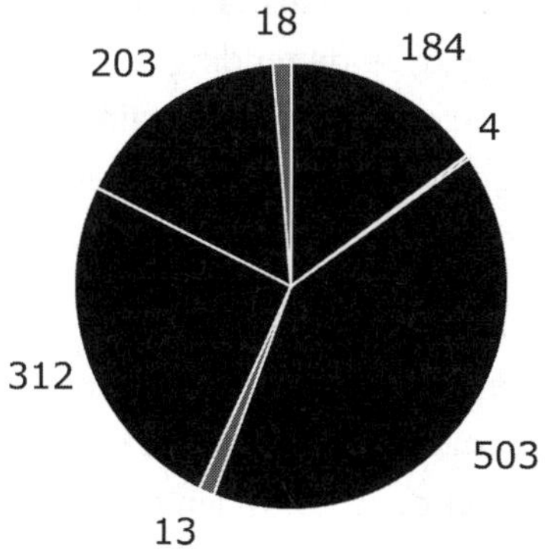

Pay attention to the main clusters and eliminate the outliers.

The mean is the average of all the answers. It is most useful for questions asked on a limited numeric scale, for example a 1–5 scale.

Medians are the mid-point value of all the answers. For example, if 5 people answered a question, the median is the third-highest number because exactly two numbers are higher and two are lower. Medians are most useful for answers on an unbounded numeric scale. For example, if you ask users how much money they make, the answer might range from $0 to $20 million, depending on who you ask. A mean can be skewed by a few people who answer very high or very low. Imagine if 20 people answer the previous question with $1 and one person answers the question with $20 million. The mean is almost $1 million, which is not very representative of the group. The median, on the other hand, would be $1.

Finally, for categorical values, where no scaled relationship exists between the categories, you need to see the percentage of people who gave each answer to this question. For example, if you asked users what their favorite color is, there would be no numeric scale for them to answer (is blue higher or lower than red?), so you just want to see what percentage (frequency distribution) of which segment answers red, blue, and so on.

The following example shows the answers to survey questions as the variables, but of course your data could also include site traffic analysis and CRM data. For this example, I've used scaled questions with mean averages.

In addition to the means, medians, and frequencies, a number of other pieces of data are interesting to analyze depending on your needs. However, two kinds of data come up again and again and they are worth asking your statistical analyst to produce for every survey question: significance and sum of squares.

Significance is a measure of how statistically significant the differences you're seeing between the different clusters are. One of the challenges in doing this sort of analysis is that sometimes just because the means or medians look different from one another does not mean that they

Question	Cluster 1 Mean	Cluster 2 Mean	Cluster 3 Mean	Overall Mean	Sum of the Squares	Significance
Q3: Appearance in local neighborhood or school web sites	1.63	1.08	2.63	1.91	82.75	1
Q3: Appearance in online city guides	2.17	1.48	3.79	2.48	72.71	1
Q3: Mentions in local blogs or discussion forums or newsgroups	1.6	1.16	2.45	1.91	71.63	1
Q3: Mentions in local newspaper web site(s)	1.84	1.3	3.3	2.16	69.41	1
Q2: Appearance in city or visitor guides	2.27	1.43	2.84	2.3	56.14	1
Q2: Sponsorship of local events or sports teams	2.29	1.35	2.25	2.14	55.22	1
Q2: Outdoor advertising	2.34	1.17	2.17	2.04	55.16	1
Q3: Appearance in classifieds web sites	1.98	1.29	3.1	2.14	53.13	1
Q3: Ratings/reviews on Web sites with ratings of local businesses	1.38	1.06	2.23	1.63	52.13	1
Q2: Newspaper and magazine advertising	2.92	1.78	2.56	2.61	50.29	1
Q6: Search engine optimization services	1.79	2.12	2.52	2.25	49.48	1
Q3: Appearance in Internet Yellow Pages	2.73	1.83	3.86	2.68	46.42	1
Q6: Advertising on web sites (all forms)	2.02	2.17	2.64	2.4	45.31	1
Q2: Loyalty programs/cards	2.76	1.26	1.7	2.04	45.08	1
Q1: Attract new customers who are visiting the area	3.66	1.84	2.5	2.78	45.07	1
Q2: Mentions in local newspapers	3.14	1.95	2.96	2.8	41.54	1
Q6: Search engine marketing	1.96	2.12	2.65	2.33	40.56	1
Q3: Appearance in industry-specific web sites or portals	2.56	1.97	3.61	2.73	40.44	1
Q9: I plan my marketing and sales programs extensively	3.02	2.46	2.04	2.83	39.92	1

Example of the output of cluster analysis, with data broken out by cluster, or segment.

actually are different in a meaningful way. A statistician can run a number of statistical tests, such as an ANOVA, to determine whether the differences you see are, in fact, real differences (at least statistically). These tests never return a simple yes or no (that would be too easy). Instead, they return a probability that the difference you are looking at is, in fact, statistically significant. When pharmaceutical companies run clinical trials on new drugs and want to see if patients taking the new drug have a different reaction than patients taking the placebo, they often look for a 95-percent significance (i.e., a 95-percent chance that what they see is not by accident). They want a high probability that the drug had a real impact. Outside of that world, you typically run 90 to 95 percent and may even go as low as 80 percent. I recommend you talk with your statistical analyst and proceed from there. In any case, do not read too much into significance. If it is above your threshold (80 to 95 percent, or 0.8 to 0.9), round it up to a 1 (good for use) and if it's below, treat is as a 0 (not good for use).

The other data of interest is *sum of squares*. Put simply, sum of squares is a measure of the amount of difference between the groups. So the greater the sum of squares, the more different they are with respect to that question. Thus, using sum of squares is a great way to rapidly identify the variables most likely to define differences between the clusters. If the variables with the greatest sum of squares make sense as the primary way to differentiate the clusters, then you are on to something and this approach to segmentation makes sense. If they do not make sense, then it's back to the drawing board.

Taken together, means, medians, and frequencies are good at describing the cluster; sum of squares is good at telling you if the clusters differ from one another; and significance tells you if anything you just saw actually matters (at least statistically). Depending on how many variables you put into the mix, this could be a very long spreadsheet, which is why sorting by significance (after rounding to 0 or 1) and then sum of squares is so useful. The most significant variables bubble nicely to the top, and now you're ready to evaluate each segmentation option.

4. Evaluate the Segmentation Options

Statistical data is one of those things you always say you want, but then when you get it, it's easy to be overwhelmed and to not know what to do with all of it. The previous spreadsheet is filled to the brim with lots of what you hope are useful numbers, but how do you turn these numbers into a story? How do you figure out whether these segments can pass the tests and become personas?

When you're ready to evaluate a particular segmentation option, I recommend that you create a quick cheat sheet like the following. Look for key differences between the segments, then document those differences in shorthand. Focus on the most significant variables and ignore all the rest to see what the key differences reveal. This document is much easier to scan and evaluate than columns of numbers.

	Cluster 1	Cluster 2	Cluster 3
Sample size	26%	57%	14%
Goals	Acquire and retain customers, brand	Retain customers, reduce costs	New customers most important, also retain customers and brand
General marketing	Owner does marketing; Less time spent, but sees value; Less marketing knowledge	No time for marketing	Dedicated marketing person; Significant time spent; More marketing knowledge
Offline marketing	Less active: radio/TV advertising, some loyalty programs	Not much: some radio/outdoor advertising, some direct mail	Active: Newspaper, city guides, directories, direct mail
Online marketing	Somewhat important: web site, industry sites, city guides; Increasing spend on own site	Least important, not on their radar	Very important: web site, email, city guides, SEM, blogs; Increasing spend on own site, ads, SEM
Technology knowledge/use	High	Medium	Medium
Customers	Many customer leads via word of mouth; Not much customer feedback	Most customer leads via word of mouth and yellow pages, very few from web; Informal customer feedback	Most customer leads via advertising, 25% from web; Formal customer feedback
Business	Very small companies; High in medical, then retail	Small companies, few locations; Highest in home improvement	Larger companies, several locations; High in medical, real estate, banking

A quick cheat sheet for identifying key differences between clusters.

Take each segmentation option and evaluate it against the tests at the beginning of this chapter. Much of the time, the segmentation option fails, for any number of reasons—maybe the segments aren't different enough or the segments don't feel like the users you interviewed. Some of the time, a segmentation option feels like it could work, but it doesn't tell as good a story as you'd like, and you wonder if there's a better alternative. In these cases, go back to steps 1 and 2, select a different number of segments or (better yet) try a different combination of attributes, and run a new analysis to see more options.

This process takes time. Don't jump at the first segmentation option that you see. And also don't feel like the numbers themselves definitively tell you what the one best segmentation option is. Statistical analysis isn't about generating the best solution but about generating a variety of mathematically valid options from which to choose. It takes science and art.

5. Profile the Segments

Once you've chosen a segmentation option, buy yourself some ice cream. Then, work with your statistical analyst to run all the data using this segmentation option. This time, instead of focusing on a subset of attributes, look at all the attributes. It's time to see how every data point you have breaks down when you slice it by segment. You already know about the key differences from step 3; now you get the full profiles of each segment. It looks something like this spreadsheet below.

	Means by segment				***% difference from***		
Question	**1**	**2**	**3**	**Overall**	**1**	**2**	**3**
Monthly Spend on Yellow Pages	$331	$272	$436	$344	-21%	27%	-4%
Question 1: How important are each of the following goals for your business?							
Retain existing customers	4.78	4.46	4.7	4.75	4%	-1%	1%
Attract new customers who are local residents	4.84	4.42	4.17	4.57	9%	-9%	6%
Increase my brand image	4.41	4.33	3.63	4.18	11%	-13%	6%
Reduce customer acquisition cost	4.53	3.33	3.63	3.99	11%	-9%	14%
Sell new products and services to existing customers	4.44	3.08	3.4	3.81	12%	-11%	17%
Attract new customers who are visiting the area	3.47	2.5	1.84	2.78	32%	-34%	25%
Question 2: How important have the following approaches been for building profitable relationships with your customers?							
Word of mouth	4.84	4.84	4.62	4.75	1%	-3%	2%
Yellow pages book(s)	3.69	3.8	3.3	3.65	9%	-10%	1%
Mentions in local newspapers	3.81	2.96	1.95	2.8	12%	-30%	36%
Participation in business networking groups or events	4.06	2.91	2.1	2.76	-3%	-24%	47%
Newspaper and magazine advertising	3.81	2.56	1.78	2.61	12%	-32%	46%
Leaflets/flyers	3.23	2.28	1.92	2.48	14%	-23%	30%
Printed directories (not yellow pages)	3.5	2.58	1.75	2.4	2%	-27%	46%
Appearance in city or visitor guides	3.63	2.84	1.43	2.3	-1%	-38%	58%
Direct mail	3.44	2	1.6	2.3	13%	-30%	50%
Sponsorship of local events or sports teams	3.38	2.25	1.35	2.14	7%	-37%	58%

Every data point broken out by segment, along with amount of difference.

For every variable, you now have the overall mean as well as means for each segment. In addition, you want to see columns showing how different each segment is from the overall mean. These percentages make it easier to scan for key differences. Better yet, use conditional formatting in Excel so that any value above a certain threshold (say, 20 percent) is green, and any value below a certain threshold (–20 percent) is red.

You're now swimming in data, but at least the data is structured in a useful way (by segments that will turn into your personas) and presented in a way that makes it easier to scan for key differences. As a result, you now have more raw material for personas than you ever could have dreamed of.

You might find it helpful to summarize the segments by expanding the cheat sheet shown earlier. This enables you to go through the data and document the key differences that you want to use in the personas. But now that you've chosen a segmentation option, you can be more thorough with each key difference, and you can also include additional variables that weren't in the cheat sheet (e.g., demographics). What you document depends on your situation, but useful categories include the much-used goals, behaviors, and attitudes, as well as demographics and a list of key features and content each segment needs.

This document can be a useful intermediate deliverable to pass around before diving in and creating the actual personas. Getting buy-in on your segmentation is a critical step, as discussed previously, and this document can help you make your case.

One additional note: If you're using the survey to prioritize site improvements or new features and content, you can generate an *opportunity score* as a key measurement. This metric uses two survey questions to identify the most important opportunities: a question about the importance of a specific item and a question about the user's current level of satisfaction with that same item. For example, you could ask users to rate how important a certain feature is, then, later on, ask how satisfied they are with the same feature. When importance is high but satisfaction is low in comparison, you have a larger gap between the two, which signals a higher opportunity.

Opportunity score is calculated using the following formula:

> Opportunity = 2 * (Importance score) – (Satisfaction score)

If the result is less than the importance score, then the importance score is used instead.

The chart below shows an example of how opportunity score plays out. The highest opportunity score goes to a feature that is fairly important, but where current satisfaction is low. Meanwhile, very important features that users are currently satisfied with are prioritized lower. In general, anything 5 or higher is a high opportunity and 4 to 5 is a moderate opportunity.

You can analyze opportunity score for each segment and thus discover what the priorities are for each persona.

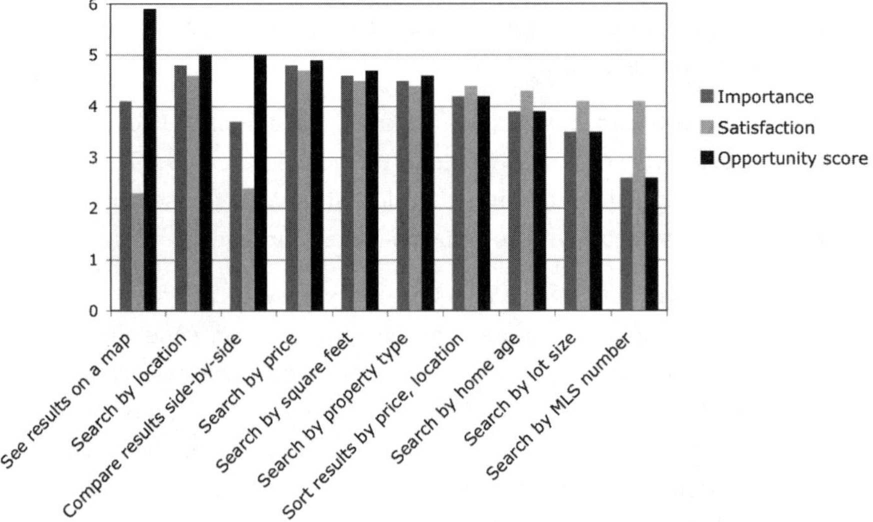

Examples of how importance and satisfaction lead to opportunity score.

A Few Examples

How this cluster analysis process plays out depends on your business, your users, and your needs. It's an iterative process that is tailored for each situation, as the following examples attest.

For one specialty retailer, my team and I knew early on how we wanted to segment users, because the company was very focused on how customers were using each channel (store, Web site, and catalog). We segmented by channel usage so that we could better understand what drove usage of each channel and so that we could explore ways of encouraging customers to shop across multiple channels. So, in this situation, we wanted to test our qualitative (or explicit) segmentation by channel usage, and our process was relatively straightforward. Following the process described earlier, we looked at all the data based on this segmentation, then we calculated significance and sum of squares to make sure that what we were seeing was statistically real. Based on the output of the analysis, we created the cheat sheet shown here, which enabled us to evaluate whether these segments were a useful approach for creating personas.

	Web-only	**Store-only**	**Store/Web**	**Store/Catalog/Web**
Shopping behaviors/ attitudes	Little time to shop for clothing; Enjoys shopping the least; Primarily a catalog browser with Web as secondary, purchase Web (with some catalog), returns through store and mail	More time to shop for clothing; Enjoys shopping somewhat; Primarily a catalog browser with store as secondary, purchases in the store, returns through the store	Little time to shop for clothing; Enjoys shopping; Browses in all the channels (catalog is the most), purchases mostly in the store (Web is secondary), returns in the store	Most time to shop for clothing; Enjoys shopping most; Browses in all the channels (catalog by far the most), purchases mostly in the store (Web is second, catalog is third), returns in the store
Relationship with Company	Shops at Company the least often; Relatively new to Company Least familiar with Company merchandise	Shops at Company somewhat regularly; Long-time customer of Company; Somewhat familiar with Company merchandise	Shops at Company somewhat regularly; Relatively new to Company; Quite familiar with Company merchandise	Shops at Company most often Long-time customer of Company; Most familiar with Company merchandise
Demographics	Slightly younger; Larger sizes	Slightly older; Largest percentage not employed or retired; Lowest household income	Youngest; Largest percentage employed; Highest household income	Slightly older
Financials	Annual value: $XXX; 4% of Company customers; 15% of Company.com visitors	Annual value: $XXX; 68% of Company customers; 14% of Company.com visitors	Annual value: $XXX; 4% of Company customers; 29% of Company.com visitors	Annual value: $XXX; 2% of Company customers; 14% of Company.com visitors

Cheat sheet for evaluating a segmentation option for a specialty retailer.

Another example is a project my colleagues conducted for Harvard Business School Publishing (HBSP). HBSP is the publishing arm of the Harvard Business School (HBS) and is world-renowned for its management and business products, such as HBS case studies, *Harvard Business Review* magazine, and the Harvard Press collection of books. HBSP has had a number of different Web properties and was in the process of developing a strategy for its next-generation Web sites.

In talking to customers, my colleagues identified a number of different ways that people were using the Web site. The first had to do with need. Sometimes a user would come to the Web site to solve a specific management problem. For example, her company had tasked her with opening a new office in China and she needed insight for a presentation to her board about how this office might be run. Other times, a user would come to the Web site simply to stay up on the latest in management thinking, expecting that HBSP would filter, sort, and present him with all he needed to know. Another variable was the type of actions these users took when they were at the Web site. Some would be very focused, with a clear idea of the book, case, or article they were looking for, while others would browse the categories, trying to find a relevant item. A third variable was the type of product that they purchased. Some customers preferred case studies, others gravitated to books, articles, e-learning applications, and so on.

After talking to customers, my colleagues had a sense for which key variables would drive the segmentation. But they sought quantitative evidence to back up their hypothesis and knew that statistical analysis would provide a richer perspective of which variables were most important. So they made sure the survey covered these issues.

Following the process described earlier, the team fed the results of these survey questions into the statistical analysis engine and tried a variety of different segmentation approaches using K-means clustering. Quickly, an effective segmentation model emerged that consisted of three segments. Once they had the segments, the team compared the users' answers in all the other survey questions to one another to get a better sense of what each segment looked like. The team used ANOVAs to identify the areas of greatest difference as a way of quickly bubbling up the key differences from a lot of survey questions. They then created a cheat sheet that enabled them to evaluate whether these segments would be useful in creating personas. The segments passed the tests, and my colleagues created a full persona for each segment. The personas provided HBSP a unique perspective on the needs of its customers and helped to refocus the strategy for its next-generation Web sites.

Applying statistical analysis to persona segmentation is an exciting development in user-centered design. It adds another level of sophistication and rigor to your goal of making user research real and actionable. Just remember that statistics will never and should never replace the machine that is best at finding the story in all the data: your mind.

7 Making Personas Real

NOW FOR THE FUN PART! You've created a world-class approach to segmentation that would make your parents proud, but segments aren't personas. Segments are boring lists of characteristics (perhaps supported by boring spreadsheets of numbers). Personas are different because they feel like real people. Personas work because teams can get to know them and think about them as real people, and thus, these teams can start making decisions about the Web site based on this realistic cast of characters.

This chapter is about how to make personas out of your segments—how to transform a quick list of facts into a story that others quickly understand, remember, and act upon. By the end of the chapter, you'll be able to build up your personas gradually in the following areas:

- Key differentiators (their defining goals, behaviors, and attitudes)
- Name
- Photo
- Personal information
- Domain-specific information
- Computer and Internet usage
- Profile
- Additional attributes
- Quote
- Business objectives
- Persona prioritization
- Scenarios

Also, Francis the First-Time Home Buyer, our example persona, returns in all her glory to show you how all these pieces might fit together in the final product. You'll learn more about various ways to document and share personas in Chapter 8.

Revealing Key Differentiators

Start with what's most important—the attributes that define your segments—and explain the key differences between them. Your segmentation is based on goals, behaviors, attitudes, or some combination thereof, and now it's time to document those key differentiators clearly.

If you're like me, you'll usually start by trying to summarize the few, most critical differentiators in two or three concise summary bullets.

Sometimes this is difficult because you have so much to say about each persona. But this is precisely why it's a good place to begin: It forces you to eliminate all but the most vital attributes that make this persona unique. Ask yourself: If you had 10 seconds to describe this persona to someone, what would you say?

For Francis, these summary bullets appear in the upper right of the page (see the figure on page 164):

- Looking for first home
- Low real estate knowledge
- Very intimidated

This list isn't brilliantly creative, but it's clear and to the point, covering this persona's primary goal as well as attributes that influence how she goes about achieving her goal. You can't count on everyone reading the entire persona, so if you have their attention only briefly, this is one of the few things you want them to read.

To make it easy to compare personas quickly, sometimes I'll make the summary bullets parallel across all personas. For example, if I were coming up with a different home seller persona, I might use the bullets in the same way: the first for the overall goal, the second for level of knowledge, and the third for attitude.

Of course, you also want to be able to go into more detail on these key differentiators, because detail helps create realism. It's helpful to reserve another part of the persona document for this information as well as integrate the differentiators throughout the document. For Francis, a persona based primarily on goals, there's a section dedicated to "User Goals" with more detailed bullets that describe why Francis comes to the site.

Let's look at a couple of other examples of how this plays out. One of the personas of Harvard Business School Publishing (HBSP) is a corporate training director. Her "User Goals" section looks like this (page 165):

Priority

PRIMARY PERSONA

Name

Francis
the First-Time Home Buyer

Quote

"I just don't know where to start!"

- Looking for first home
- Low real estate knowledge
- Very intimidated

Key differentiators

Profile

Personal Profile

Francis and her husband Michael have dreamed of owning their own home for years, and love to look through real estate listings together on Sunday mornings. Now that Michael's promotion has come through, they can finally get serious about it. The only problem is, Francis has no idea where to start.

She has ideas about what they want: newer home, closer to the city, 3 bedrooms, pool. But she knows she has a lot to learn about real estate, and she's intimidated by the number of factors and decisions. What can they really afford? How can they avoid buying a home in an area they won't like? Francis simply doesn't know all the steps involved in buying a house, and is reluctant to ask her home-owning acquaintances dumb questions.

What Frances wants is a site that will explain the whole process without drowning her in confusing jargon. But she also wants it to have everything she needs to actually begin the process and look for houses, so she doesn't have to go to multiple sites. She likes sites that are friendly and straightforward, especially the ones that remember who she is so she doesn't have to enter her information each time. But most of all, she wants to use a site that she can trust to give her good advice and good information.

User Goals

Francis comes to the site to…

- Learn more about the home-buying process, including jargon, realtors, mortgages, insurance, and how to evaluate houses
- Find out what they can afford based on current rates and first-time buyer programs
- Discover what areas of Atlanta are desirable, taking into account schools, taxes, mass transit, crime, etc.
- Find a house that matches their criteria
- Find the best mortgage lender
- Find the best homeowners insurance

Business Objectives

We want Francis to…

- Visit the site often (ad revenue)
- Register for email alerts and newsletters
- Subscribe to premium services
- Follow through on individual listings by contacting realtor
- Follow through on mortgage and insurance by contacting partner
- Recommend the site to others

Key differentiators

Business objectives

Personal Information

Personal information

Profession: Registered Nurse, Northside Hospital

Location: Atlanta, GA

Age: 33

Home life: Married to Michael (pharmaceutical sales); no children, but planning to start a family soon

Hobbies: Cooking, matchmaking among her many friends, tennis

Favorite TV shows: Oprah, The Apprentice

Personality: Outgoing, friendly, a bit meddling, detail oriented

Real Estate Information

Domain-specific information

Current home: Apartment south of downtown (for 6 years)

Household income: $70,000

Savings: $10,000

Credit: Good

Purchase timeframe: 3-6 months

Real estate knowledge: Low

Internet Usage

Computer and Internet usage

Internet experience: Intermediate (online 2 years)

Primary uses: Shopping, email, horoscope

Favorite sites: Coolsavings, Peapod, GAP, E Online

Hours online per week: 3

Computer: iMac, 56K modem, Internet Explorer 5

The various components of a persona come together.

Carrie comes to the site to...

- Research a particular management challenge
- Find subject matter experts in certain topics
- Find recommendations related to the pharmaceutical industry specifically
- Find support to clarify questions she has about the material
- Print records of past transactions

Note that each bullet begins with a verb. If you're segmenting based on goals, document them as actions. Verbs make personas feel more realistic, and give a sense of urgency to what the personas need. Verbs are also most helpful later when you're using the persona to drive features and functionality and decide how things should work.

Sometimes it helps to think about this list as comprising the sub-goals of the persona's overall goal, if you recall the hierarchy of goals from the previous chapter. By going to a deeper level of detail, you can make the persona realistic and specific rather than generic, as you are simply stating a more general, overarching goal such as, "Show the value of corporate training."

Depending on your segmentation approach, you might devote a section to behaviors and/or attitudes. You may even consider including a section on goals as well, because what users are trying to do is often the most valuable piece of information that drives decision-making.

For VistaPrint, my team created a section called "Goals & Motivators." The following examples show how we used this section for two personas:

Patricia comes to the site to...

- Find the perfect template and customize it exactly the way she wants it, including uploading images
- Upload her own design

- Proof her work carefully before printing
- Check on the status of her order

Patricia cares most about...

- High quality of color, paper, and finish
- Freedom to customize anything she wants
- Low prices and fast delivery

Howard comes to the site to...

- Create professional business cards quickly
- Find a template that's unique
- Reorder his cards

Howard cares most about...

- Getting "good enough" results *fast*
- Having a unique professional image
- Finding ways to make things easier
- Working with someone reliable that he can trust

Even with just this small amount of text, you can start to get a feel for these two very different personas. In this case, the key differentiators are just as much about what's important to each persona (behaviors and attitudes) as they are about goals. Patricia is driven primarily by perfectionism, and Howard by speed and convenience.

You don't have to document these key differentiators in the form of bullets, of course. You might find that a paragraph or two can describe more powerfully the most important aspects of each persona. I usually create both a dedicated section with a bulleted list that's easy to scan and a more narrative approach that creates the persona's overall story (see the "Writing a Profile" section later on).

Regardless of your approach, documenting key differentiators involves some level of simplification, and in some cases oversimplification, which can be a good thing. For example, VistaPrint data told us that the Patricia and Howard segments both cared about being able to proof their business cards before printing. But because Patricia cared about it more, and because proofing wasn't critical to describing the core differentiators of Howard, we didn't include proofing in Howard's persona. By honing in on the differences that mattered most, we made the personas crisp and easy to understand. It's often useful to sacrifice just a little complex realism for the sake of making the personas more memorable.

This being the most important part of actually writing the personas, treat it iteratively. Write a rough draft of key differentiators, move on to the other components of the personas, and then come back to your text as the persona becomes more and more real in your mind. All of these components build upon each other to make your personas feel real.

Creating a Name

A persona is not a persona without a name. It might seem silly, but a name that everyone can refer to can make all the difference in viewing the persona as being real rather than just a segment or user type. Talking about Francis is more effective than talking generally about first-time home buyers.

A first name is usually enough, to avoid stretching everyone's recall capacity. When you're picking a name, use a real name that this particular person could have. You might even want to use the first name of a specific person you met during user interviews—one who fits this segment well. However, steer away from the names of any colleagues, since using such names is more distracting than helpful.

Make sure that the names of your personas are considerably different from each other to avoid any confusion. You don't want the team to mistake Amy for Annie, for instance. When each name is distinct, they're easier to recall.

Also think about personalities when you choose names. In the VistaPrint example earlier, one persona was motivated by quality and perfectionism, so my team chose the name Patricia rather than Patty, because Patricia felt more appropriate for someone who cared about detail and a refined self-image. Make a conscious effort to think about what this type of person would want to call themselves: Bill or William, Becky or Rebecca, and so on.

Diversity is also critical, as you'll see in later sections. What you don't want is a set of homogenous, white-bread personas, who don't reflect the diversity of your audience. This is another area where art meets science, because even though you might have data that shows that every one of your segments is more male than female, or more white than minority, or more American than not, you don't need to be shackled to that data. Making one or more of your personas female or Latino or German is valuable because doing so helps the team think about all users, not just the stereotypes in their minds. If you have data, look for which segments are the best candidates for diversity.

When I'm looking for names used in the United States, one of my favorite sites is the NameVoyager at iVillage, found at www.babynamewizard.com/namevoyager. Through an interactive interface, you can explore how names have shifted in popularity over the decades and find unique names easily.

The only name I'd suggest staying away from is Jesús. After all, you don't want your team running around asking, "What would Jesús do?" (My apologies, I've been saving that groan-inducing joke for many pages now.)

When naming personas, consider adding a descriptor to the name so that everyone automatically associates the name with the primary differentiator. Like the summary bullets discussed earlier, this descriptor becomes a shorthand version of the persona. Find one word or a few that capture best what sets this persona apart from the others.

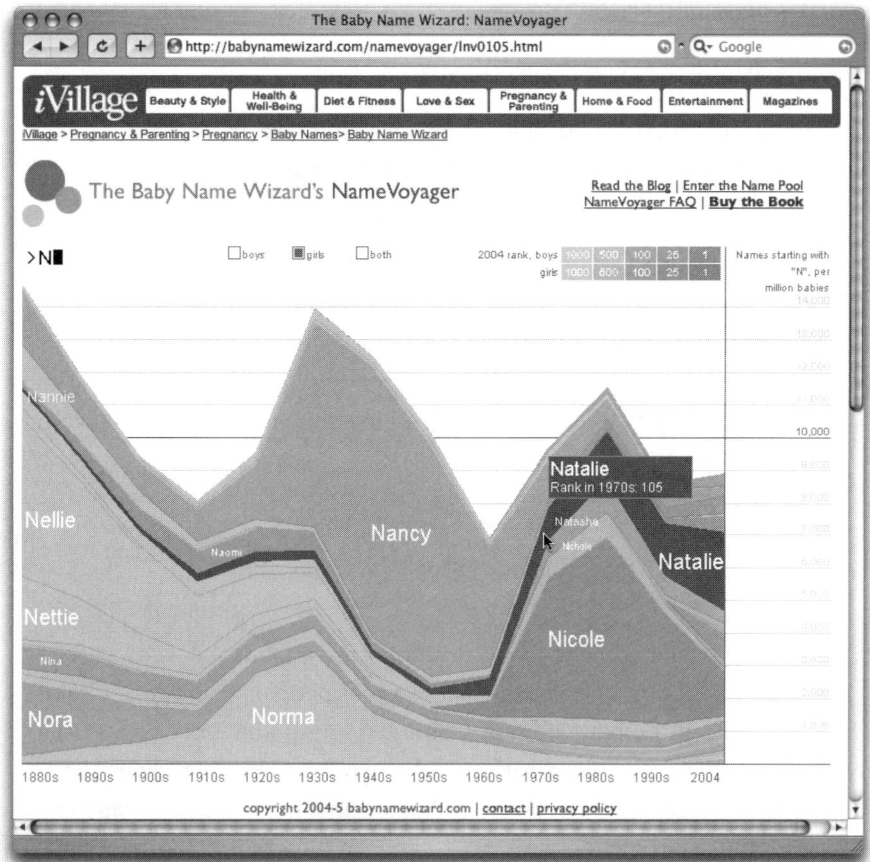

Exploring persona names with NameVoyager (created by Martin Wattenberg and Laura Wattenberg).

Here are a few examples from various personas:

- Patricia the Perfectionist
- Howard the Hurried
- Hal the Hyperactive Trader
- Henry High Touch
- Larry the Conservative Laggard

- David the Delegator
- Harry the High Geek

You'll notice I've used alliteration to help make the names more memorable. It can be a helpful trick, as long as it doesn't make the name sound silly (e.g., Mary the Merry).

Choosing a name is an iterative, collaborative process like everything else. People have instinctive responses to different names, so it's important to find a name that everyone feels is right for that persona. You know your personas are working when team members start referring to them by name, saying things like, "But Francis wouldn't do that!"

Finding a Photo

Personas don't come to life without photos. You absolutely must *see* these characters before they feel like real people. And if you think your colleagues have opinions about names, wait until you start looking at photos. Even early on when you're working on your segmentation approach, everyone will start forming a mental image of what these people look like. So it can take time to find a photo that everyone agrees as being truly Francis or Patricia or Howard. Picture selection is often a very subjective process—you tend to know it when you see the right one.

The most important thing about selecting photos is to use real people.

The most important thing about selecting photos is to use *real people*. Do not use shots of people who are models or, in any way, can be viewed as models. Also, avoid traditional stock photography and photography approved for marketing uses. The whole point of personas is to create realistic characters who represent your *actual* users. If you select photos that don't look like real people with real flaws, you'll end up creating idealized user profiles that may be misleading when they're used for decision-making. Don't worry about choosing photos that aren't perfect, because they're for internal use only. However, whatever image you use, make sure you have the legal rights to use it as you intend.

To make sure your photos look like real people, avoid overly posed photographs. A face smiling at the camera is fine, but if the photo looks too carefully planned or unnatural, it's not useful for a persona. For this reason, photos with something in the background look more real, compared to those obviously taken in a studio. The more your persona photo looks as if it were taken in the actual environment of your users, the better. Just make sure the focus of the photo is the person; sometimes the background can be overwhelming.

Just as with names, photos of the personas should be appropriate to the personality you're trying to create. Think about the clothing this particular person would wear, the hairstyle, the makeup, and so on. Patricia the Perfectionist's photo won't contain ratty hair or a baggy sweatshirt. Choosing a photo means choosing an age range as well, so look at any data you have on age, but don't feel confined by it. You don't want four personas all of the same age.

Diversity is important in other areas as well, particularly race. Don't end up with an all-white cast of characters. This simply reinforces stereotypes rather than helping colleagues think about the true diversity of your user base.

When you're choosing photos, remember that they'll be viewed as a set, so you want some consistency—not in terms of the people in the photos, but in terms of the treatment. For example, you don't want three head shots and one full-body shot or one profile shot. Nor do you want some color and some black and white. Look at them as a set.

I recommend using face-and-shoulders shots for persona photos, because the face captures an excellent level of detail and personality, and you also get just enough clothing to get a sense of it. Make sure to get shots in which the people are looking in the general direction of the camera and are not in profile. You should be able to see their faces clearly and not be too distracted by other people or objects, or anything else that feels overly odd or eccentric for this person, such as a hideous Christmas sweater or a parrot on his or her shoulder.

Because you'll use these photos in various ways (printed, in presentations, etc.), use color photos and find photos that are high resolution and won't break up when you print them.

Where do you find such photos? Traditional stock photo sites can still work if you're careful to avoid anything posed or model-like, but I like the following sites:

- stock.xchng (www.sxc.hu) is a free photo sharing site that's growing constantly and enables you to browse portraits of women, men, and seniors.
- morgueFile (www.morguefile.com) is a similar (and also free) site.
- iStockphoto (www.istockphoto.com) is practically free ($5 or less per photo) and is also full of great head shots.

In theory, online dating sites would be great sources of photos of real people, but no, you can't use them. Besides, can you imagine presenting your personas and looking up to see one of your personas staring back at you?

And now for some good examples of persona photos:

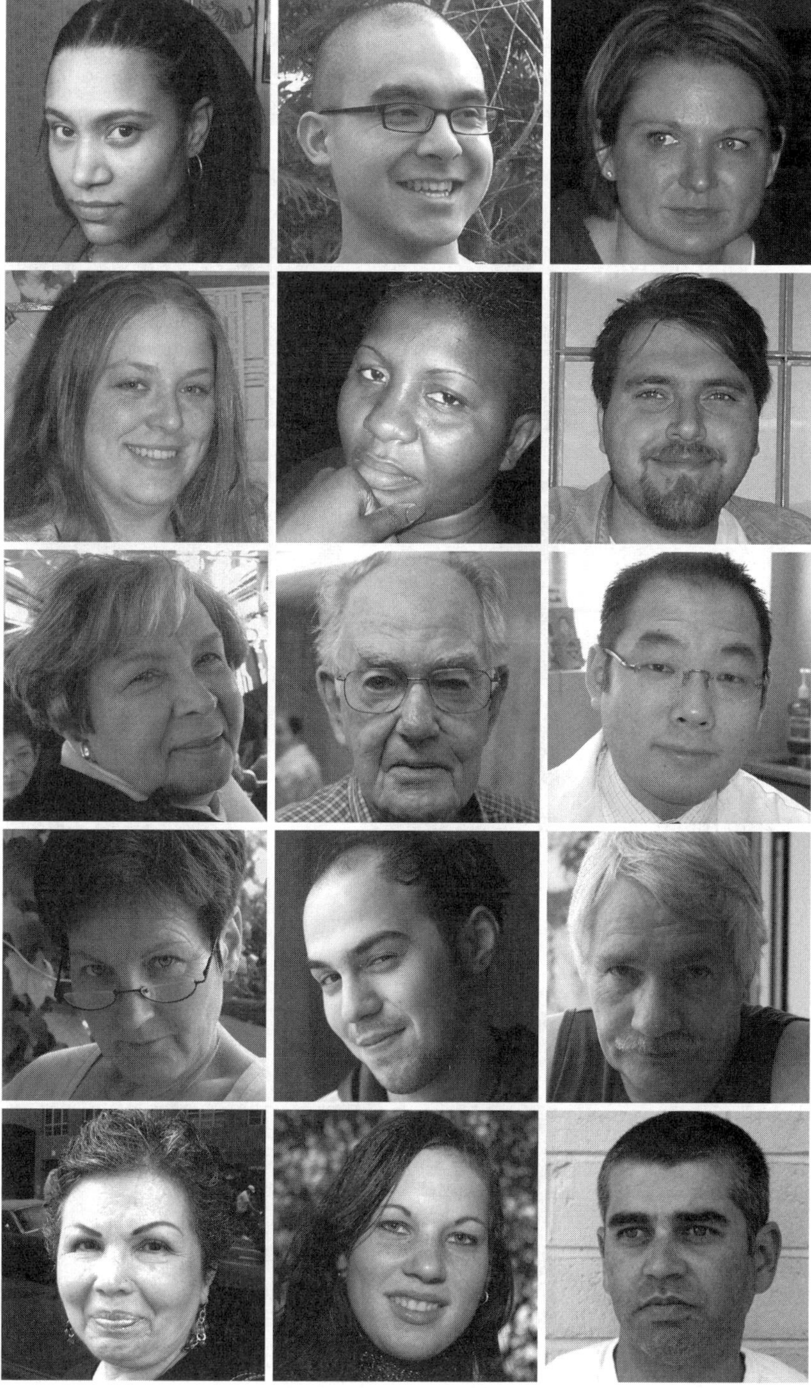

The photo you choose will have a huge impact on how others view the persona. Look at the photo in the lower left and the one above it. Apply either photo to the same written persona, and immediately her entire personality changes. Choose wisely, young Jedi knight.

Just for fun, here are a few examples of bad persona photos.

Too beautiful and/or posed:

Too hidden:

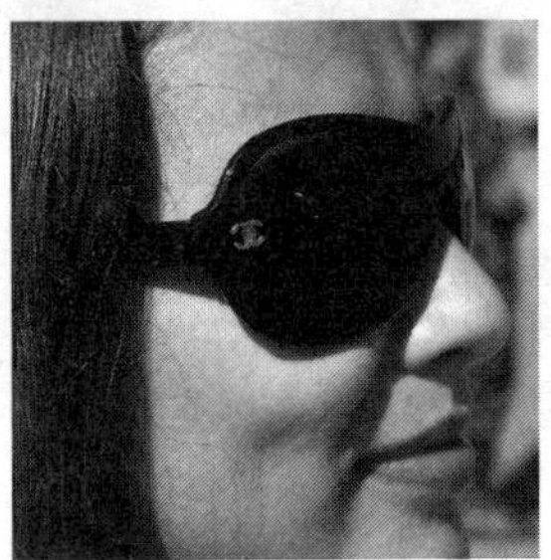

Too much distraction:

Too much expression:

Too much stereotype:

Remember, it's about real people, not caricatures.

Showing Personal Information

Once you have a name and a photo, it's time to add the details that bring the persona to life. And so we come to a rather curious thing about personas: Precision is more important than accuracy.

What that slightly odd statement means is that *details* are what make people real and memorable. Look at the following images and ask yourself this question: Which one looks more like a real person to whom you could relate, and why? The more details we see, the more the person moves away from being an abstraction (e.g., a smiley face) and toward being a real person in our minds.

What makes images of people feel more real?

Because personas are all about inventing realistic people, details make all the difference. Francis the First-Time Home Buyer is only a vague cartoony figure until we give her an age, a job, a location, and a personality. Sometimes, of course, you don't have hard data on these types of details. But that's okay, because including these details is so important that you shouldn't worry that they might not be 100-percent correct. Precision is more important than accuracy.

So, make it up! Be creative as you invent this cast of characters. Make an educated guess. Choose details that reinforce the story you're trying to build about each persona. Got a perfectionist? Give her a hobby like beaded jewelry making. Got an adrenalin-driven personality? Maybe he likes watching the television series, *24*.

Here are some details to include:

- **Job and company.** What your persona does for a living (whether by choice or not) says a lot. Find a vocation appropriate to the persona's goals, attitudes, and behaviors, based on whatever data you might have. Be specific by creating an actual job title and an actual company name (I like using real companies). If it's useful, you can list core job responsibilities.
- **Age.** Choose an age that corresponds to the photo you've selected. In most situations, a range of ages among personas is a good idea.
- **Location.** Put a stake in the ground on where your persona lives. Think internationally if it's appropriate for your business.
- **Personality.** List a few adjectives that this persona's friends would use to describe him or her. Friendly, shy, emotional, meticulous, egotistical, fearless, articulate, whatever. Find the two or three words that support the story building in your mind for this persona.
- **Home/family life.** Establish whether your persona is single, married, and whether she or he has kids. What about living

arrangements? Depending on the purpose of your personas, you might not need to go very deep on this one.

- **Hobbies.** Look for non-work activities that reinforce the persona's character. One or two hobbies can help round out the persona.
- **Favorite TV shows or music.** Sometimes this can be helpful for supporting a personality. Does he like *American Idol* or *Nova*? Does she listen to Mary J. Blige or Celine Dion? It can make a difference.

Sometimes this step can feel awkward, like you're creating a stereotype or an archetype rather than a real person: balding suburban alpha male Republican NASCAR dad with two kids and beer in the fridge! Although you don't want to create a caricature or a cartoon character, there's something to be said about leveraging archetypes. Archetypes are oversimplifications of types of people who, in many cases, exist in great numbers in the real world. When I sense that a persona I'm creating is similar to an archetype, I'll often run *toward* that pattern rather than away from it, because I know that more people are likely to recognize my persona and think, "Oh, yeah, I know someone like that." The minute they recognize the persona, the persona becomes real for them and thus effective.

Remember Patricia the Perfectionist? Here's her personal information, which I tend to document as a bulleted list of facts:

- Profession: Jewelry designer
- Location: Seattle, WA
- Age: 34
- Home life: Married, renting in historic district
- Hobbies: Writing fiction, biking, singing
- Favorite TV shows: *The Apprentice*, *Antiques Roadshow*
- Personality: Creative, detail-oriented, passionate

Presenting Domain-Specific Information

For every set of personas, there's always information you want to establish about them that is specific to the domain in which you're working. If it's the real estate industry, you'll want to specify facts such as where the persona is currently living, when she might want to buy or sell, what her financial situation looks like, and so on. These additional facts contribute to making the persona more realistic, of course, but they also make the persona more understandable to colleagues, who are no doubt steeped in the jargon and facts that are specific to your industry. These details put the personas in their language.

Find the domain-specific information that is most important for differentiating the personas from each other. Here are some ideas to get you started:

- **Past experience with your domain.** How long have they been functioning in this area? How experienced are they? What do they know? How do they typically behave? What competitors do they use?
- **Current status.** What attributes describe them right now? What things affect how they go about achieving their goals? This could be information about them personally or about the organization they're part of.
- **Future plans.** When are they going to act, and how? How will future behavior change from current behavior?
- **Motivators.** Which types of things motivate them and affect their likelihood of doing business with you?
- **Pet peeves and pain points.** Where are they currently experiencing problems? What things drive them crazy?

Some of these details could overlap with the main goals, behaviors, and/or attitudes you're using to define your personas. In that case, you might not want to repeat the primary differentiators here; instead use this space to document secondary differentiators.

Here are a few examples that show how differently domain-specific information can be used. The first is the financial information for a frequent trader persona at BrownCo. Each attribute would get a specific value, which is not shown here.

- Annual income
- Assets
- Trades per year at BrownCo
- Trades with margin
- Trades without margin
- Years investing
- Online investing experience
- Years with BrownCo

For R.H. Donnelley, the following data points were used for the personas of the marketers who would list their businesses on the site:

- Business name and category
- Type of customers (e.g., locals versus visitors)
- Number of employees
- Locations
- Years in business
- Offline marketing programs
- Online marketing programs
- Access to and use of customer feedback

Finally, here's organizational information for a university IT administrator who makes purchases from a computer reseller:

- Size: 350 staff and faculty, 2000+ students, 4000+ alumni and parents
- Yearly spending: $250,000

- Spending with the company: 45 percent
- Years purchasing: 10+ years
- Preferred method of purchasing: Phone and Internet
- Method of purchase with the company: Phone
- Sites used for purchases: CDWG.com, OEM sites
- Purchases: Computer systems, peripherals, accessories, consumables, software, software licenses
- Number of tech purchasers: Decentralized, 2000+

Although I tend to document domain-specific information as quick bullets like the ones here, I also incorporate these important details into the narrative profiles, which are coming up in a bit.

Specifying Computer and Internet Usage

Computer and Internet experience and setup are less important than domain-specific information, but they still help make personas real. This is a good opportunity to make sure the team is thinking about the range of knowledge users will have about computers and about the Web. It's also helpful to remind colleagues about the reality of Macs, Web browsers other than Internet Explorer, and dial-up connections. Here too, diversity is important.

You could include the following attributes:

- **Computer setup.** What operating system and Web browser do they use? What is their connection to the Internet?
- **Computer experience.** How long have they used a PC? What is their level of knowledge?
- **Internet experience.** How long have they been online? How many hours per week do they spend online? What is their level of knowledge?

- **Primary uses of the Internet.** What do they use the Internet for? What activities are primary and secondary?
- **Favorite Web sites.** Which sites do they rely on?

Our friend Patricia the Perfectionist looks like this:

- Internet experience: High
- Primary uses: Email, IM, shopping, music
- Favorite sites: eBay, Google, Gloss.com
- Hours online per week: 15
- Computer: Mac, Safari, cable modem

Writing a Profile

Personas are stories, and the last thing you want your persona document to look like is a long list of bullets. Bullets are useful for facts that you want people to be able to scan quickly, but they can't take the place of the narrative profile of your persona. The profile is the meat of the persona; it summarizes all the key differentiators and attributes, while telling the story of who this person is and how he or she interacts (or wants to interact) with your company.

Profiles work well when they provide context for who these people are—the story of how they got to where they are today and what they need from here. It's important to relay not only the facts, but the psychological and emotional side as well. Attitudes are particularly important to blend into your profiles.

In addition, make the profiles as specific as possible—again, to make the personas realistic. For example, one of the things Francis the First-Time Home Buyer wants is a pool. That's not something that came directly from the data about the first-time home buyer segment; it's something I made up that's consistent with the type of wish that this person would have. These types of details are specific and they're representative of the entire segment. If I had instead made Francis a realtor, that would have been specific as well, but it would have made Francis an edge case rather than a representative sample of her segment.

Think of profiles as psychologically based mini-biographies.

These profiles aren't scenarios, that is, detailed stories about how the persona will actually interact with the site to accomplish their goals. I'll talk about scenarios at the end of this chapter. Think of profiles as psychologically based mini-biographies.

Persona profiles are better understood through example, so let's look at a couple. The first is from a VistaPrint persona named Howard the Hurried:

> Howard has been a realtor long enough to know that he has to project a professional image to be successful. But he simply doesn't have the time to make his printed materials really stand out—and it's not something he enjoys much either. So when Howard needs to create any materials, he finds someone that will make the process easy, fast, and painless so that he can get "good enough" results without wasting a lot of valuable time.
>
> A few years ago Howard saw an ad for free business cards at VistaPrint and gave it a try. The quality was good enough that he has stuck with VistaPrint ever since, mainly because he can conveniently order cards from them anytime he wants. He later upgraded to premium business cards so that he could add his own logo, though he wished that process had been easier. He has no idea what else VistaPrint might offer and doesn't want to take the time to find out since he's happy with his current process. He currently creates letterhead and labels from his own printer and hires a student to design his occasional newsletter, which he prints at a local print shop. The newsletter still takes more time than he'd like, but he knows it's

> an important marketing tool. He uses OfficeMax for his ever-changing collection of house sell sheets.
>
> He visits the site only when he needs to reorder and finds it's fast and efficient. He has the site bookmarked and goes straight for his portfolio. He likes how easy it is to quickly reorder his cards, and the price is right. He emailed customer service once about a typo on his card, and he now tries to be a little more careful before placing an order. Overall, he's interested in anything that makes the process faster and easier.

Notice that the profile covers his high-level goals and his behavior, but it also covers Howard's attitudes toward the process and the company. You may also find it useful to integrate into the story the improvements that this persona wants.

The next example is from R.H. Donnelley, a company that focuses on helping small business owners such as Iris better market themselves:

> Iris is very proud of her small dental practice, which is doing well thanks to good word of mouth. She knows she could probably grow her business even more, but she simply doesn't have the time for the kind of marketing that she sees competitors doing. Her days are already full of managing all aspects of the business. Someday she wants to take a marketing course and learn more about what she should be doing. Word of mouth has been great for her, but she feels she hasn't done a good job of getting her name out there in the community.
>
> She's advertised in the yellow pages since starting her practice, but in the last few years, she's focused more on other offline marketing efforts, such as appearances in local community directories, ads in local magazines and school yearbooks, and occasional direct mail pieces. Just recently she was happy with how many calls came in after she sent out postcards to part of the community.

> Iris sees online marketing as becoming more important in the future, and she is glad to have her own Web site, even though she knows it's very basic and never has time to update it. She plans to invest more in the site next year. She does spend some time making sure she's on some of the sites that list Orlando dentists, including online city guides and industry sites that help consumers find a dentist. Unfortunately, there are so many sites out there that she doesn't get to all of them. Often she has her receptionist look for more of these sites, since she's not the most tech-savvy person.
>
> The only feedback she gets from patients is informal, during their visits. To Iris, the most important feedback a patient can give her is to recommend her to someone else. She knows that her patients like her and wishes she could better publicize their loyalty, but isn't quite sure how. She likes the idea of an online local directory with consumer reviews, as long as the site results in a lot of new calls to her office.

I find it useful to structure profiles so that they cover the same topics across all personas. For R.H. Donnelley's personas, the first paragraph of the persona always provided an overview of the business and the persona's attitude toward marketing. The second paragraph covered offline marketing activities, and the third covered online marketing. The final paragraph discussed the importance of customer feedback and word of mouth.

Using Additional Attributes

You can give many other attributes to your personas other than those I've discussed so far. Adding realistic details is a creative and fun activity, but tread carefully. Remember that the key differentiators of your personas are what should stand out the most. Someone picking up a persona document should be able to understand the basics of that person within seconds. Keep the emphasis on what's most important and make sure everything else (including the realistic details that add flavor) supports your main messages about that persona.

For example, the fact that Francis wants a pool is a representative detail that reminds us about other types of needs, and thus it is helpful. But talking about her orange tabby shorthair, Eliot, probably isn't going to affect decisions we make about the Web site on her behalf. Find the few details that best support the overall story you're creating. Don't feel that just because you have data on something, you have to use it in the personas.

One additional attribute worth considering is a persona's disabilities. If your site serves users with disabilities, then giving one of your personas a disability can be an excellent way to keep that objective front-of-mind for everyone in the company.

If you want to explore other attributes to give personas, an excellent resource is George Olsen's "Persona Creation and Usage Toolkit," which is available at www.interactionbydesign.com/presentations/olsen_persona_toolkit.pdf. Here, George provides a valuable list of persona characteristics that is worth examining, including social class, lifestyle motivations, brand relationship, emotional goals, language proficiency, organizational politics, and much more.

Crafting a Quote

One of the last things I do when fleshing out a persona is add a quote. Like the summary bullets, a quote from the persona's own mouth (so to speak) can capture his or her essence and serve as one of the initial things that people read to get a quick sense of that persona.

I recommend creating a quote toward the end of the process, because after you dive into all the detail, a quote forces you to look at the big picture and figure out what the *one thing* is that this person would say that would summarize where he or she is coming from. Keep it simple and short and focused on one or two points that set this persona apart from the others. Be sure to use the natural language of the persona—after all, this is supposed to be the persona talking to you, not jargon-filled marketing copy.

Here are a few examples:

- "I think I'm getting good at this."—Connor Up'n Comer, a relatively inexperienced financial trader who's eager to grow
- "I'm always in the hot seat to prove Training ROI. I need partners who read my mind and don't waste my time."—Carrie the Corporate Training Director
- "I was late to the game, and now I'm playing catch up."—Bob, who didn't start saving for retirement early enough
- "I want you to want me!"—Henry High Touch, a B2B customer who needs lots of handholding
- "I buy a yellow pages ad and that's enough."—Larry the Conservative Laggard, who doesn't put much effort into marketing his business
- "My work is who I am, so everything has to be just right."—Patricia the Perfectionist

Adding Business Objectives

After you've finished a rough draft of your persona and you've included the bits of realistic detail that make your persona come to life, there's one more important piece to add: the business objectives you have for the persona. Just as the personas have things they wish to accomplish on the site, so too do *you* have things you want the *personas* to do in order to achieve business results. The whole point of most Web sites is to serve users in a way that encourages desired user behavior, which then leads to business results. It's time to document just what you're hoping to get out of all of this.

In a way, this part of your personas represents your success metrics for each one. Ask yourself what you want and expect the persona to do for your business, given what you know about him or her. Because you know Francis the First-Time Home Buyer so well, you should be able to serve her needs successfully, so it's only appropriate to document what you can expect from her in return. For this reason, I preface user goals with "Francis comes to the site to...." and then business objectives with "We want Francis to...."

Just as with goals, think of business objectives in terms of verbs. What actions do you want the persona to take that are measurable in terms of business results? What does success look like if you serve this persona perfectly? Personas will likely have business objectives in common (e.g., "Tell a friend about the site."), but you should also look for the business results that are specific to each persona, since you want to target them individually.

Just as the personas have things they wish to accomplish on the site, so too do you have things you want the personas to do in order to achieve business results.

Also like goals, find the right level of specificity for your business objectives. If your objective for a particular persona is simply "Be a loyal customer," that's overly broad. What does that mean exactly, and how are you going to measure it? On the other hand, objectives can also be too narrow, such as "Send emails to 12 friends about the site's great search engine." Find a happy medium: objectives that are specific and measurable but that you can cover in a few bullets or a paragraph.

Check out the business objectives for Francis.

We want Francis to:

- Visit the site often (ad revenue)
- Register for email alerts and newsletters
- Subscribe to premium services
- Follow through on individual listings by contacting realtor

- Follow through on mortgage and insurance by contacting partner
- Recommend the site to others

Remember Carrie the Corporate Training Director, a customer of Harvard Business School Publishing?

We want Carrie to:

- Come to HBSP first for her training topic research
- Consider HBSP a valuable corporate resource
- Partner with consulting services who use HBSP products in their courses
- Recommend HBSP conferences and products to her company

By documenting business objectives for each persona, you make an explicit connection between the users you're targeting and the business models that you're focused on. Without a roadmap to show where you want each persona to end up, there would be no way to see if they're helping. Look for more on measuring success in the final chapter of this book.

Prioritizing the Personas

Imagine you have a set of personas and you're making decisions about the features and content to improve for the next Web site release, when suddenly you realize that the needs of two of your personas conflict on a certain feature. One persona needs it to work one way, and another needs it to work very differently. You can't please both. What do you do?

All personas aren't equally important to satisfy, which is why it's critical to *prioritize* your personas so that you know how to resolve possible conflicts like this. Before using your new personas, ask yourself which one or two are most important to satisfy. The most obvious way to decide this is to look at the value each persona brings to the business. Which one is the most financially valuable to the company? Or, which one do you *expect* to be the most valuable in the future? If you were able to tie CRM data to your segments, you have information to make this decision easily. Otherwise, you might need to do a little analysis to determine the likely value of each persona.

You might also want to add each persona's influence into the mix. Does one persona have extraordinary influence over the others, or over your company's reputation? He or she might deserve more weight when you're prioritizing.

Don't assume that the persona who has the most needs is automatically the most important to satisfy. It's easy to get sidetracked and spend a lot of time focusing on the squeaky wheel, when there are probably more important needs to satisfy first.

Give each of your personas one of these priority levels:

- **Primary.** The primary persona is the one for whom you'll optimize the site. This is the persona most valuable to the business and worth satisfying above all others. If you ever have a conflict between what different personas need, this persona's needs always win. This is the persona you have most in your mind as you make decisions. Often you have only one primary persona, but you could have two.
- **Secondary.** The rest of your personas are probably secondary personas, who are also important to the business. Your goal is to satisfy these personas wherever possible, unless, of course, their needs conflict with those of the primary persona.
- **Unimportant.** You might want to create a persona for a certain segment that is worth thinking about but is less important when it comes to decision-making. For example, if you know that the press is coming to the site and you want to keep them in the back of your head as you work on it, you might create a press persona and label it as unimportant.

- **Excluded.** This rare type of persona is someone you're specifically *not* creating the site for. The idea is to create a persona to remind everyone not to focus on him or her. This seems like a lot of work to me, but you might find situations in which this persona is useful.

Most of the time, you'll end up with one (or possibly two) personas labeled as primary personas and the rest as unlabeled secondary personas.

This prioritization can vary depending on which area of the site you're working on. For example, your real estate site might focus primarily on the home buyer but also support for-sale-by-owner sellers on the side. In the section of the site devoted to home selling, the home seller persona would suddenly become the primary persona for decision-making.

Make sure everyone on the team buys into your prioritization, and, for that matter, all of the details you've added to make your personas real. A particular detail that feels right to you might feel out of place to someone else, and it's important to remove as many obstacles as possible so that everyone can internalize these personas as real people. Be prepared to iterate the personas during this stage until everyone is comfortable with them.

Writing Scenarios

A completed persona is like a marionette: Until you pull its strings and make it move, it has no chance of looking realistic and telling a story.

Scenarios put personas in motion. They are the stories of how a persona interacts with a Web site (and/or other channels). The persona is the character, and a scenario is a plot. The persona has specific goals, attitudes, and behaviors that set up what he or she wants to do and how he or she likes doing them. The scenario tells what could actually happen when the persona visits the site.

User research ➤ Segments ➤ Personas ➤ Scenarios ➤ Task analysis/ Use cases ➤ Feature design

Scenarios connect the dots between user research and detailed decision-making.

Scenarios are idealistic visions of the persona's interaction with the site. If you could serve the persona's needs perfectly, what would that look like? Knowing what the persona wants to accomplish, how would he or she try to do it, and in an ideal world, how would your site respond? Scenarios help create the long-term vision of the experience your site should offer, so everyone has a common objective for the future.

Personas can exist without scenarios, but often these stories are a useful first step toward actually using personas, a process the remaining chapters cover in detail. Scenarios create another link in the chain between user research and the decisions you'll make using your personas. The goal of using personas is that every decision your team makes can be linked back to users in a defendable way. If you're debating how a particular feature should work, you can go back to your task analysis or use case (more on this in Chapter 11), which was based on a scenario, which was based on a persona, which was based on segmentation, which was based on user research.

Be sure to write at least one scenario for each primary persona, focusing on the core goal(s) each persona is trying to accomplish. Of course, you can also write scenarios for secondary personas, and if it's helpful, you can have multiple scenarios for each persona, with each story covering a different usage of the site. Often I'll write the one most important scenario for each persona up front, and then I'll write more scenarios as needed during the design process. However, I seldom end up with more than three scenarios per persona.

For each persona, start with the most important situation in which he or she would use the site. This could be the most common way the persona will repeatedly use the site, or it could be that critical first visit and first impression. You probably already know exactly what the key usage is for each scenario, because you referred to it in your persona profile or key differentiators. Now it's time to flesh out the story.

Your mission is to document that experience from the persona's point of view. I like to use the classic components of good storytelling when doing this.

1. **Set the scene.**

   Where is the persona when he or she first discovers the need that will lead him or her to the Web site? When does it happen? Who else is around possibly influencing his or her decision? What else is going on at the time? Be as specific as possible to create a realistic story, just as you were with the persona details.

2. **Establish the goal or conflict.**

   Visits to the site are triggered by goals, so something must have happened to prompt your persona to go to your site. What was it? Perhaps it occurred in typical narrative fashion, based on a conflict with someone else or an inner conflict that he or she needed to resolve. Be very clear about what your persona is trying to achieve by visiting the site, keeping in mind that he or she could have multiple goals.

3. **Overcome crises along the way.**

   When the persona comes to the site, how does he or she enter? What decisions does he or she make along the way? How does the persona find what he or she's looking for? Are there intermediate steps to describe? What challenges does the persona face along the way that the site helps with? Does the action all take place on your site, or does the persona use other sites, email, IM, phone calls, meetings with others, store visits, and so on? Even though this is an idealized story about how your site could satisfy this persona's needs perfectly, be realistic about what he or she would actually do. How does the persona feel about the experience while going through it?

4. **Achieve resolution.**

   How does the persona ultimately achieve his or her goal? What are the persona's attitudes at the climax of his or her story? What are the most critical factors in helping the persona achieve his or her goal?

5. **Reach denouement.**

   What does the persona do after succeeding? How does the persona leave the site? How does this story affect his or her work or life? What's his or her perception afterward? How does the persona's success impact your business?

Scenarios don't have to cover all of these questions. Use whatever is most helpful for your particular persona and story. Your goal isn't to write a novel, but only one or a few paragraphs that dive into a particular usage scenario and make the persona's interaction with the site as realistic as possible.

Think of scenarios as documented journeys through the Web site, if everything were to work as it should. Each persona, because of his or her unique goals, attitudes, and behaviors, will take a different journey through the site. If you can document the most critical journeys of each persona, you'll have documented all of the most critical paths through the Web site. As you'll see in Part III, this makes designing the site easier later on.

Each persona, because of his or her unique goals, attitudes, and behaviors, will take a different journey through the site.

As always, examples show what I'm talking about better than my own prattling on can do. Let's begin with our friend Francis the First-Time Home Buyer. She and her husband are eager to start the process of house hunting, but they have very little real estate knowledge and don't know where to start. So one scenario for Francis could describe her first visit to the site.

> Francis and Michael have agreed that she'll take charge of learning more about the home-buying process. She goes online, does a Google search for "Atlanta real estate," and follows a link to the site's home page. She sees that she can search for houses from the home page, so just for fun, she does a quick Atlanta search to see what kinds of houses show up. There are lots of houses in many different neighborhoods, and she easily narrows her results down to the area where she and Michael live, using a map. There are still many results, and she's not quite sure which search options to use to narrow the search further. Then she notices a link for first-time home buyers and follows it, hoping for basic how-to information.
>
> The link takes Francis to a step-by-step tutorial that explains the whole process, and she immediately feels like she's found the right site from which to begin her house search. She carefully reads some articles for first-time home buyers, taking notes as she reads. She bookmarks other articles she wants to go back and read later. She also comes across the site's calculator and starts trying different combinations of numbers to find out what she and Michael can afford. She particularly likes the glossary of terms so that she can finally figure out what "points" are and learn more about different types of mortgages. After an hour and a half of reading, her brain is full, and she shuts her computer down for the day, feeling like she got an excellent start.
>
> The next day, she comes back to the site to look up information specific to Atlanta neighborhoods and finds lots of information on each. She's able to focus on five neighborhoods that look particularly good. The fun begins that night, when she takes Michael through all that she has

> learned, and they set up a regular schedule for looking at online house listings.

In this scenario, Francis has a rather vague initial goal (to learn about the home-buying process), and the Web site helps her refine and satisfy that goal. Like many people, Francis is tempted from the beginning to try a house search, even though she doesn't really know what she's looking for yet. During her visit, specific features are pointed out, some of which she knew she wanted and others she didn't realize she needed. Overall, her experience is a positive one, as all scenarios should be, since they describe the ideal story of a persona interacting with the future site.

Now let's look at a different Francis scenario—one that describes her routine usage once she's learned the basics.

> About twice a week, Francis goes online for about an hour, checking for new listings. She sets up email alerts so that the site tells her when new houses are available that match her criteria, and she absolutely loves how this works. She also likes how her realtor can set aside certain listings for Francis to browse through at her leisure. She does her own searches on the Web site, trying different combinations of criteria, hoping new homes will show up in the results. When she finds a house that looks interesting, she adds it to her Wish List, marking especially promising candidates as Important.
>
> If the homes she's interested in are nearby, Francis drives over to check them out, after printing a map from the site that shows all the houses on her Wish List in a certain area. If the homes aren't nearby, she creates a different list of houses she and Michael can drive to the following weekend. If a house looks good, she checks the Web site to see if it will be having an open house, and then she adds that date to her Google calendar. If no open houses are scheduled, she calls her realtor to ask him about setting up a personal tour.

> She's happy with how efficient the whole process is and feels like she's seeing a lot of houses and being thorough in her research. She still feels like she's in a bit over her head sometimes, but the site and her realtor are making the process easier week by week. She can't wait to find the perfect home.

As you can see, scenarios lend themselves to proposing new features, based on an understanding of what the personas need and how the site could best serve them. None of these ideas are locked in stone; scenarios evolve over time as you develop new and better ways of satisfying your personas' goals.

Finally, here's a scenario for Stan, a persona who values time and convenience when using his company's intranet.

> When Stan is out of the office and working at a client's location, the last thing he feels like doing at the end of a long day is entering his hours into his company's time tracking tool. So he usually puts this off until Friday and then grimaces to himself at 6:00 as he launches the VPN tool, logs in, and then points his Web browser to the intranet home page. Fortunately, there's a link to the time tracking tool right on the home page, along with other commonly used tools.
>
> Once in the time tracking tool, he's happy to see that it remembers his activities from the previous week, so all he has to do is enter new hours for this week for the same activities. He started a new project this week, so he clicks New Project and selects his client from the list that appears, then easily enters his hours. Soon he's finished, and what used to take a half hour now takes ten minutes. He glances at the total to make sure all the hours are there, then clicks Submit.

> After the confirmation message appears, the Web browser redirects Stan to the intranet home page, where he immediately notices that yesterday's company presentation is now available. He missed the meeting, so he quickly downloads the presentation to look at while he's on the flight home tomorrow. While it's downloading, he sees from a dashboard on the home page that the company message board has come to life with a discussion about what Web 2.0 means to the business. He can't resist clicking to see what Riccardo has to say on this topic, and before he knows it spends 15 minutes reading various posts. He even posts a quick URL of a Google Maps mashup he just found.
>
> Before leaving the intranet, Stan remembers that he promised his client a white paper on Rich Internet Applications, and so does a quick search. The results page enables him to filter the list by document type and author, so he easily finds the white paper and downloads it. Happy that he got so much done so quickly, Stan shuts down his laptop and leaves his client's office, heading toward the local bar he knows will be showing the Red Sox game.

Scenarios can be shorter and more targeted, or they can be more detailed like these examples. As always, the details can help bring a sense of reality to the story so that the empathy they feel leads to solid decision-making based on Stan's situation.

Scenarios can affect a great many decisions made about a Web site, from overall business strategy and scope down to the details of information architecture and design. That's what Part III is all about.

PART III USING PERSONAS

8 Keeping Personas Alive

THE THIRD-CENTURY PHILOSOPHER Plotinus once said, "Knowledge, if it does not determine action, is dead to us." The whole point of personas is to make your knowledge about users actionable so that they have a real impact on the decisions you make about your Web site.

You have personas and you're ready to use them. How do you present your personas to others? How do you make them a living part of your everyday process so that people remember to use them? The last thing you want is to spend time creating personas only to see them rot in the corner and never be used.

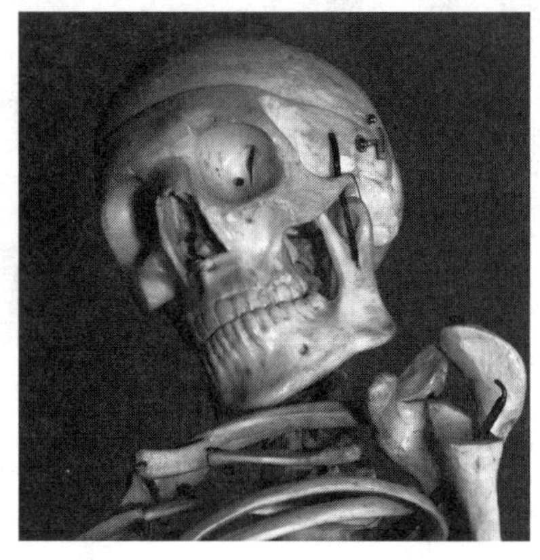
What happens to a persona who's not used.

This chapter explores various ways to present and deliver personas to your colleagues so that they make an initial impact, are remembered, and are used regularly within the organization. The goal is to *socialize* the personas within the company so that everyone knows them and thinks about them as real people—as real members of the team that is responsible for the Web site. How you do this depends on your organization. In a culture that responds well to stories that induce empathy, scenario role-playing might be effective. In a number-crunching analytical culture, something less cutesy is probably better. What follows is a collection of tools from which to draw as you see fit.

Creating the Persona Document

Personas can take many forms, but you want to have one version that represents the complete information on each persona. The full persona document was presented in Chapter 7, with components such as key differentiators, name, photo, domain-specific information, profile, business objectives, and so on.

You can design this document in many ways, but I've settled on a template that has the following information hierarchy:

- The persona's name, photo, quote, and key differentiator bullets have the most emphasis and serve as the quick snapshot of the persona.

- The narrative profile, full key differentiators (often a list of user goals), and business objectives for this persona are the secondary block, occupying most of the page.
- Details that flesh out the persona, such as personal information, domain-specific information, and computer and Internet usage, fill the remaining space.

Keep this document within one page if it's possible. Although it's important to add enough detail to make the personas real, when each becomes multiple pages, there's simply too much content for others to remember. Prioritize what needs to be in the persona and eliminate the unnecessary. Your goal isn't to say everything about each persona, but to provide just enough detail to make each persona feel real.

Connect the persona to the company visually by including the company logo—ideally a high-resolution version to ensure quality prints. You can use the company's colors when creating the persona document (for the background of the snapshot area and the text headers) so that the personas feel like part of the corporate family.

Design your persona document to be the most effective within your organization. Think about where you want to give emphasis and what visual elements will help people accept the personas easier.

Presenting Personas

Introducing the final personas to your colleagues and decision makers can be a tricky affair. Don't assume that, since you have your main persona documents finished, you're all set and can simply hand them over. It's important to set aside time to walk people through the personas; this is a critical step in socializing the personas throughout the organization.

An example of a persona document for VistaPrint.

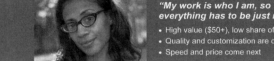

VistaPrint
BEST PRINTING. BEST PRICE.

PRIMARY PERSONA

Patricia the Perfectionist

"My work is who I am, so everything has to be just right."

- High value ($50+), low share of wallet (<50%)
- Quality and customization are critical
- Speed and price come next

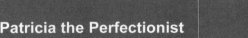

Personal Profile

For Patricia, if you're not going to do something well, why bother? If her business cards, price tags, and invitations don't look as stunning as her jewelry, she knows it will hurt her one-woman business. Her customers will judge her based on the complete package, so she puts in the effort to get it right – though because she doesn't have a lot of money to spend, most often that means hours and hours of her own work.

She found out about VistaPrint last year through another vendor at a street fair, and spent quite a while going through the site. She didn't think there were enough design choices at first, and had some difficulty finding a template for her. Eventually she picked one and started playing around with everything she could customize. (She used her neighbor's PC since the site didn't fully work on her Mac.) It took her a couple of visits to get the business card perfect, with her logo and an icon she created, and she used the PDF proofing just to make sure. She was impressed at how flexible the site was, and the prices were great. When she received the cards, she was disappointed that the colors didn't exactly match what she had seen on-screen, but maybe she can fix that when her supply runs out and she needs to order more.

She hasn't tried VistaPrint for anything else yet, mostly because she's not fully convinced the quality is good enough. She also thinks shipping is a bit slow and pricey. She uses Shutterfly to create invitations and holiday cards using photographs of her jewelry, and hasn't found a good way to custom print price tags the way she wants them, so she creates all of those by hand. She'd love to be able to upload her own designs from Photoshop.

Goals & Motivators

Patricia comes to the site to…

- Find the perfect template and customize it exactly the way she wants it, including uploading images
- Upload her own design
- Proof her work carefully before printing
- Check on the status of her order

Patricia cares most about…

- High quality of color, paper, and finish
- Freedom to customize anything she wants
- Low prices and fast delivery

Business Objectives

We want Patricia to…

- Be reassured about VistaPrint quality
- Use VistaPrint for other printing needs
- Recommend VistaPrint to others

Personal Information

Profession: Jewelry designer

Location: Seattle, WA

Age: 34

Home life: Married, renting in historic district

Hobbies: Writing fiction, biking, singing

Favorite TV shows: The Apprentice, Antiques Roadshow

Personality: Creative, detail-oriented, passionate

Business Information

Works out of: Home

Age of business: 3 years

People: 1

Printing Information

Products: Business cards, price tags, invitations, holiday cards

Competitors: Desktop color printer, Shutterfly, handcrafted

Total two-year spend: $200

VistaPrint two-year spend: $20

Internet Usage

Internet experience: High

Primary uses: Email, IM, shopping, music

Favorite sites: Ebay, Google, Gloss.com

Hours online per week: 15

Computer: Mac, Safari, cable modem

Created in partnership with Molecular.

This example is for a community-driven yellow pages for R.H. Donnelley.

PRIMARY PERSONA

Lewis

Active Leader (7% of population)
Consumer

"My community is online. I love being part of it."

- Very tech savvy and socially active online
- Uses Yelp, Yahoo Local, Google, and friends to find businesses
- Reads reviews and contributes regularly

Profile

For Lewis, the Internet is about connecting with people. He loves meeting new people online, whether it's new connections through Friendster or Evite or great discussions in the comments area of his blog or his friends' blogs. He's technically savvy and loves to multi-task: At any given moment, he has two IM conversations going, iTunes playing, sports scores streaming across his monitor, and RSS feeds coming in from his favorite blogs.

Lewis knows his community quite well, but when he needs to find a local business, he usually turns to Google first, although recently he's started using Yelp and Yahoo Local because he's heard good buzz about them. He particularly likes how the sites are integrating business information, reviews from people like him, and better mapping. If he can't find a business quickly enough online, he uses the yellow pages book or sometimes SuperPages.com. He also likes doing business person-to-person through sites like eBay and Craigslist, a site he visits daily. Lewis prefers sites with multiple ways to search, comprehensive information, current offers from businesses, and support for cell phone access.

He's used product rating and review sites for years, and relies on ratings at Amazon and Cnet before buying anything. He reads both expert and consumer reviews to get the complete picture. He's proud of the 10 thorough reviews he's written at Cnet and enjoys being able to give something back to the community that helps him find the best products. For local businesses, Lewis has used restaurant reviews on Citysearch, but didn't write any reviews until a friend told him recently about Yelp, where he's already written 10 reviews of favorite local spots. He only tends to write reviews on positive experiences. He enjoys it when his friends ask him for advice, which is happening more and more. He wants sites with expert and consumer reviews, personalization and email alerts, and more community features.

User Goals

Lewis comes to the site to…

- Find a local business for a particular need
- Browse for new places to try
- Read reviews of a particular business he's heard about
- Check for new promotions from favorite businesses
- Check for reviews from his favorite reviewers
- Write reviews on businesses

Business Objectives

We want Lewis to…

- Visit the site often
- Sign up for alerts
- Contribute ratings/reviews often
- Recommend the site to others

Personal Information

Age: 28

Location: Winter Park, Orlando, FL

Knowledge of community: High

Profession: Media Producer, Pearson Publishing

Home life: Married, 4-year-old son, large network of friends

Hobbies: Running, writing, going out to hear local bands, board game night with friends

Favorite TV shows: The Apprentice, Alias

Personality: Outgoing, funny, adventurous

Internet Usage

Internet usage: Very high (50 hours/week)

Primary uses: Email, IM, blogs, music, shopping, online magazines, entertainment news

Favorite sites: Google, Craigslist, Flickr, Friendster

Computer: Windows XP, cable modem, Firefox

Ratings & Reviews

Reads: Product reviews several times a month (Amazon, Cnet, Epinions), business reviews once or twice a month (Yelp, Citysearch)

Trusts: Consumer and expert (nationally known slightly more than local expert) reviews

Contributes: Product reviews several times a month (Amazon, Cnet), business reviews once or twice a month (Yelp)

Reasons for contributing: Give back to the community, and secondarily build his reputation as an expert and get some compensation when possible

Created in partnership with Molecular.

First, decide to whom you should present the personas. Likely, various groups within the organization can benefit from the new personas, including the executive team, product teams, sales, marketing, and, of course, the folks in charge of user experience and design. It's often wise to present the personas to each group separately, because each group wants different information so they can understand the personas and accept them as decision-making tools.

Know your audience before you present. Are they looking for the evidence behind the personas before they buy into this potentially cutesy design tool? Bring your supporting data along. Are they skeptical about how the personas will actually be used? Bring examples of how the personas can be applied to common situations. Are they likely to forget the details as soon as they leave the room? Make the meeting engaging and interactive.

When you present the personas, make sure to review what personas are (and what they're not) and how they're useful. Provide some information on how they were created, although the level of detail should depend on your audience. Then go through the personas one at a time. Spend enough time on each so that people get to know each one well enough before you move on to the next. Spend more time on the primary persona(s), who are the most critical to the business. Refer to the personas by name throughout the presentation.

The most important people in your audience to already know about the personas, because you've involved them from the beginning. You have involved them, haven't you? This is important, because people who feel they've been involved in creating the personas are far more likely to accept the personas, move forward with them, and evangelize them to others.

People who feel they've been involved in creating the personas are far more likely to accept the personas, move forward with them, and evangelize them to others.

When walking people through personas, you might not want to simply hand over the full persona documents, which can be overwhelming at first glance. A PowerPoint presentation can help you step through each persona gradually so that you tell each story the most effectively. Remember to focus on the most important differentiators and not overwhelm your audience with secondary details.

One way to emphasize what's most important to each persona is to first introduce each one, and then talk briefly about how to build a relationship with him or her. While creating personas for a bank, my colleagues uncovered one persona, Scott the Skeptic, who was cynical by nature, unimpressed by banks in general, and unlikely to ask for financial advice or seek out new products or services. After introducing Scott's persona, my colleagues recommended the following approach for building a relationship with Scott:

Relationship goals

- Maintain his level of satisfaction
- Opportunistically address his life event concerns to improve the relationship
- Establish our site as a source of unbiased information

What works

- Finding channels that he frequents and is apt to pay attention to (e.g., ATMs)
- Quoting independent sources of statistical information (e.g., census information and independent studies)
- Reinforcing his interest in background research by giving him factoids and useful info
- Using informational content to target life events

What to avoid

- Unsolicited contact of any kind
- Overt sales-oriented content

- Over-promising by setting high expectations and then not meeting them

In addition to the primary persona documents and good old PowerPoint, you can use other formats to present personas. Portable versions can help you when you want widespread distribution and can also help you boil down the personas to their most important attributes so that they're easier to remember. In the vein of sports cards, you can create persona cards, with name, photo, and perhaps a quote on the front, and key differentiators and a wee bit of a profile on the back. Since they represent a fresh way of seeing a document, persona cards can feel more interesting and more memorable.

CNN.com has also created a portable version of its personas. Its "persona cheat sheet" summarizes all the personas on one convenient sheet so that the most critical aspects of each persona are easily recalled. This cheat sheet has been distributed throughout the

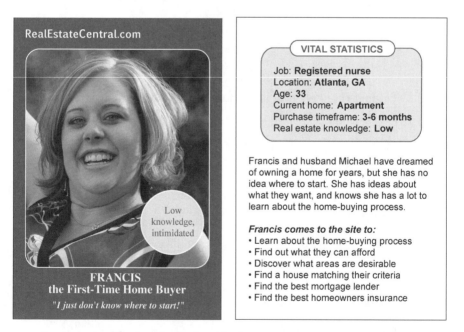

VITAL STATISTICS

Job: **Registered nurse**
Location: **Atlanta, GA**
Age: **33**
Current home: **Apartment**
Purchase timeframe: **3-6 months**
Real estate knowledge: **Low**

Francis and husband Michael have dreamed of owning a home for years, but she has no idea where to start. She has ideas about what they want, and knows she has a lot to learn about the home-buying process.

Francis comes to the site to:

- Learn about the home-buying process
- Find out what they can afford
- Discover what areas are desirable
- Find a house matching their criteria
- Find the best mortgage lender
- Find the best homeowners insurance

A persona card for Francis, front and back.

Life-sized cardboard cutouts can be a bit creepy, but also effective.

organization and is brought to meetings so that everyone keeps the personas in mind as decisions are made.

You can also create a large poster for each persona, which can potentially include more of the personas' content. Posters can help keep the personas front-of-mind because they serve as a visual reminder—the personas are literally looming overhead in hallways and/or meeting rooms.

Another idea is to create cardboard cutouts of the personas so that they are even more physically present in the room. A few hundred dollars is a valuable investment if it makes the personas come to life.

Then, of course, we have the ubiquitous T-shirt. Perhaps you could create one per persona, emblazoned with the eternal question, "What would Francis do?"

And for crying out loud, don't forget all the possibilities with other tchotchkes:

- Persona mugs
- Persona mouse pads
- Persona desktop wallpaper
- Persona screensavers
- Persona hats
- Persona Halloween face masks for scaring children

In addition to printed materials, bring in multimedia to make your personas real. Audio or video clips from user research can drive home key points about each persona. There's nothing like hearing the voice of the user or seeing users talk about their needs to encourage empathy in the room. These clips reinforce that the personas represent real people, not just vague abstractions of the user base.

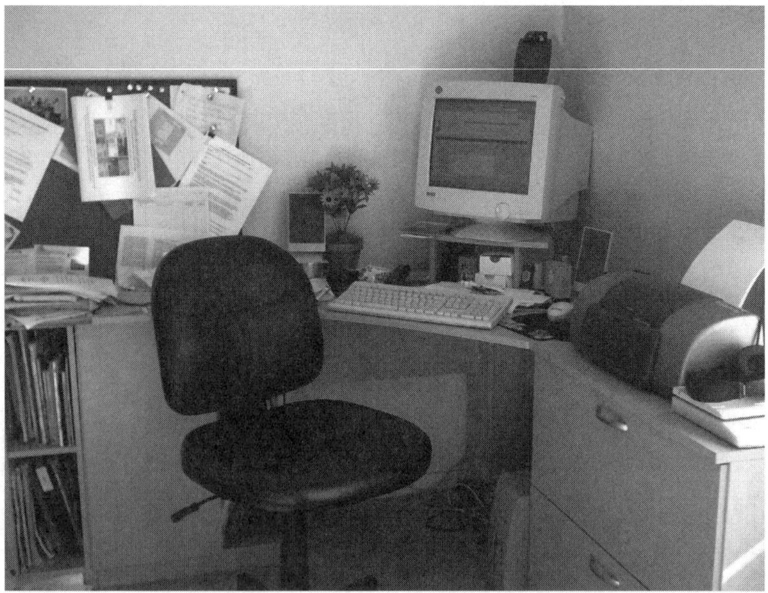

A desk for each persona can bring many details to life.

You might also take this idea up a notch by creating day-in-the-life photo essays or audio/video diaries for each persona. Find someone to play the role of each persona, and take pictures of them as they perform those personas' daily tasks and talk about what they need. Make sure the story you tell echoes the primary differentiators of each persona so that your message is consistent.

If you want to create something that immerses people even more in the world of the personas, try creating an actual physical environment. Set up an office or cubicle for each persona that shows exactly what would be on their desks, on their walls, on their bookshelves, and on their computer screens. Which persona is organized, which is messy? What applications are open all day long? What phone numbers are written down? What's on their to-do lists? If you can create an environment that enables someone to literally walk into this persona's life and feel what it's like to be him or her, you've made huge progress toward making the persona real. An executive can sit down in Howard the Hurried's chair and start asking questions about what he sees.

Presenting personas isn't just about the objects you've created; it's also about interacting with your audience. When you're initially presenting your personas, think about ways to engage the audience and have them interact with the persona information, rather than simply absorbing it passively.

One idea is to quiz the audience after presenting the personas. Outline a particular situation, then ask which persona they think it describes given what they already know. Which persona is most likely to work late hours? Which one is the most frustrated when he or she is behind schedule? Which one least enjoys talking to people on the phone? Which one sleeps in the nude? Okay, maybe not that last one, but you get the idea.

I mentioned earlier that my colleagues delivered personas recently for a bank. At the end of the presentation, to drive the personas home, they quizzed the audience on which persona (or personas) were most likely to:

- Apply online
- Look for the features and benefits of the bank's loans, accounts, and services
- Use the bank's calculators
- Take online tours
- Use the bank's ATM and branch locator tool
- Read articles on the site
- Listen to the bank's podcasts

You could also go through the current Web site and ask your audience how each persona would react to certain pages or certain tasks. What features on the current site best satisfies each persona? What frustrates each persona the most?

When people are asked to imagine the persona in action, the persona is more likely to become real in their minds. Give them a specific scenario and ask what they think the persona would do. How exactly would Francis find out what areas of Atlanta are desirable? What sites would she use, and when might she use yours?

Or, instead of having your audience imagine what the personas might say or do, draft some folks to role-play the personas. They can walk into the room (dressed as the personas, of course), sit down, and talk as the personas. The group can ask each persona questions to flesh out who the person is. To do this, you need people who are familiar with the personas up front and can improvise the answers to various questions. It's a lot of fun, and it implants the personas firmly in the minds of everyone in the room.

Living with Personas

After you've introduced everyone to the personas, your job is to keep the personas from becoming like those people who work at your company but whose names you never bothered to learn. To be useful, personas should remain alive in everyone's mind so that they come right to the fore when a decision needs to be made about the Web site.

Many companies rely on the human brain for this, trusting that the right people will remember the personas when the situation demands it. Sometimes this reliance on memory works fine, but often the human brain is too tempted to revert back to its habit of making decisions based on what *it* wants rather than on what real users want.

That's why you should always look for ways to make personas explicit at every step in the process, whether it's driving overall business strategy, defining the scope of a project, or making detailed decisions about information architecture, content, visual design, testing, and so on. If you can embed an obvious reminder about personas into these activities, it helps everyone take a moment to ground themselves in thinking about the personas rather than about themselves. The more blatant the reminder, the better.

The next few chapters cover various ways of making personas more visible as you go about your ordinary working life, so that they're put to good use throughout the entire lifecycle of your Web site. These ideas work for all types of projects, from small site enhancements to crazy, big site redesigns.

In order to keep personas alive at all times, you can do a few things regardless of your current activity. You can, distribute your persona materials far and wide. Put posters on walls so that personas hover over everyone like Big Brother. Leave persona documents or cards in conference rooms as gentle reminders, or staple them to documents that need reviewing. Give refresher presentations of the personas occasionally to remind veterans of their existence and to introduce them to new folks. Get regular coverage of your personas in the company newsletter.

As mentioned earlier, have team members role-play the personas in meetings so that as you're talking about a potential new feature or as you're evaluating a design, you can listen to the voices of the personas. Role-playing takes a little practice and might feel odd at first, but once you start, it's easy to get into it. This role-playing can also be useful for ramping up new team members. Another option in meetings is to begin the discussion with a short audio or video clip from the user research that reminds the gang about the personas. These techniques work when you're presenting personas for the first time as well as when you're using them throughout your typical process.

It can be challenging to create visual reminders of your personas, so one thing you might try is to associate each persona with an object (maybe funky glasses for Patricia the Perfectionist) or a symbol (a house with a question mark for Francis the First-Time Home Buyer). Then, you can use these symbols in all manner of documents as forms of visual shorthand for the personas. When people see the house icon, they'll think of Francis.

Here's one of my favorite strategies: Create email addresses for your personas so that they can individually send emails to the team members. One persona might send out an email about something a competitor site has done successfully, and another persona could send a complaint about a new bug on the site. Email is yet another tool you can use to make the personas feel like real people that demand to be heard. (Just hope that your colleagues don't put your personas on too many spam lists.)

If you have the time, you can even create a fake blog for each persona as another way to help others immerse themselves in the worlds of the personas.

If your audience for the personas responds better to offline reminders, you can also leave them voicemails from your personas on the same topics just discussed. This works well as long as your personas don't try to sell people magazine subscriptions.

This is the point in persona creation when personas are at most risk of dying. It's very easy to create personas, then think your work is done. But just having personas doesn't mean people will accept them. Just accepting the personas doesn't mean people will remember them. Just remembering the personas doesn't mean people will actually use them. Your job is to keep the personas alive so they show their worth. The first time you hear someone say, "What would Francis do?" without you prompting them, go buy yourself something nice, because you've earned it. Then get back to work.

9 Directing Business Strategy

IN 2004 THE DISCOUNT brokerage BrownCo, which I discussed in earlier chapters, was trying to develop its two-year business strategy. The discount brokerage industry was undergoing some upheaval at the time: The stock market had recovered from much of its contractions of 2001–2003, investors and traders were coming in droves, and this had ignited a price war and a wave of consolidations, as the various brokerage firms jockeyed for position and market share.

BrownCo had a longstanding reputation for catering to an experienced crowd of stock traders who valued simplicity and the lowest commission fees in the industry. Now, BrownCo was coming under increasing threat from big players such as Fidelity, that had aggressively lowered their commissions in an effort to peel off some of BrownCo's customers.

BrownCo embarked on an effort to develop its next-generation strategy and trading platform in order to retain existing customers and acquire new ones. As with many companies developing a strategy, it started by launching a study on its target market (active traders), performing a segmentation study, and identifying the target segment to go after. The BrownCo team identified its most important customer segment: slightly older active traders whose significant investable assets are almost completely concentrated in stocks.

Yet, it was what BrownCo did next that set it apart from its competitors. The company took the information about this segment, added to it data from customer interviews and studies with people who fit this segment, and created a persona called Frank the Frequent Trader. Frank represented his segment; he was an active trader focused on stocks. But unlike typical, dry segmentation models, Frank also had a personality that was representative of his group. Frank valued simplicity over bells and whistles. He did not want every trading tool under the sun. He knew how to use a few tools well and made good money for himself in the process. He was not interested in a huge basket of product offerings such as foreign exchanges, loans, or mutual funds. He knew how to do one thing well in trading—stocks—and he wanted a broker who understood that. He wanted a broker with whom it was easy to do business, who provided quick and easy access to knowledgeable customer service, offered low trading prices, and otherwise left him alone.

As the primary persona, Frank became BrownCo's strategy. Instead of running after competitors in features and functionality (and in the process running up huge development costs that would have to be passed on to Frank in the form of higher trading fees), BrownCo could differentiate itself by focusing on Frank, and providing the simplest, most bare-bones, elegant interface suited completely for an active trader with Frank's needs. In doing so, BrownCo could keep its development costs and trading fees low, and satisfy a niche customer base that larger companies such as Fidelity, that were trying to be all things to all people, could not possibly reach.

Frank was developed by the user experience group at BrownCo, but was quickly taken up and championed by the product marketing group which consistently pushed his needs and goals both up the corporate ladder and across to other groups. At the senior levels of the organization, the leadership team members were very interested in Frank, and in how they could craft a differentiation strategy around his needs. They rallied the organization around Frank the Frequent Trader and encouraged employees to internalize Frank's needs in everything they did. Frank's face started to make an appearance in meetings; it got to the point where you would hear members of the trade desk (which provided customer support for trading issues) describe the "Frank" they had just spoken to. Eventually, posters sprouted around the organization saying, simply, "What would Frank do?"

BrownCo is an example of one of the most exciting new applications of personas: bringing them into the field of business strategy. The same factors that have made personas so useful for Web site design and development are applied in the organization on a much broader scale.

Why Apply Personas to Business Strategy?

First things first: What do I mean by *strategy*? One of the best definitions I've heard (although I long ago forgot who coined it) is that strategy is the sum of decisions a company makes about where it should apply its resources (such as people and money) in order to maximize business benefit. As I think through this definition, I notice a number of similarities to Web site design.

First, both Web site design and strategy refer to making decisions about scarce resources. In Web site design, scarce resources usually include time and money, as well as page real estate and number of clicks. You can't put too many links, images, and copy on one page without confusing everyone, and you never have enough resources to design and build everything that your users might desire. As a result, the Web site design process is about making decisions based on the best opportunities worth pursuing. In business strategy you face similar challenges. Whether you are Bob's Backyard Toaster Repair or IBM, companies never have enough time, money, resources, or attention to follow up on every potential marketplace opportunity. Companies must decide which are the best opportunities to pursue with the resources they have.

Second, Web site design and strategy are, ultimately, about making your Web site/company successful. This point is extremely important. The ultimate goal of both Web site design and business strategy is not making users happy, it's making the Web site or company successful. Of course, in Web site design, many of us subscribe to the belief that by serving your users best, you serve your Web site best. But this is not always the case. Many business strategies that were not centered around users have been enormously successful. For example, for years, Dell has pursued a business strategy of cutting costs from its supply chain in order to keep a price and margin advantage over its competition. Procter & Gamble aggregates many popular consumer brands into one company in order to give itself a strong negotiating position for shelf space and prices with grocery stores, supermarkets, and others. There is nothing insidious or wrong with these corporate strategies; they are simply not centered around the user. However, many businesses today believe that a strong focus on users—understanding their needs and finding unique ways to deliver products and services—is the key to business success. For those businesses, personas can be of tremendous help.

Finally, both Web site design and business strategy require a framework by which to make decisions. This framework must create focus and allow trade-offs between opportunities competing for the company or Web site's scarce resources. Personas can provide that framework. On Web sites, personas allow you to internalize the needs of users, and prioritize the features which would provide the most value to them. For business strategy, a similar version of personas can help internalize the needs of your customers, and prioritize the features which would provide the most value to them, and thus achieve your business goals.

However, the mere fact that the challenges involved in Web site design and development are similar to those faced in business strategy does not, in and of itself, explain why personas should be used for business strategy. Instead, it's important to look at the biggest gaps or challenges in business strategy today and to understand how personas can help each of them. There are three gaps:

- **User gap:** Businesses are beginning to understand that they cannot just execute strategies "on" their user base and expect users to be passive participants. In many industries, users have a lot more power and a lot less loyalty now than they used to have. Companies that take their users for granted often find that they lose users rapidly. As a result, many businesses are seeking a better understanding of their users and a way to weave them into their business strategies.
- **Communication gap:** Once a strategy has been assembled, the next step is to communicate it throughout the organization. The best strategies are not insightful, carefully researched PowerPoint presentations that sit collecting dust on some shelf in the CEO's office. They are living things that have been embraced and internalized by the entire organization, from the senior management to the clerks in the mailroom. Unfortunately, too many strategies stay close to the vest of senior management, only partially communicated to the rest of the organization. Management teams worry that if they communicate too broadly, some word of the strategy might get back to their competition. So, they sacrifice broad acceptance of the strategy by their own organization for the sake of secrecy, and often find that the strategy fails because not enough people are working to implement it.
- **Execution gap:** Coming up with a good strategy is substantially easier than executing it—in fact, execution can be the

> toughest challenge businesses face in this process. Once a strategy has been developed, the team in charge of executing it inevitably runs afoul of time, cost, priorities, and politics. Project teams can get so focused on managing these constraints that they forget why they set out to execute this strategy in the first place. By the time they deliver, the core business value of their work has been completely lost.

Let's look at ways personas can help bridge these three gaps.

First, personas lead to tighter integration between user needs and strategy, helping bridge the user gap. Fundamentally, a persona is a story about a user—or, more accurately, an archetype representing the goals, behaviors, and attitudes of many users. Businesses are at their best when they understand how to align their products and services to their users' goals, behaviors, and attitudes. By starting with the user goals and needs, then layering on products and services to best meet those goals and needs, businesses develop strategies that close the user gap.

In the previous example, BrownCo had traditionally been the low-cost provider. But a price war in the brokerage industry was chiseling away at its competitive edge. The company needed to find another strategy. By focusing on Frank the Frequent Trader and leveraging its traditional strengths with this user, BrownCo could maintain its differentiation and increase its market share, without having to enter a features and functionality development war against much better funded competitors such as Fidelity Investments.

Second, personas provide common stories that are easy for people to digest, helping you bridge the communication gap. Harley Manning at Forrester Research has a way of describing personas that I have always liked. He calls personas a "user-friendly interface" to a lot of data about users. He's exactly right. A well-developed persona tells a story about a person, his or her needs, goals, and processes. At our core, human beings are storytellers. We like to tell stories and we like to hear stories. So when it comes time for an organization to cross the communication gap, wrapping a strategy in a series of stories about users is an extremely effective way to do it. Not everyone can swallow 200 slides' worth of financial analysis, or table after table of market research and competitor analysis. However, just about everyone can relate to a story about a user the organization is making a priority to serve, and about that user's unique goals and needs.

In the previous example, BrownCo's strategy was to acquire more Frank the Frequent Traders, so a relatively simple story could be distributed throughout the organization to align the direction of the business. "What would Frank do?" is the most succinct way I have ever seen to deliver a corporate strategy to the employees of a company.

Wrapping a strategy in a series of stories about users is an extremely effective way to cross the communication gap.

Finally, personas work because they are reusable across the process, from strategy to execution, helping us cross the execution gap. This is the greatest challenge most organizations face and, happily, the one for which the personas are best suited. By providing employees with well-developed personas that articulate users' needs, a business communicates the strategy more effectively and provides it in a way that employees can easily execute. Personas are a framework for making the day-to-day decisions that make or break the successful execution of a strategy.

For BrownCo, this is where personas paid off. By leveraging Frank the Frequent Trader across all its groups, BrownCo could extend its high-level business strategy down to the most minute tactical decisions. For example, during the redesign of BrownCo's multiple-order entry screen, several developers pushed for a screen that supported up to 20 orders. Others countered with the reminder that Frank the Frequent Trader only placed an average of eight trades per day. Clearly, providing room for up to 20 orders was overkill, and added unnecessary complexity. The multiple-order entry screen was simplified accordingly. By using personas, BrownCo had achieved alignment at all levels, from the CEO deciding how to differentiate in the marketplace, all the way down to the folks deciding how many orders can be placed in the order entry screen. Few organizations can claim such depth of internal strategic alignment.

Hopefully, by now you have a good understanding of the similarities between Web site design and business strategy, and of how personas can help with some of the key issues faced by businesses. The next step is to understand what you need to do differently when applying personas to business strategy, versus applying them to Web site design.

Using Personas for Business Strategy

You can do a few things to optimize personas for directing business strategy, but there aren't many differences between using personas for Web site design and using them for business strategy. For the most part, you can take the same tools and methodologies discussed in earlier chapters of this book when creating personas, and apply them to business strategy. There are, however, a few guidelines that you'll find helpful when developing personas for business strategy.

Business strategies require a wider range of information than you need for Web site design. Business strategy is concerned with the entire length and breadth of user interactions, across all the channels in which the business is involved (and even channels in which it might not yet be involved). When you develop business strategy personas, it is often useful to start by analyzing the entire user lifecycle: awareness, intent, purchase, and service. Then, identify the key needs in each stage of the user lifecycle. Next, identify the key channels used in each step: Web site, catalog, store, phone, and so on. Finally, identify the key weak points in the process where either you're not meeting user needs, or you are missing new opportunities to interact with the user.

Developing a business strategy with personas also requires an increased focus on competitors. Since many business cases may involve companies acquiring new customers or increasing share of wallet with existing customers, you want to understand the other businesses seeking to meet those users' needs. Once you've completed that research and assessed the competitors' strengths and weaknesses, you can weave these details into the narrative of the persona, to make a particular point that is important to the business strategy.

As I said in Chapter 7, one of the most important components of a business strategy persona is a "business objectives" section. This section details the goals you have for the persona, or what you want the persona to do. This could be increased use of a product, cross-selling or up-selling of a new item, increased customer satisfaction or loyalty, and so on. The important thing is that anyone looking at this persona will have a clear understanding of *your* goals for the persona, not just the persona's goals.

Once you have specific business objectives, it's important to have a way to measure your success or failure in achieving those objectives. Most strategies have metrics such as increased market share, increased share of wallet, increased revenue, higher margin, and reduced cost of service, as well as soft metrics such as increased customer satisfaction or loyalty. Personas are a great place to include these metrics.

Finally, scenarios (described in Chapter 7) are a must-have for business strategy personas and are used in a special way. At its heart, a business strategy represents a path that the business uses to achieve a business goal. But that line of thinking puts the user in a passive role and the business in an active role. Strategy becomes something you "do" to the users. A better way to look at it is that strategy is a way to fulfill a user's needs that no one else is able to fulfill. This way, the balance of power between business and user becomes more equal. Scenarios are a great way of taking a business strategy initiative and describing it as a story of user needs met by new business offerings.

Strategy is a way to fulfill a user's needs that no one else is able to fulfill.

For example, let's take our friend Francis the First-Time Home Buyer. If you were a large residential mortgage company (let's call you Best

Bank) instead of a real estate Web site, you might look at her goals and develop a strategy based on the premise that, if you can be a trusted partner for Francis in all her goals, you can convince her to give you her mortgage business, even if you are not the lowest mortgage product around. If there are enough Francises around, it might mean millions in additional income.

In order to drive this point home in the persona, you might write the scenario as follows:

> Francis first finds out about Best Bank through the Web site. There, she gets an explanation of the steps to home buying, some tools to help her find out how much of a home she can buy, and an agent locator to find the nearest Best Bank Realtor and schedule an appointment. (You created Best Bank Realtors through a series of acquisitions of Realtor offices in the area, and provided them with training customized for Francis, as part of this strategy.) At the Best Bank Realtor office, she meets Wilma the broker, who is a Best Bank employee, and operates on a mixture of commissions from house sales and a commission on the sale of Best Bank mortgages. Wilma takes her step by step through the home-buying process, and answers any questions she may have that the Web site did not answer. Wilma also spends some time helping Francis understand how much of a home she can afford, and is even able to qualify her for a Best Bank loan (at a reasonable rate, but not the lowest in the industry).
>
> Over the next few weeks, Wilma sends Francis the latest listings via email, which Francis can then check out on a Best Bank Web site personalized with Francis's listings. For the listings in which she is interested, Francis can automatically schedule a showing, or get visit times for an open house. Wilma goes out with her to view the properties, providing valuable advice about what to look for and what to stay away from. This is particularly helpful at one property that Francis had fallen in love with. Although the

> property has a fresh coat of paint and remodeled kitchen and bathrooms, Wilma notices some rotting wood on the side of the house that looks like recent termite damage. She warns Francis that the house might be infested. It turns out that it is infested and the cost to fix the damage is substantial. Armed with this knowledge, Francis demands a better price, but the deal falls through as the owners and Francis are unable to agree.
>
> Eventually, Francis finds the house of her dreams at a price she can afford. But she has to move fast, as there are several other offers. Since she is already pre-approved by Best Bank, she decides to stay with its product and has Wilma draft the offer. The owners accept, and the house goes under agreement a few days later. Francis has a great experience purchasing the house and recommends Wilma (and Best Bank) to her friends and family.

As you can see, the mechanics of adapting personas to business strategy are not too difficult. You must, however, shift your mindset from tactical Web site improvements to thinking holistically about your organization and your relationship with your customers. Next, I'll discuss one potential process that you can use to develop business personas and business strategies.

A Framework for Directing Business Strategy

A few years ago, Ziv found himself working with the services division of a large scientific instruments manufacturer. This manufacturer sold instruments at prices ranging from tens of thousands to millions of dollars per installation. The service division sold service contracts; if the instrument ever broke, it would send a service engineer to fix it. The company sought a better understanding of its users' needs in order to gain competitive advantage, and appealed to Ziv for strategic advice.

The process Ziv used can be broken down into nine steps:

1. Start by developing your personas. You can use any of the methods described earlier in this book, both qualitative and quantitative, although I recommend quantitative when dealing with big make-or-break-the-company decisions. Along the way, use market research to understand the relative business value of each persona, the size of the market, and growth opportunities that the organization might have.

   In the case of this manufacturer, Ziv conducted a series of qualitative user interviews followed by a survey of the customer base. He generated a quantitative, emergent segmentation based on the users' goals for purchasing a service contract, and then developed a series of personas based on this information. He found that one persona (I'll call her Sally Saver), representing 26 percent of the customer base, had a primary goal of saving money on the service plan costs, while another persona (I'll call her Marcia Maintainer), representing 29 percent of the customer base, had the primary goal of minimizing instrument downtime. Clearly these are two very different goals.

2. Once you have your personas, it is useful to share them with a small group of people representing the various parts of the organization (sales and marketing, operations, finance, service, etc.) for a few days of strategic visioning and prioritizing of business goals. Spend the first part of the meetings presenting and discussing each persona. You may choose to prioritize the personas based on fundamental business value or growth opportunity.

   In the group meetings with the manufacturer, Ziv discovered that, while the company had service plans designed to keep the prices low for users like Sally Saver, it lacked plans to address the quick service needs of Marcia Maintainer. In fact, many of the cost-saving processes built into the service plans were in direct conflict with the quick turnaround time needed by Marcia Maintainer. For example, in order to keep prices low, the company shared a group of service engineers among several clients, dispatching the first available service engineer whenever a client had a problem with its instrument. This was great news for Sally Saver, as it kept her service plan costs low, since the company was not holding a resource specifically for her. However, it was lousy for Marcia Maintainer, as the service engineer who showed up might not have any familiarity with her particular instrument and its particular quirks. As one Marcia Maintainer told Ziv during user interviews, "I have $40 million dollars of venture capital tied up in these two machines running 24/7. I cannot go back to the VCs and tell them their investment is at risk when these machines go down because I am too cheap to spend $40,000 on a good service plan."

3. During these strategic visioning meetings, use a large easel pad to list the key goals, behaviors, and attitudes of each persona, and ask the group to brainstorm potential solutions your company can provide to satisfy each persona. Focus on solutions that are truly differentiated in your industry, instead of improvements that are more incremental in nature and won't set you apart from competitors. Each solution should be written on a sticky note and hung up on the easel pad under the appropriate issue.

   As Ziv did this with his manufacturer, an idea emerged—a new series of premium service plans targeting the Marcia Maintainers of the world. These service plans would be more expensive than the clients' existing service plans, but would offer a higher level of service and faster turnaround time for problem resolution by providing, among other things, a more dedicated service engineer.

4. Next, have the groups go through each solution and develop a business case that would help quantify the business benefit of the solution. This can be in hard metrics such as increased revenue, higher product margin, or reduced costs,

or soft metrics such as increased customer loyalty, retention, customer service center wait time, and so on. Write up the business case "formulas" on a different color sticky note than you used in step 3 and stick it directly under the idea sticky notes.

As Ziv's team brainstormed solutions, it also developed a business case that juggled the incremental costs of providing better services with an estimation of the higher price, and the percentage of the market they could capture.

5. Have the group go through each of the sticky notes in step 4 and create two new sticky notes: one describing information for the business case that you need to gather from your users, the other describing information for the business case that you need to gather from within the company or from third-party sources. Put each of these sticky notes under the sticky notes from step 4.

   As Ziv did this with his manufacturer, the two key pieces of information needed were: the incremental costs in lower employee productivity, if dedicating staff to a client account was offered; and the increased price that customers were willing to pay, in order to have fully or partially dedicated staff available. Provided that the price the clients were willing to pay was significantly higher than the cost of providing those employees, the company had a new offering that would not only increase customer satisfaction, but also increase the business margins.

6. If you end up with too many ideas, ask the group to prioritize or vote on the top ideas and kill everything else.

   When Ziv was working with his manufacturer, a great many ideas came up in the process. One was to provide the service engineers more sales training so that they could help the instrument sales process instead of relying exclusively on the sales team. This was shelved because the cost of providing this training was very high.

7. Take the research sticky notes from step 5 and assign them to various members of the team, who may have to do additional user research and surveys. Once you have the information, assemble the business cases and prioritize those ideas according to which have the highest impact in terms of hard and soft benefits. Prioritizing is a key step—there are never enough resources to chase every potential opportunity.

8. Develop action plans for executing each of those top ideas with timelines, dependencies, implementation, and operating costs (as well as development, marketing, staffing costs, etc.) and add these plans to your business cases.

   In Ziv's case, the product manager for the manufacturer's services organization was made responsible for collecting this information and developing a product and marketing plan.

9. Finally, take those top ideas and re-incorporate them into the persona narrative. For each idea (or group of related ideas), create a separate scenario that describes the user's goals and needs and how the company can meet them through the ideas proposed.

   Eventually, the Marcia persona and her story about $40 million in VC funding became a powerful scenario within the manufacturing organization. Ziv told the story to dozens of people within the organization, and heard it relayed back to him from employees he hadn't met during the initial engagement. The scenario captured the essence of Marcia Maintainer's dilemma in a way that company employees could quickly relate to. It became easy for employees to sympathize with Marcia and her plight, develop effective products for her, and rally around them when executing the many details necessary to make her happy.

This chapter provided an overview of applying the tool of personas in the larger context of an organization's business strategy. As you can see, developing a business strategy is not a simple thing, with or without personas. The use of personas for business strategy is an exciting new field and some of the best work is yet to be done. Personas give you a valuable framework for creating and prioritizing business initiatives, and a way to enable more effective distribution and alignment of a strategy throughout the organization. They are well worth the effort when your organization is developing its next strategic plan.

10 Scoping Features and Functionality

YOU'RE SEATED AT the conference room table, surrounded by colleagues, ready to talk about the next release of the Web site or the next big redesign. A lot of chefs are in this kitchen, and therefore a lot of different opinions are floating around about what features and content should be built next. Your neighbor Susan is convinced that it's time to create more how-to content for the site, while Andy is adamant that a product selector tool is most important. Meanwhile, you're wondering if *any* of these ideas are really the best way to invest time and money.

Perhaps you're hearing in your head the voice of Karl Malden from that old commercial for traveler's checks: "What will you do? What *will* you do?"

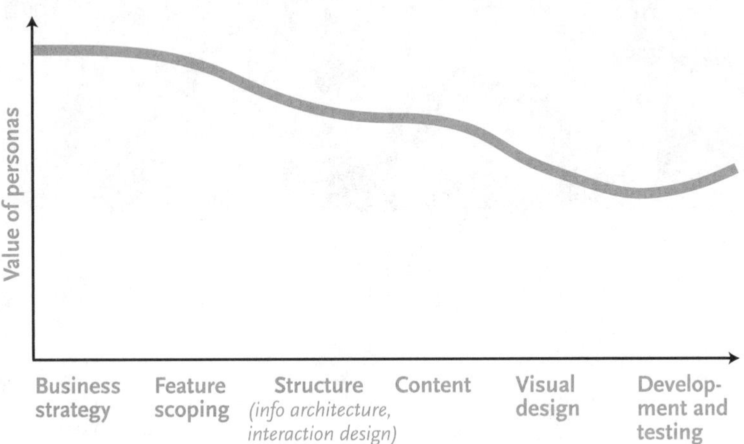

A speculative graph of how the usefulness of personas varies depending on the task at hand.

For many organizations, personas are the most useful at this stage in the process—when you're figuring out what to build in the first place. Even if you don't use personas to direct your overarching business strategy, they become critical when you're deciding on the scope of features, functionality, and content that should be created. Personas are valuable every step of the way, of course, but using them upstream in the process helps you avoid wasted effort downstream.

This chapter explores two ways in which personas can be used to establish the scope of a project:

- **Brainstorming** potential features, functionality, and content based on the personas' goals, attitudes, and behaviors
- **Prioritizing** what should ultimately be in scope, based on (at least in part) what's important to the personas

Brainstorming Scope

Using personas is a no brainer when you are thinking about all the potential features, functionality, and content that you could create for your Web site. Remember the diagram from the first chapter that shows the fundamental conversation that takes place between your user and your business? The logic is simple:

- Users come to the site with at least one goal in mind.
- Personas help you understand and document those goals for each type of user.
- Each goal will be met by specific features or content (and thus ideally lead to business results).

One method for using personas to brainstorm features and content is to simply keep them in the back of your mind as you come up with a long list of possible scope items. The idea is that you and your colleagues internalize the personas well enough to be able to brainstorm, without having them right there in front of you.

I'm not a big fan of this method. As mentioned in Chapter 8, the more you can make the personas a visible part of your process, the better. If they're not visible, they're too easily replaced by your personal opinion (or your colleagues') about what features and content would be the best. With this method, you also run a risk of everyone on the team having different ideas of what the personas want, and then everyone, essentially, revising the personas in their heads, according to their own preconceived notions. We humans are very good at rationalizing our own desires.

Every goal of every persona leads to ideas about content and features that could satisfy that goal.

Make the personas an explicit part of your brainstorming process, whatever that might be. My favorite method of directed brainstorming is to facilitate a group workshop, where I take one persona at a time to blue-sky everything that could potentially satisfy each one of that persona's goals.

Here's how it works: On a whiteboard, or one of those ultra-large sticky notes, list one persona's goals down the left side. Then list the business objectives for that persona on the right side, using every potentially relevant objective for each user goal. (You may encounter a lot of repetition, so consider making a duplicate list of objectives on a separate sheet so that they're always visible.) Leave plenty of blank space in the middle.

Now you can brainstorm one goal at a time. What are all the possible features and content that could help Francis learn about the home-buying process? You know Francis, and you know she doesn't understand much about real estate and that she's intimidated by its complexity. What would help her?

This is blue-sky time, and no idea is a bad idea. You can prioritize the long list later. The goal is quantity—as many different ideas as you can come up with as a group. Brainstorm now, evaluate later. Remember to refer back to your qualitative research; chances are your users have already told you about some of the content and features that would be useful.

When you're done brainstorming around the first user goal, look at the business objectives related to that goal. Is there any other feature or type of content that would encourage Francis to visit the site more often, or register, or subscribe? The idea is to approach the middle column from both sides, and find potential sweet spots—features and content that satisfy users *and* business objectives.

Then, of course, it's time to move on to Francis's second user goal and keep the ideas flying. The table on page 238 shows just the beginning of what might come out of such a session.

FRANCIS THE FIRST-TIME HOME BUYER

User Goal	Possible Features and Content	Business Objectives
Learn about the home-buying process		Visit the site often Register for email alerts and newsletters Subscribe to premium services Recommend the site to others
Find out what she can afford		Visit the site often Register for email alerts and newsletters Subscribe to premium services Recommend the site to others
Discover what areas of Atlanta are desirable		Visit the site often Register for email alerts and newsletters Subscribe to premium services Recommend the site to others
Find a house that matches her criteria		Visit the site often Register for email alerts and newsletters Subscribe to premium services Recommend the site to others
Find the best mortgage lender		Visit the site often Register for email alerts and newsletters Subscribe to premium services Follow through by contacting mortgage partner Recommend the site to others
Find the best insurance		Visit the site often Register for email alerts and newsletters Subscribe to premium services Follow through by contacting insurance partner Recommend the site to others

FRANCIS THE FIRST-TIME HOME BUYER

User Goal	Possible Features and Content	Business Objectives
Learn about the home-buying process	Introductory how-to articles Glossary of jargon Videos and podcasts Success stories Q&A with experts Message board Blogs Rent vs. own calculator Links to other content resources Local experts to call/meet Checklists to print Book recommendations Interactive quizzes Common mistakes Animated cartoons Call an expert Email content to a friend Bookmark content	Visit the site often Register for email alerts and newsletters Subscribe to premium services Recommend the site to others
Find out what she can afford	Introductory how-to articles Glossary of jargon Affordability calculator Step-by-step wizard Rich Internet Application Local experts to call/meet Call an expert Example stories	Visit the site often Register for email alerts and newsletters Subscribe to premium services Recommend the site to others

And so on for the remaining goals....

Go through this exercise for each persona. I usually begin with the primary persona(s), while minds are fresh. This process can take a while, so you might want to split the workshop up into multiple meetings.

Yes, you end up with a very long list. No, you don't actually build all of these items. Yet, it's important to take the time to open the floodgates, because this directed brainstorming might reveal new ideas that emerge as high priorities. It's often the case that one person's idea incites another person to expand on it, or take it in a new direction, and the final result is greater than what any one person could have conceived.

If the process of establishing the scope of your projects is less democratic, with your list of features and content being driven by a small number of decision makers, you might try a different approach. Rather than facilitating a group workshop, it may be more profitable for you to interview key stakeholders, in order to establish their requirements. Try structuring these interviews around the personas. Instead of launching into a discussion about the stakeholders' favorite features or pet peeves, start with your primary persona, and ask each stakeholder what the requirements should be to better satisfy this user. By reframing the conversation, you're more likely to get them thinking outside of themselves and focus on one user-type at a time.

Prioritizing Scope

Directed brainstorming with personas is a rich method for generating ideas that you know will satisfy your users. But now that you have a long list of what you could build, how do you winnow that list down to what you *should* build? How do you prioritize features and content to render them, ultimately, in scope?

Conducting a Competitive Feature Analysis

Many companies find it helpful to look at their competitors when prioritizing new features and content for their sites. Keeping an eye on competitors is always wise, since users build up expectations based on what they see other Web sites doing. Thus, a common tool is the competitive feature analysis, a spreadsheet that lists every feature seen on competitors' sites, with information on the current features present on each site. This approach enables one to scan which features are baseline expectations (because everyone has them), and which are potential opportunities (because few or no competitors have them).

Here is part of a competitive feature analysis I created for a Web search engine a few years ago. I used a filled circle to denote which sites had each feature, and an empty circle for sites that had the feature to some degree, but perhaps not implemented as soundly as on other sites. The spreadsheet went on for many pages, but from this preview, you can see how certain features were more common across competitors (e.g., query refinement) and others were rare at the time (e.g., recent queries).

When you're conducting a competitive analysis such as this, consider adding personas into the mix. Add a column for each persona, and then rate how well each feature would satisfy the needs of each one of them. Since you know who each persona is, and what types of features or content each would find helpful, you'll find this is a relatively easy exercise.

I find it's most effective to take one persona at a time when doing this prioritization. When rating each feature for a particular persona, ask yourself the following questions:

- Would the persona consider this feature a baseline expectation, without which the site wouldn't be worth using? Or is the feature simply a nice-to-have addition that wouldn't affect this persona's loyalty?

Feature	Description (Ability to...)	Web Search Competitors														
		AllTheWeb	AltaVista	Dogpile	Google	HotBot	iLOR	Lycos	MetaCrawler	MSN	ProFusion	SurfWax	Teoma	Vivisimo	WiseNut	Yahoo!
Catalog filter	Choose which search engine will be used for your search (e.g., Google, Altavista, Ask Jeeves, etc.)			●				●	●		●	●		●		
Recent queries	See a list of your most recent search queries; click to perform that same search with those settings															
Customized filters	Choose which advanced search filters appear on the main search page	○				●										
Query refinement	See a list of related searches done by other people who did the same search you did	○	●	●		●	●	●	●	●			●		●	
Adult content filter	Tell the search engine to block offensive content from search results	●	●		●			●						●	●	
All/any/exact filter	Tell the search engine to search for all the words, any of the words, or the exact phrase you enter	●	●		●	●			●	●	●		○	●	●	●
Word filter	Specify which words must be included, should be included, or must not be included	●	○		○	●		●						●		○
File type filter	Specify the type of file to be searched: image, audio, Java, PDF, etc.	○			○	●				●						
Domain filter	Specify which domains should be searched or excluded: .com, .net, .edu, .uk, etc.	●	●		●	●		●		●				●		
IP filter	Specify which IP addresses should be searched or excluded	●														
Languages filter	Select which languages should be included in your results	●	●		●	●		●		●				●	●	
Spelling recommend-ation	Have the search engine spell-check your search term and suggest an alternative search		●		●											
Spelling correction	Choose whether the search engine should try to automatically correct your spelling									●						
Region filter	Specify which regions should be searched: North America, Europe, Africa, etc.		●			●			●	●						
Word stemming filter	Choose whether or not the search engine should show partial word matches (e.g., "movies" for a "movie" search)					●				●						
Query rewriting fiilter	Turn on or off the engine's capability to try to improve your query based on what it thinks you're looking for	●														
More from this site	Do the same search but only within one of the sites listed on the results page	●	●		●	●										
Related pages	View the pages the search engine finds are related to a particular result		●						●		●		●			
Search within results	Search within a current set of results to refine those results													●		
Thesaurus	Narrow or broaden your search by clicking on related terms to add them to your search											●				
Sort by	Choose which of your search terms will be ranked highest		●													
Occurrence filter	Specify where the search terms can occur: entire document, title, URL, etc.	●			●			●		●				●		

A competitive analysis is a helpful tool for prioritizing features and content.

		Personas					Web Search Competitors														
Feature	Description (Ability to...)	Harry	Ping	Kip	Sally	Ray	AllTheWeb	AltaVista	Dogpile	Google	HotBot	iLOR	Lycos	MetaCrawler	MSN	ProFusion	SurfWax	Teoma	Vivisimo	WiseNut	Yahoo!
Catalog filter	Choose which search engine will be used for your search (e.g., Google, Altavista, Ask Jeeves, etc.)	●		●	○	○			●				●	●		●	●		●		
Recent queries	See a list of your most recent search queries; click to perform that same search with those settings	●	●	○	●	●															
Customized filters	Choose which advanced search filters appear on the main search page	●	○	●			○				●										
Query refinement	See a list of related searches done by other people who did the same search you did	○	○	○	○	○	○	●	●		●	●	●	●	●			●		●	
Adult content filter	Tell the search engine to block offensive content from search results			○			●	●		●			●						●	●	
All/any/exact filter	Tell the search engine to search for all the words, any of the words, or the exact phrase you enter	●	○	●	○		●	●		●	●			●	●	●		○	●	●	●
Word filter	Specify which words must be included, should be included, or must not be included	●	○	●	○		●	○		○	●		●						●		○
File type filter	Specify the type of file to be searched: image, audio, Java, PDF, etc.	●	○	○	●		○			○	●				●						
Domain filter	Specify which domains should be searched or excluded: .com, .net, .edu, .uk, etc.	●	○	●			●	●		●	●		●		●				●		
IP filter	Specify which IP addresses should be searched or excluded	●		●			●														
Languages filter	Select which languages should be included in your results	○	○	○	○		●	●		●	●		●		●				●	●	
Spelling recommend-ation	Have the search engine spell-check your search term and suggest an alternative search	○	○	○	●	●		●		●											
Spelling correction	Choose whether the search engine should try to automatically correct your spelling	○			○										●						
Region filter	Specify which regions should be searched: North America, Europe, Africa, etc.			○				●			●			●	●						
Word stemming filter	Choose whether or not the search engine should show partial word matches (e.g., "movies" for a "movie" search)	○	○	○							●				●						
Query rewriting fiilter	Turn on or off the engine's capability to try to improve your query based on what it thinks you're looking for	○		○			●														
More from this site	Do the same search but only within one of the sites listed on the results page	○	○	○	○	○	●	●		●	●										
Related pages	View the pages the search engine finds are related to a particular result	○	○	○	○	○		●						●		●		●			
Search within results	Search within a current set of results to refine those results		○		○														●		
Thesaurus	Narrow or broaden your search by clicking on related terms to add them to your search	○	○	○	●	○											●				
Sort by	Choose which of your search terms will be ranked highest							●													
Occurrence filter	Specify where the search terms can occur: entire document, title, URL, etc.	○					●			●			●		●				●		
Updated filter	Limit your search to pages updated within a certain time period		○	○			●	●		●	●				●						

A competitive analysis with new columns that show how important each feature is to each persona.

- Would the persona consider this feature a differentiator compared with other sites, something that would cause him or her to use this site repeatedly? Or would it be important enough to make a real difference in which site he or she uses?
- How often would this persona use this feature? On a regular basis, or rarely?
- How effectively would this feature drive this persona toward the appropriate business objective? Would it encourage this particular user to register or make a purchase? Would it lead him or her toward some other goal? Or, would it have little impact at all?

You can use any type of rating scale. For the Web search engine analysis, I used a 1–3 scale. Features that were most important to the persona got a filled circle, features that were somewhat important got an empty circle, and the rest got no circle. The result is an easy-to-scan list of features that provides more useful information than a typical competitive feature analysis. You can quickly visualize which features are more important and get a sense of where competitors are lagging behind on satisfying certain user needs. From this type of analysis, a feature such as recent queries suddenly looks like an opportunity worth exploring.

Creating a Scope Matrix

Even if you don't do a competitive analysis of features and content, you can embed personas in your normal prioritization process. I often create a scope matrix early in a project, to list all the discussed features and content. Like the competitive feature analysis, this spreadsheet lists all the potential features and content down the left side. Typically, such a scoping tool encourages people to discuss the overall priority and level of effort for each feature so that they can decide which features are in scope and which are not.

By adding personas to this tool, you can keep the users constantly present in everyone's minds, while analyzing the importance of each feature. Shown here is part of the scope matrix for VistaPrint, the online design and printing company. The VistaPrint team was considering a variety of improvements to the site; this excerpt shows possible features for the Gallery, where users select a design template for their business cards, brochures, or other printed material.

My team rated each potential feature (shown in the figure here as placeholders to preserve confidentiality) based on how important it was to each of the four personas, with a full circle meaning very important, an empty circle meaning somewhat important, and an empty cell meaning not important. This prioritization enabled us to give an overall Priority rating to each feature (using the familiar High, Medium, and Low) based on its importance to the personas and its importance to the business. We ranked Effort in the same way,

		Personas						
ID	**Scope Item**	**Nancy**	**Patricia**	**Howard**	**Lee**	**Priority**	**Effort**	**Phase**
4	**GALLERY**							
4.1	A description of the feature would normally appear here.	●	●	●	○	H	H	**1**
4.2	A description of the feature would normally appear here.	●	○	○	○	M	H	**3**
4.3	A description of the feature would normally appear here.	○	○	○	○	M	L	**1**
4.4	A description of the feature would normally appear here.	●	○	●	○	M	M/H	**2**
4.5	A description of the feature would normally appear here.	○	○	○		M	M	**2**
4.6	A description of the feature would normally appear here.	○	○	○	○	M	M	**3**
4.7	A description of the feature would normally appear here.	●		●	○	H	L	**1**
4.8	A description of the feature would normally appear here.		●		○	M	L	**1**
4.9	A description of the feature would normally appear here.		●	○	○	H	L	**1**
4.10	A description of the feature would normally appear here.	●	○	●	○	M/H	M	**3**
4.11	A description of the feature would normally appear here.	●	●	○	○	M/H	M/H	**1**
4.12	A description of the feature would normally appear here.		○		○	L/M	M/H	**3**
4.13	A description of the feature would normally appear here.		○	●	●	M/H	M	**1**
4.14	A description of the feature would normally appear here.	●	○	●	●	M/H	M	**1**
4.15	A description of the feature would normally appear here.		●	●	○	M/H	M/H	**1**
4.16	A description of the feature would normally appear here.	●	●	●	○	H	H	**1**
4.17	A description of the feature would normally appear here.	○	○	○		M	M	**1**
4.18	A description of the feature would normally appear here.		○	○		L/M	L/M	**2**
4.19	A description of the feature would normally appear here.	○	●		○	M	M	**3**
4.20	A description of the feature would normally appear here.	●	●	○	○	M/H	L/M	**1**
4.21	A description of the feature would normally appear here.	○	●		○	M	M/H	**3**
4.22	A description of the feature would normally appear here.	●	●	○		M/H	M/H	**1**
4.23	A description of the feature would normally appear here.	○	○	●	●	M/H	M/H	**1**
4.24	A description of the feature would normally appear here.	○	○		○	M	M	**2**
4.25	A description of the feature would normally appear here.	○	○	○		M	H	**1**

Add personas to a scope matrix to help prioritize features and content.

		Personas						
ID	Scope Item	Nancy	Patricia	Howard	Lee	Total	Priority	Effort
4	GALLERY							
4.1	A description of the feature would normally appear here.	4	5	4	3	33	H	H
4.2	A description of the feature would normally appear here.	5	2	4	3	30	M	H
4.3	A description of the feature would normally appear here.	4	3	3	2	26	M	L
4.4	A description of the feature would normally appear here.	4	4	5	3	33	M	M/H
4.5	A description of the feature would normally appear here.	2	4	3	1	21	M	M
4.6	A description of the feature would normally appear here.	3	4	3	3	26	M	M
4.7	A description of the feature would normally appear here.	5	1	5	3	30	H	L
4.8	A description of the feature would normally appear here.	1	5	1	3	18	M	L
4.9	A description of the feature would normally appear here.	1	5	2	3	20	H	L
4.10	A description of the feature would normally appear here.	5	3	5	3	34	M/H	M
4.11	A description of the feature would normally appear here.	4	5	3	3	31	M/H	M/H
4.12	A description of the feature would normally appear here.	1	2	1	2	11	L/M	M/H
4.13	A description of the feature would normally appear here.	1	3	5	4	23	M/H	M
4.14	A description of the feature would normally appear here.	5	3	5	4	35	M/H	M
4.15	A description of the feature would normally appear here.	1	4	4	3	22	M/H	M/H
4.16	A description of the feature would normally appear here.	4	4	5	3	33	H	H
4.17	A description of the feature would normally appear here.	2	3	2	1	17	M	M
4.18	A description of the feature would normally appear here.	1	3	3	1	16	L/M	L/M
4.19	A description of the feature would normally appear here.	3	5	1	3	24	M	M
4.20	A description of the feature would normally appear here.	4	5	3	3	31	M/H	L/M
4.21	A description of the feature would normally appear here.	2	4	1	2	18	M	M/H
4.22	A description of the feature would normally appear here.	4	4	3	1	27	M/H	M/H
4.23	A description of the feature would normally appear here.	3	3	5	4	29	M/H	M/H
4.24	A description of the feature would normally appear here.	3	3	1	3	20	M	M
4.25	A description of the feature would normally appear here.	4	3	2	1	23	M	H

A more mathematical approach provides a different weight to each persona's rating so you can calculate a total value.

taking into account all levels of effort involved, from required organizational changes to technical development. Finally, after an iterative process, we decided in which phase to launch each feature.

A simple rating scheme such as this can go a long way toward making personas an active part of the decision-making regarding the scope of the project. You can also make this process a wee bit more scientific. Let's say Nancy is the primary persona, and you want her rating to count more than that of any other persona. Let's say that Patricia and Howard are also important, and Lee is the least important persona. Instead of using a 1–3 scale shown as circles, you can make the ratings a little more specific using a numerical 1–5 scale. To give the appropriate importance to each persona's ratings, you can add a weighting mechanism to the spreadsheet. In this example, a simple Excel formula makes Patricia and Howard's ratings count twice as much as Lee's, while Nancy's rating is thrice as much. The new Total column shows the sum of these weighed ratings and provides a quick summary of the importance of each feature, relative to the weight of each persona.

Don't be seduced by numbers: This is still a qualitative process. The numbers might give a little more detail about the value of each feature, but you're not required to follow the output verbatim. Prioritizing the scope is still a very human process.

Whatever method you use to prioritize features and content, whether it's a formal, documented process, or an informal chat around a conference room table, find a way to make your personas an explicit part of that process. Deciding what to create for the site is a critical moment with vast downstream implications. No one wants to waste time developing features or content that isn't important to users and to the business. Personas are immeasurably useful for helping you make the right decisions early, before you dive into the design and development process.

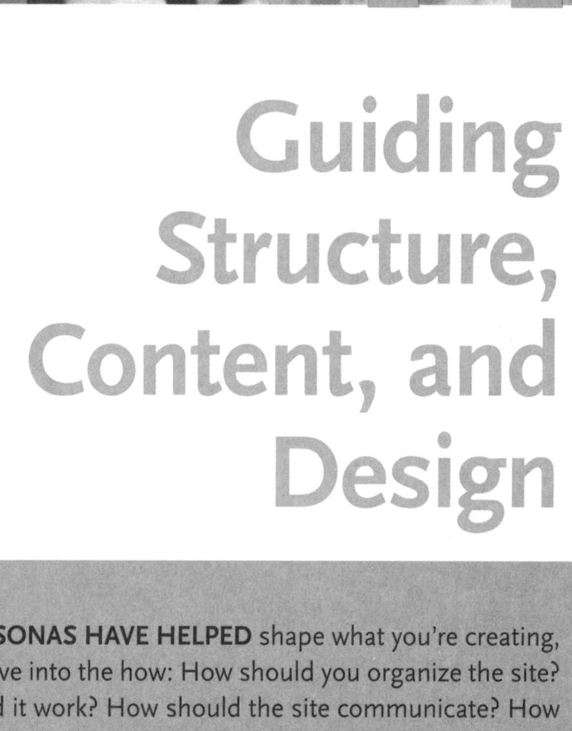

11 Guiding Structure, Content, and Design

ONCE PERSONAS HAVE HELPED shape what you're creating, you can move into the how: How should you organize the site? How should it work? How should the site communicate? How should it look?

When it comes to day-to-day decisions about design (I'm using *design* in the broadest sense here), everyone has his or her own methodologies and tools. You and your colleagues have a lot of expertise in your area, and as a result, it's easy to revert to designing based on what you think will work, and to forget about the personas. Don't be tempted. Personas are incredibly valuable for guiding design decisions, regardless of which methodologies and tools you call your own.

This chapter delves into how to use personas throughout the design process, including:

- **Structure:** If you're organizing content, personas can help with information architecture, navigation, and search. If you're working on a Web application, they can guide the interaction design and help structure the flow of the experience.
- **Content:** Personas are the readers for whom all content is written, and thus they can inform what you say and how you say it.
- **Visual design:** How you communicate visually can be critical to informing or persuading your users; personas keep visual designs focused on who matters most.

Establishing Structure: Information Architecture and Interaction Design

Whether you're designing the high-level structure of a site or application, or working on the detailed structure of individual pages or screens, the foundation of your creativity is your personas. No matter how formally you use them, personas should guide the basic structure of the user experience you're building.

Why? Because persona goals, attitudes, and behaviors point you to exactly what users want to do on the site and how they want to do it. When you know that, you can begin to organize everything so that users can accomplish their goals. It's that simple, and that hard.

Recall the diagram from Chapter 7 on page 191. User research is broken down into segments, which become personas. Personas have goals, some of which you might bring to life in scenarios, but all of which can be investigated through task analysis or use cases. This analysis tells you what you need to know in order to design any particular feature or content, including how to structure it.

User research ➤ Segments ➤ Personas ➤ Scenarios ➤ Task analysis/ Use cases ➤ Feature design

Each decision in the chain is based on the step before it.

Performing Task Analysis

Let's take a scenario from Chapter 7 and see how this works. Here's the scenario for Francis the First-Time Home Buyer:

> Francis and Michael have agreed that she'll take charge of learning more about the home-buying process. She goes online, does a Google search for "Atlanta real estate," and follows a link to the site's home page. She sees that she can search for houses from the home page, so just for fun, she does a quick Atlanta search to see what kinds of houses show up. There are lots of houses in many different neighborhoods, and she easily narrows her results down to the area where she and Michael live, using a map. There are still many results, and she's not quite sure which search options to use to narrow the search further. Then she notices a link for first-time home buyers and follows it, hoping for basic how-to information.
>
> The link takes Francis to a step-by-step tutorial that explains the whole process, and she immediately feels like she's found the right site from which to begin her house search. She carefully reads some articles for first-time home buyers, taking notes as she reads. She bookmarks other articles for later reading. She also comes across the site's calculator and starts trying different combinations of numbers to find out what she and Michael can afford. She particularly likes the glossary of terms that allows her to finally figure out what "points" are, and learn more about different types of mortgages. After an hour and a half of reading, her brain is full, and she shuts her computer down for the day, feeling she had an excellent start.

> The next day, she comes back to the site to look up information specific to individual Atlanta neighborhoods, and finds plenty of it. She's able to focus on five neighborhoods that look particularly good. The fun begins that night, when she takes Michael through what she has learned, and they set up a regular schedule for looking at online house listings.

Let's break down this scenario into the discrete tasks Francis performs during this story. The task analysis might look like this:

1. **Search for houses from home page.**
   a. Enter location by city and state, or zip code.
   b. Enter price range.
   c. Enter number of bedrooms and/or bathrooms.
   d. Submit search.
2. **View and narrow results.**
   a. Browse first page of results: photo, price, address, basic stats, and description.
   b. Click to show results on map.
   c. Click map to narrow results to one neighborhood.
   d. Browse new results.
3. **Read tutorial.**
   a. Click link for first-time home buyers.
   b. Read landing page for learning area.
   c. Click teaser for step-by-step tutorial.

   And so on . . .

You get the idea. A task analysis drills down into the scenario to identify its smallest components. What you get is a to-do list for defining the structure of this particular experience: First, enable users to search for homes from the home page, providing filtering based on clicking a map. Then, make sure a welcoming link for first-time home buyers appears on the results page, and so on. Before you know it, you're creating a site map or flow diagram of this part of the site.

Now, go back and do the same thing for other scenarios and other personas. You might not have scenarios for every goal of every persona, but you can still do a task analysis even without scenarios. Take the goal and, knowing how the persona would want to accomplish it, break down the experience the persona would want to have.

Whereas scenarios describe ideal experiences, now is the time to inject reality, because, as a famous bard once crooned, you can't always get what you want. Your task analysis should reflect what's possible, given constraints in terms of the business, content, and, of course, technology.

The output of this exercise is a multitude of separate task analyses. Your next job is to create one structure to support all of these individual journeys. Think of this as the superset of all the needs of all your personas. For example, the process of searching for houses on the example real estate site needs to support different personas, and so the site contains some features for the first-time home buyer Francis, other features for an advanced, experienced buyer, and so on.

By the time you've added up all the analyses of all the personas, you should have accounted for all the content and features of your entire site, because you have covered all probable journeys through it. If you have content or features left over that aren't covered in any task analysis, you might want to ask yourself if they're absolutely necessary. Why waste effort creating something that doesn't satisfy a goal, and therefore won't be used?

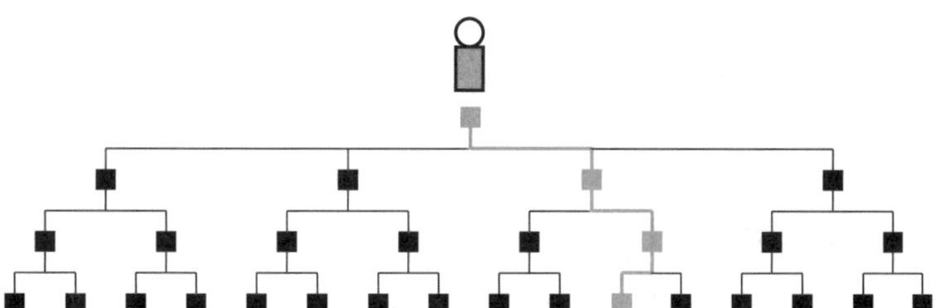

Each persona goal or scenario is one path through your eventual site structure, whether it's a content-heavy site map, such as this, or a flow diagram for a Web application.

Over time, you might find that you don't need to create explicit task analyses; instead, you can go straight to sketching out high-level structure based on your deep understanding of your personas and scenarios. But if you're looking for a way to make sure your personas are at the center of this process, persona-based task analysis is an excellent step.

Producing Use Cases

If you're familiar with use cases, you can see how a task analysis can easily evolve into a use case. Use cases have long been valuable for documenting requirements for software or a Web site in the form of back-and-forth interaction between user and system. Whereas task analyses focus on the user's perspective of the experience, use cases include the system's perspective and actions as well. Most use cases begin with a generic *actor*—a user who performs all the actions.

Personas take this to the next level. Rather than use cases talking about a generic user, you have personas as specific users, each with his or her own set of use cases. As with task analysis, each persona goal becomes a use case. Rather than providing you with a sterile interaction between the user and the system, use cases gain personality and flavor, because you know exactly how and why each persona behaves as he or she does. As use cases become more realistic, they also become more useful in defining the structure and requirements of the user experience.

Here's a quick example of a use case based on just the first small part of the Francis scenario earlier:

> **Search for Houses**
>
> *Scope:* RealEstateCentral.com
>
> *Level:* User Goal
>
> *Primary Actor:* Francis the First-Time Home Buyer

Preconditions:

- Francis arrives at home page or House Search landing page.

Main Success Scenario:

1. Francis enters city and state or zip code.
2. System uses auto-completion to show options below search field as Francis types. System shows up to 10 matching city names in order of number of homes for sale in each city. Francis can click a city name to select that city.
3. Francis selects minimum and maximum price values from drop-down menus.
4. System validates selected values.
5. Frances selects number of bedrooms and bathrooms from drop-down menus.
6. Francis submits search.
7. System validates required fields before submitting query.

In this use case, because you know Francis can use all the help you can give her, step 2 is particularly useful. The system is proactive in helping Francis select a city quickly.

A typical use case would continue with alternative flows (other actions Francis could take within the same process, along with any system responses, including error conditions and resolutions), postconditions (what happens when the task is completed successfully or failure occurs), assumptions, and open issues about this particular use case. A use case is a very detailed type of documentation that isn't always relevant to projects, but when your system is very complex and you want to document every potential flow, it can be extremely helpful. Make sure to cover all the goals of all of your personas.

Creating Site Structure and Page Structure

Task analyses and use cases provide an ingredients list for the structure of your Web site or Web application. You know all the components and can now assemble them into an overall structure. One technique I use is to begin with my primary persona and create a site structure just for him or her. After I've created the optimal experience for my primary persona, I move on to the next most important persona, adding to the existing site map or flow diagram to satisfy this persona—as long as what I add doesn't interfere with the needs of the primary persona. I continue in this manner with the third persona, the fourth, and so on. The site structure gradually comes together as I layer on each persona's needs.

One side note here: Your primary persona might vary depending on what area of the site you're working on. For example, Francis might not be the primary persona for the entire real estate site, but for the section containing how-to content, she would be. That means you need to start with Francis for this particular section and prioritize her needs above the other personas.

No matter how you arrive at a high-level structure for your content-based Web site or interactive Web application, remember that personas are useful not only for creating the structure but also for presenting and explaining it to others.

Let's face it: Site maps and flow diagrams are pretty boring. You might love the complexity and thought behind your giant map of boxes and arrows accounting for every page, but the people you're presenting to probably won't. To them, a site map is a complicated abstraction, not something that describes what the site will actually be like.

Personas bring storytelling to these diagrams and create interest and clearer understanding among your audience members. When you present your site map or flow diagrams to others, do so in the context of the personas. Rather than overwhelm your audience with everything at once, start with your primary persona's goals and describe how he or she would achieve them. Show how Francis begins on the home page, moves to the results page, clicks to a map view of the results, narrows the results by neighborhood, and then moves to another page of results. Then, show how she achieves another goal. These stories bring an otherwise dry site map to life.

I often show the entire site map, but with the primary persona's core goals highlighted, so that people can see exactly what paths through the site the primary persona takes. You can show the paths of other personas as well, but this can get overwhelming quickly, so be careful.

After talking through the primary persona's experience on the new site, you can move on to the other personas. Gradually, the people you're presenting to come to understand the overall structure. It builds up in their minds slowly as they hear the stories of personas traveling through it. This method is often much more effective than overwhelming people with the entire structure all at once.

A similar approach is to label each section of the site with the personas who are its primary users. Refer to personas by number for this technique, because otherwise the site map rapidly becomes overwhelming. You can also label every page with every persona who uses it. The goal is to identify who uses what content or feature so that you can make better decisions when you're creating that content or feature.

You can also use personas to create and present wireframes or other documentation about specific pages. Task analyses and use cases help you map out what should be on each page and how it should work based on how you've prioritized your personas.

For example, when my colleagues were creating wireframes to define the structure and content on each page for BrownCo, the discount brokerage, they based many small decisions on the primary persona, Frank the Frequent Trader. They knew, for instance, that margin was critical for Frank, so when they created the wireframe for the trade ticket, they placed margin balances directly on this page so that Frank would have the information he needed at the point of transaction. In addition, my colleagues knew that Frank doesn't like losing control

This site map highlights a couple of paths one persona takes.

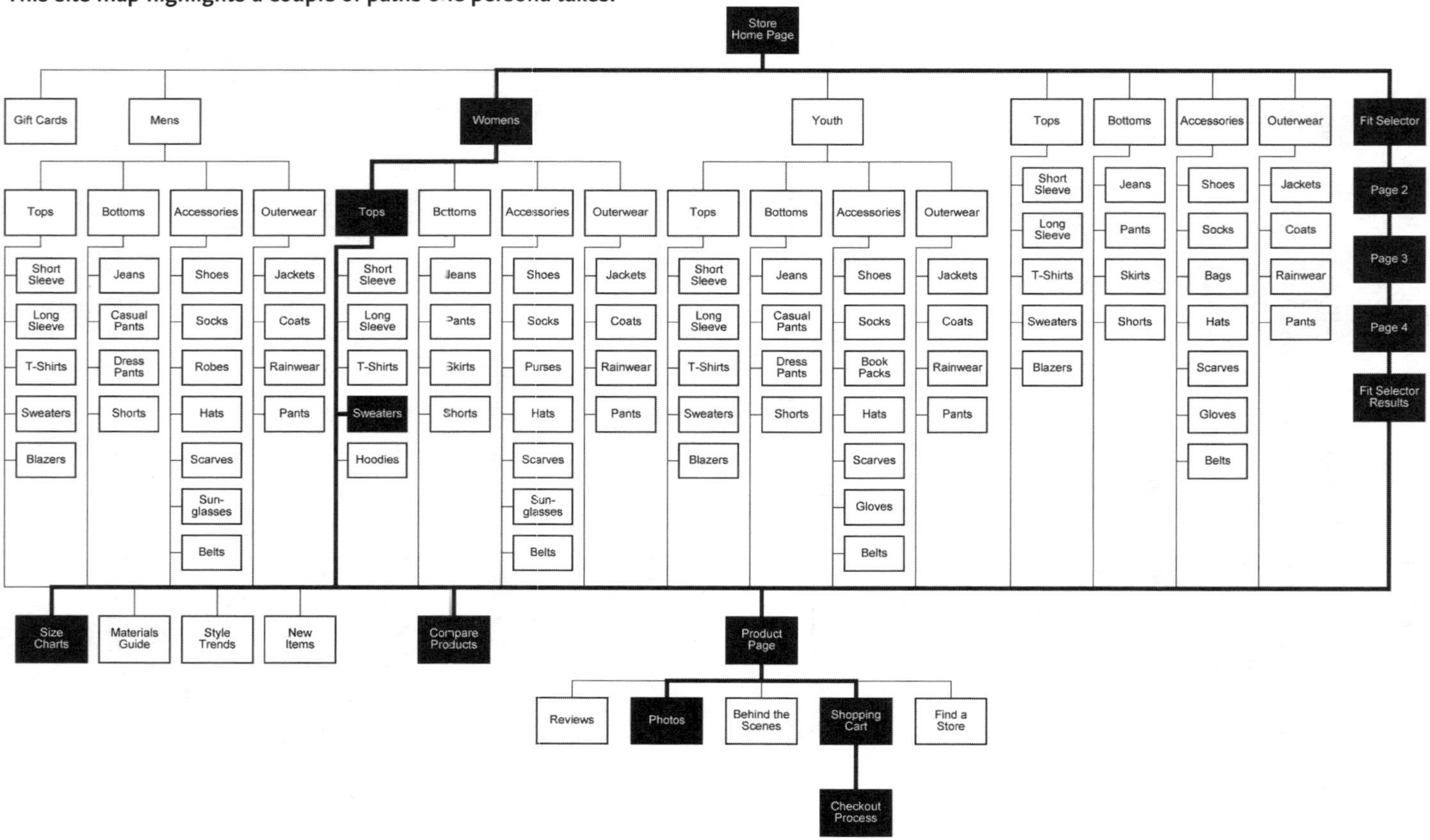

Store Home Page

Gift Cards
Mens
Womens
Youth
Tops
Bottoms
Accessories
Outerwear
Fit Selector

Tops
Bottoms
Accessories
Outerwear
Tops
Bottoms
Accessories
Outerwear
Tops
Bottoms
Accessories
Outerwear

Short Sleeve
Long Sleeve
T-Shirts
Sweaters
Blazers

Jeans
Casual Pants
Dress Pants
Shorts

Shoes
Socks
Robes
Hats
Scarves
Sun-glasses
Belts

Jackets
Coats
Rainwear
Pants

Short Sleeve
Long Sleeve
T-Shirts
Sweaters
Hoodies

Jeans
Pants
Skirts
Shorts

Shoes
Socks
Purses
Hats
Scarves
Sun-glasses
Belts

Jackets
Coats
Rainwear
Pants

Short Sleeve
Long Sleeve
T-Shirts
Sweaters
Blazers

Jeans
Casual Pants
Dress Pants
Shorts

Shoes
Socks
Book Packs
Hats
Scarves
Gloves
Belts

Jackets
Coats
Rainwear
Pants

Short Sleeve
Long Sleeve
T-Shirts
Sweaters
Blazers

Jeans
Pants
Skirts
Shorts

Shoes
Socks
Bags
Hats
Scarves
Gloves
Belts

Jackets
Coats
Rainwear
Pants

Page 2
Page 3
Page 4
Fit Selector Results

Size Charts
Materials Guide
Style Trends
New Items
Compare Products
Product Page

Reviews
Photos
Behind the Scenes
Shopping Cart
Find a Store

Checkout Process

This wireframe includes a persona's comments about her needs from the page.

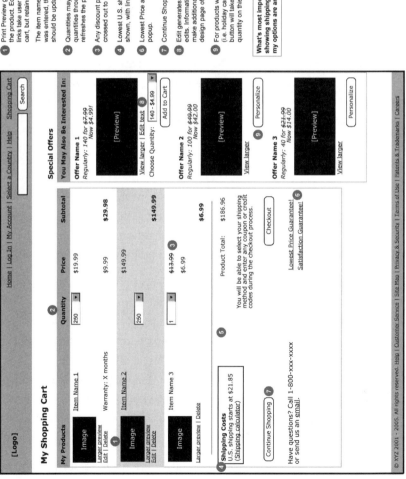

[Logo]
Home | Log In | My Account | Select a Country | Help Shopping Cart
Search

My Shopping Cart

My Products		Quantity (2)	Price	Subtotal
Image Larger preview Edit | Delete (1)	Item Name 1	250	$19.99	
	Warranty: X months		$9.99	**$29.98**
Image Larger preview Edit | Delete	Item Name 2	250	$149.99	**$149.99**
Image Larger preview | Delete	Item Name 3	1	~~$13.99~~ (3) $6.99	**$6.99**

(4) **Shipping Costs**
U.S. shipping starts at $21.85
(Shipping calculator)

(5) Product Total: $186.96

You will be able to select your shipping method and enter any coupon or credit codes during the checkout process.

Continue Shopping (7)

Checkout

Have questions? Call 1-800-xxx-xxxx or send us an email.

Lowest Price Guarantee!
Satisfaction Guarantee! (6)

Special Offers

You May Also Be Interested In:

Offer Name 1
Regularly: 140 for ~~$7.99~~
Now $4.99!
[Preview]
View larger | Edit text (8)
Choose Quantity: 140 - $4.99
Add to Cart

Offer Name 2
Regularly: 100 for ~~$49.99~~
Now $42.00
[Preview]
View larger
(9) Personalize

Offer Name 3
Regularly: 40 for ~~$21.99~~
Now $14.00
[Preview]
View larger
Personalize

 Help | Customer Service | Site Map | Privacy & Security | Terms of Use | Patents & Trademarks | Careers

1. Print Preview generates popup displaying larger image of the product. Edit, or clicking on the product image or name links take user to the design page. Delete removes item from cart, but retains the item as an In Progress item.

   The item name should be the saved item name, or if none was entered, the first entry field in the template. Name should be updated if that entry field is updated.

2. Quantities may be changed from this page. Changing the quantities through the drop-down menu immediately refreshes the page with updated quantities and pricing.

3. Any discount prices is first displayed with the original price, crossed out to display the new price.

4. Lowest U.S. shipping cost for items currently in cart is shown, with link to pop-up shipping calculator.

6. Lowest Price and Satisfaction Guarantee links generate popup.

7. Continue Shopping takes user back to homepage.

8. Edit generates popup that allows user to make any textual edits. Information is pre-populated. User may also choose to make additional changes. Personalize will take user to design page of product.

9. For products where information can not be pre-populated (i.e. holiday cards), user can Personalize product. This button will take user to the design page. User may not select quantity on this page.

What's most important to me in the Shopping Cart is showing shipping information. If I can't quickly get to what my options are and what they cost, I won't start checkout!

Carol the Controlling

when margin calls come in and his account is locked, so they added prominent messaging that explains what's happening, and they designed it in such a way that he has to see the message before he continues. Having a deep knowledge of Frank made it easier for my colleagues to decide on the page-by-page details of the experience.

When presenting wireframes, show how personas justify the structure you're proposing. As with the site map, start with your primary persona and walk through the pages he or she visits to complete each goal. Tell a story—don't overwhelm your audience with scores of wireframes all at once.

To make the personas come to life in the wireframes themselves, try exposing the personas in the document. Include the persona's name and/or photo, along with the persona's comments about this particular page. I often annotate page wireframes anyway, and adding the voice of the key persona into the annotations makes the pages feel more real.

Defining Navigation

As you know, any Web structure needs a navigation system to help users move through it. Personas come to the rescue here as well. Where you might otherwise create a navigation system based on one generic user, now you have personas to guide your decisions.

First, ask yourself what the core paths through the site are for each persona. You're already familiar with these because you know the personas' goals and you've thought through task analyses and/or use cases. Design the navigation from page to page for these flows, making them clear and prominent. This is what the personas are here to do, so don't assume that small text links across the top of the page will suffice. Make core tasks easy by using the main part of the page, big text, buttons, and the like. As always, give the primary persona the most attention.

The next critical step is to figure out where each persona needs to go from each page. After you've done this, create the system of rules that defines which navigation links are available from each type of page on the site. Are your personas likely to travel from one section to an entirely different section at any point? If so, make sure links to top-level sections are always present. Even if the personas aren't likely to do this, one of your business objectives for them might be to understand the breadth of features and content within the site—sitewide navigation can help accomplish this.

Working with one retailer in particular, my team uncovered a persona who used the site largely for gift giving. On other Web sites, she browsed the product categories looking for gift ideas, which took a lot of time. What she really wanted was an area with gift recommendations, so my team created a new Gifts link in the site navigation just for her. This didn't require significant new products; it was simply another path for accessing existing products. We knew the word she was looking for (Gifts), and she was important enough, as a persona, to warrant a new navigation item.

Figure out where each persona needs to go from each page, and create the system of rules that defines the site's navigation, based on that persona.

Personas are particularly useful when you're deciding what local navigation should appear within the current section. If your primary persona is an explorer who deeply understands the domain and is eager to try a variety of features or content to accomplish his or her goals, then exposing more navigation links is appropriate. But if you're designing for Francis, it's more important to guide her through key paths on the site rather than risk overwhelming her with each and every feature. In Francis's case, you're better off reducing the number of navigation links.

The question of consistency often comes up for Web site navigation. In one camp are those who argue for complete consistency across the site, so navigation always behaves the same way and contains the same links. I used to be in that camp, and when it's appropriate, I still visit quite often. But I no longer live there. Personas' needs can be different enough that you need to bend the rules, depending on where you are in the site and who the primary persona is at that time.

I'd rather sacrifice some consistency in site navigation (which few users ever notice anyway) than risk losing a particular user because the navigation links aren't suited to what he or she is doing.

Finally, use personas to establish the labeling of your navigation links. I'll cover content creation in more detail later in this chapter, but since content is an essential aspect of an effective navigation system, I'll touch on it here as well. If you were creating a section of how-to tutorials for Francis, would you call it "Tips for First-Time Home Buyers" or "FAQs for Real Estate Sharks"? Tailor navigation labels to the personas who will use them.

When working on a cosmetics site a few years ago, I learned all I ever needed to know about applying foundation. I also became fluent in the lexicon of cosmetics. For the site navigation, we had no choice but to use this standard terminology, since all of our personas already understood and expected it. But I remember wondering what would happen if I were to design a cosmetics site for a very different persona: men buying gifts for women. What might the navigation labels look like on this imagined site?

NAVIGATION OPTIONS FOR COSMETICS SITE

Actual site navigation	**Imaginary site navigation**
Foundations	Spackles
Powders	Dusts
Blush	Fake Color
Concealers	Paint
Lipsticks	Lip Paint
Gloss	Sparkly Slime
Eye Shadows	Black Eyes
Mascara	Scary Lashes
Nails	Varnish

It's probably better that I never had the opportunity to try this navigation system. I can't imagine that my client would have embraced this clearly brilliant solution.

By the way, navigation labeling can encourage users to select the correct path through the site. For example, if you're working on the search interface for Francis, you know she wants a few straightforward criteria, such as price range and number of bedrooms and bathrooms. Another persona, Thomas the Tycoon, craves more advanced search functionality, and so you might create a separate search page for him with more robust options. What do you call the navigation link to this page? If you call it "More Search Options," Francis might check it out, but you know she would likely be confused by the jargon there. If you call it "Advanced Search," the label would likely scare her away, but appeal to Thomas. Thus, "Advanced Search" works well for both personas. Words are powerful tools for guiding behavior and for helping personas use the site most effectively.

Related to the idea of self-selection is the idea of exposing the personas on the Web site. Users visit the home page and are greeted by the site's personas, with names, photos, the works. Each user then selects to which persona he or she is most similar; then you can serve him or her the appropriate experience. A real estate site, for example, might show Francis's photo and key differentiators, as well as those of a few other personas.

I'm not a big fan of this approach to site navigation. First of all, when users come to your site, they have a goal in mind. They're looking for trigger words to satisfy that goal: "Search for Homes," "Tips for First-Time Home Buyers," "Refinance Your Mortgage," and so on. Forcing them to change their plan, and instead figure out which persona they resemble, is likely to leave a bad taste in their mouth. Second, users are likely to misunderstand the concept of personas and not identify with the appropriate one. A guy coming to the site is simply less likely to associate with Francis, even if they're both first-time home buyers in need of advice.

Personas are great decision-making tools for you and your team behind the scenes, but it's risky to expose them to your users in the interface. This doesn't mean that all navigation by user type is a bad idea. "Home buyers start here" can be useful, but including full personas probably isn't.

Designing Site Search

Site search is as important to be tailored to your personas as site navigation is. Both are critical to helping users find what they need, and both are too often designed for a generic or ideal user, rather than for real users. When you're designing a search system, the place to start is not with the interface, but rather with how a search works.

Start with relevancy. When your primary persona performs a search, what kind of results does he or she expect to see? People often think of search as a solved problem, with best practices (created by Google) that everyone should follow, yet search interfaces that look the same can't possibly be optimized for personas, which inevitably vary from site to site.

Here's a simple example. Go to Cosmeo.com and search for "Saturn." What do you get for results? Videos, pictures, articles, brain games, and events. The content and the interface are perfect for the personas coming to this site, which I'll let you figure out on your own. Now go to the NASA Astrophysics Data System at adswww.harvard.edu and do the same search (assuming you can figure out the search interface). What do you get? Abstracts of scientific articles with titles such as "Latitudinal variation of Saturn photochemistry deduced from spatially resolved ultraviolet spectra" (which I hear someone is making into a movie starring Emma Thompson). It's the same search, but very different targeted personas translate into very different search results.

Figure out what type of results your primary persona wants to see. Then think about what content should appear for each result. Does he or she want simpler results, with less content for each one and more showing above the fold? Or are the details important? Also, in what order does the persona want the results to be sorted? Does he or she want advanced search filters on the results page for further refinements? Would editorially selected "Best Bets" links at the top of the results help this persona?

Run every decision through the filter of your primary persona. Then add features to satisfy your other personas, as long as they don't hurt the experience for the primary persona.

Creating Content

Writers have known for millennia that you can't create effective content without knowing your readers. It's not enough to create content that is good. It also has to be appropriate for what your readers want and how they want it.

Personas make your readers explicit, so that you know exactly for who you're creating content. When you know your personas' goals, you understand what type of content will help users accomplish their goals. One of the most common mistakes you are apt to make when writing content is that you might create it from the site's perspective rather than the user's perspective. To avoid this, rather than telling users about the product, tell them what they will be able to do with the product. Rather than organizing instructional text based on how features work, write it based on what users want to do. Start with user goals and put yourself in your users' shoes before creating content. That's what personas are good for.

By content, I mean the whole variety of textual content on a site, as well as nontextual content:

- **Articles or product descriptions:** These are the first kinds of content that are apt to come to your mind when you're designing a site. That's why it's a no-brainer to spend time and effort ensuring that this content effectively serves your personas. You know what personas need to learn and what they're interested in when you write an article. And you know what your personas need to know about products and services.

- **Instructional text:** Most of the words that users read on your Web site are not the articles and product descriptions on which you've spent so much time. Most of what they read are small bits of text scattered on every page—content telling them where to go and what to do. It's the teaser for the article that appears on the home page, or the quick sentence that describes how to zoom in on a product image, or the labels next to the form fields on the registration page. It's all the text you write quickly while creating a complicated page wireframe.

  Whenever you're faced with writing a quick sentence, phrase, or label, don't be tempted to dash it off without thinking about your personas. If you don't get these bits of instructional text right, your personas will never reach the content or products that you want them to. Take some time to think about which persona is most important for each bit of content. What does he or she need to know right here, right now? Then consider how the other personas will respond to this text, and optimize that content for all the personas who need it.

- **Documentation and help:** Beyond instructional text on your pages, use personas to plan ahead for where users will need additional help. Will they need quick contextual help, which could consist of short tips on the page? Or will they need appropriately placed links to a more comprehensive help section with full documentation? You know your personas, so you know how much text they need and, more importantly, how much they're likely to actually read.

- **Error messages:** When users encounter errors on your site, the experience is at risk. The site is not responding as they expect, and if you don't supply an error message that tells them what they need to know, you might very well lose some business. Personas tell you exactly what each user wants to hear when something goes wrong. You know what information to share about the current error event, you know what to tell them about what they can do next, and you know what style to use when writing the error message.

- **Imagery:** Content isn't just about text. When you select an image to accompany an article, or when you decide between product shots, you make a critical communication decision that should be based on your personas. The content of the image is important, as is its visual style and the way it is used. If Francis the First-Time Home Buyer is reading an introductory article on mortgage options, which image will she respond better to: a complex and artistic collage of numbers, or a friendly and colorful picture of a lender in front of a house?
- **Sound:** If you decide to use sound on your site—whether interface sounds or music—base your selection on your personas. What sounds will reinforce the experience your primary persona wants to have, and you as well want him or her to have?
- **Video and more:** By now it's obvious that personas are useful for creating all types of content, including video, animation, or other multimedia. As with other types of communication, consider the substance as well as its style.

Style is critical to creating content that works for your personas. How you say things is just as important as what you say. First, consider the vocabulary you use. Given the persona with whom you're communicating, should you elevate your language or stick to common words? Should you use jargon or keep it simple? In an introductory article for Francis, it would be unforgivable to use the term ARM without explaining it as Adjustable Rate Mortgage. On the other hand, if your persona expects complex vocabulary and appreciates the communication shortcuts that jargon provides, go for it.

In addition to vocabulary, consider the tone of your content. Will your persona respond better to a formal, or an informal tone? Will he or she want you to be authoritative and objective, or approachable and friendly? Keep in mind that personas' expectations could vary depending on where they are in the site. An informal, approachable tone that works well on the home page might seem disconcerting when the user reads your privacy policy.

Not long ago, I conducted a usability test on a prototype of a financial services site. My client wanted approachable content that would help users plan for retirement. The site was filled with casual language to put users at ease with this complex and somewhat scary topic. On one page that addressed worst-case options of borrowing against a retirement plan, the site included the following sentence: "Our Loan Ranger has lassoed options for your perusal." Participants in the usability test rolled their eyes at this language, commenting that it was inappropriately goofy for such serious content. The personas wanted something approachable, but this site took the tone too far.

Here's another example: VistaPrint enables users to design their own marketing materials for printing. When working on the design page, I knew that the content had to explain the various printing options. One of the personas, Nancy the Nervous, was likely to be intimidated by too many options for customizing her design. Meanwhile, Patricia the Perfectionist, whom you met earlier, wanted as many options as possible. My goal was to serve both personas with content appropriate for each.

For Nancy, I created a prominent link to VistaPrint's free phone-based help. I used text that I knew would appeal to Nancy in content and tone:

> **Free Design Help**
>
> 1-800-555-1212
>
> We'll help you design the perfect brochure. It's free and easy. Learn more.

For do-it-all-myself Patricia, I added a button to help her fully customize her design. If she clicked the button, all the advanced options would be revealed, including font control, drag-and-drop layout control, more colors, and so on. I wanted text that would appeal to Patricia's goals but also scare Nancy away, since Nancy was overwhelmed enough already:

> **Customize** [button text]
>
> Change fonts or colors, move things around, and use more advanced options. Only $9.99!

Creating effective content is about providing the right content to the right persona at the right time. Know what each persona needs and when they need it.

How do you ensure that your content is appropriate for your personas? As you conduct your task analyses or create use cases, note where each persona needs content to help achieve his or her goal. Based on where personas are in the task and what they're trying to do, you know what content they need and how they need it for any particular moment. You can integrate these content needs into your task analyses or use cases, or you can create a separate content audit document to identify all the content needs for each persona.

Another strategy is to create a communication plan or style guide for each persona that includes more general guidelines about how to write for each one. You can list the vocabulary that each persona is familiar with or is expecting to see, perhaps as a guiding "word cloud" (see figure on next page) for anyone who creates content for this persona. You can also specify tone and style guidelines to use for each persona.

However you involve your personas in creating content, make them as explicit as possible in your normal writing process, as I've discussed before. There's nothing better than having your personas visible to remind you of exactly who you're trying to satisfy.

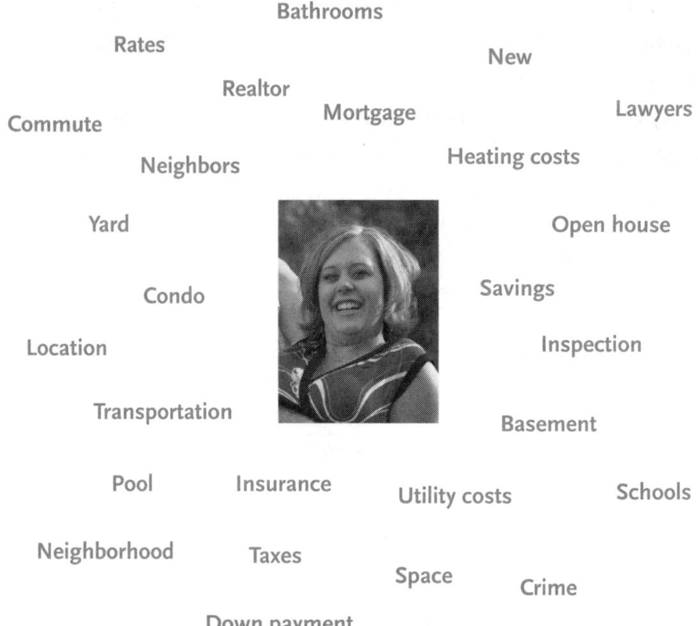

This word cloud includes vocabulary that appeals to Francis the First-Time Home Buyer.

Shaping Visual Design

I know I'm preaching to the choir when I say that how you communicate visually to your users can be just as important as what content you use. People respond to visual stimuli instinctively; it either works or it doesn't. For better or worse, if a user is turned off by your visual design, you often don't get a second chance.

The flipside is also important: You have a brand to communicate visually and you need to be as certain as possible that your users experience your brand as you intend them to. It's impossible to guarantee this, of course, since you can't really control user behavior. But anything that helps you know what design elements more successfully communicate your brand is a good thing.

I doubt you are shocked to hear me saying that personas are useful for decisions about visual design. As I've said before, personas bring the abstraction of "user" to life in very specific ways that help you make better design decisions. Your knowledge about Francis puts you on solid footing, as far as understanding to what she may respond to visually, and what best communicates the brand to her.

Earlier, I suggested that you create a style guide for each persona. This technique is helpful for visual design as well. Typically, a style guide or creative brief summarizes the brand attributes that any site design must communicate. For the imaginary RealEstateCentral.com, you might settle on brand attributes such as "expert," "comprehensive," "friendly," and "current." You want all users visiting the site to come away with these perceptions.

When you add personas into a style guide or creative brief, it becomes even more useful. Illustrate what the brand attributes mean to each persona. How does Francis interpret "expert"? What design elements make her perceive the site as "expert"? For Francis, clean page layout and sturdy, reliable colors (e.g., no hot pink) help. So do more traditional fonts and straightforward imagery. Obviously, the content communicates expertise, but the visual design needs to reinforce that message. Another persona might interpret "expert" in very different ways, so it's important to think through the brand attributes from the perspective of each persona.

Personas bring the abstraction of "user" to life in very specific ways that help you make better design decisions.

You can also use the style guide or creative brief to document what each persona tends to like and notice on other sites; this provides you with a way to explore which visual design elements are more effective with him or her. Frank the Frequent Trader, primary persona for BrownCo, loves Yahoo!'s Web site for many reasons, including the simplicity of its design. Knowing this helped the BrownCo team model its page layout on Yahoo!'s straightforward, clean approach. Find what works for each persona, and use it to your advantage.

A mood board explores visual elements that a particular persona would respond to. (Courtesy of Andy Clarke.)

Another technique for using personas to shape visual design is to create a mood board for each persona. A mood board is an exploration of which visual elements or visual tone users are likely to respond to. In this case, you create a mood board for each persona, since each one may be attracted to a different style. Think of a mood board as a collage of design elements, not as a completed design system that you use for your site. It consists of imagery, shape, color, typography, composition, and even, potentially, multimedia and interactivity. A mood board reveals a variety of design options from which you can choose in order to appeal to each persona.

Here's a challenge: How do you take four mood boards for four different personas and create one visual design that works for all of them? As I discussed earlier with structure and content, the key is to begin with your primary persona. Optimize the entire experience, including the visual communication, for him or her. This persona's creative brief and mood board should take precedence, because he or she is most critical to the business. Then look for ways to appeal to your other personas without negatively impacting the primary persona. What you don't want to do is create a lowest common denominator design that no persona likes, so keep the focus on the primary persona.

This is clearly an art, which is why I enjoy working with talented visual designers so much. The ability to take potentially competing

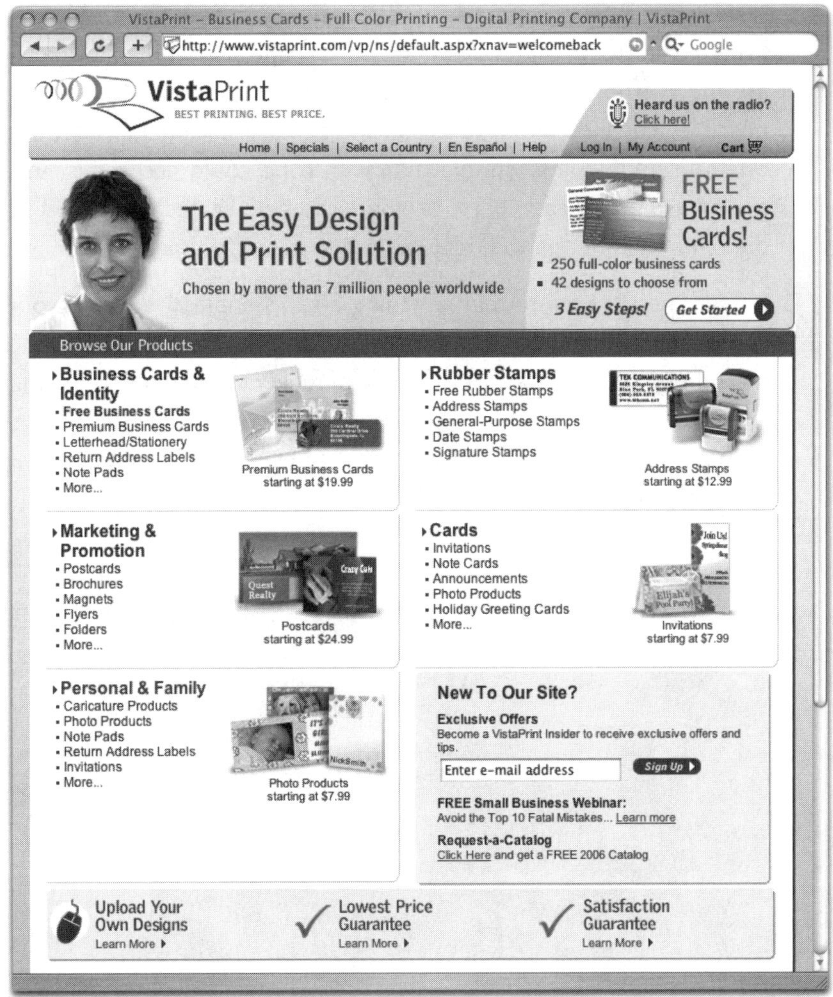

The VistaPrint home page meets the needs of all of VistaPrint's personas.

requirements and create a unified visual system that works within all of them is inspiring.

For VistaPrint, the final design my team and I created appealed to all the VistaPrint personas. For example, we knew that Nancy the Nervous wanted a site she could trust, a site that would make it easy for her to create marketing materials for her business. Her first impression of the home page was critical. Through color, shape, typography, and the straight-on photo of a person, we drew attention to VistaPrint's differentiators so that Nancy would feel reassured right from the start. Simultaneously, the home page also worked for Howard the Hurried, who wanted to create his materials as quickly as possible. For him, we exposed all the types of products VistaPrint offers in a clean and simple manner, so he could accomplish his goals quickly. For each persona, there is a path that is supported by the right content and the right design, at the right time.

Design, perhaps more than anything else, is subjective. All of your colleagues probably have an opinion, and all have reasons for liking what they like. Personas bring a dose of reality to the table by forcing everyone to think outside of personal opinion. The more you focus on personas for design decisions, the more likely it is that the final result will actually work.

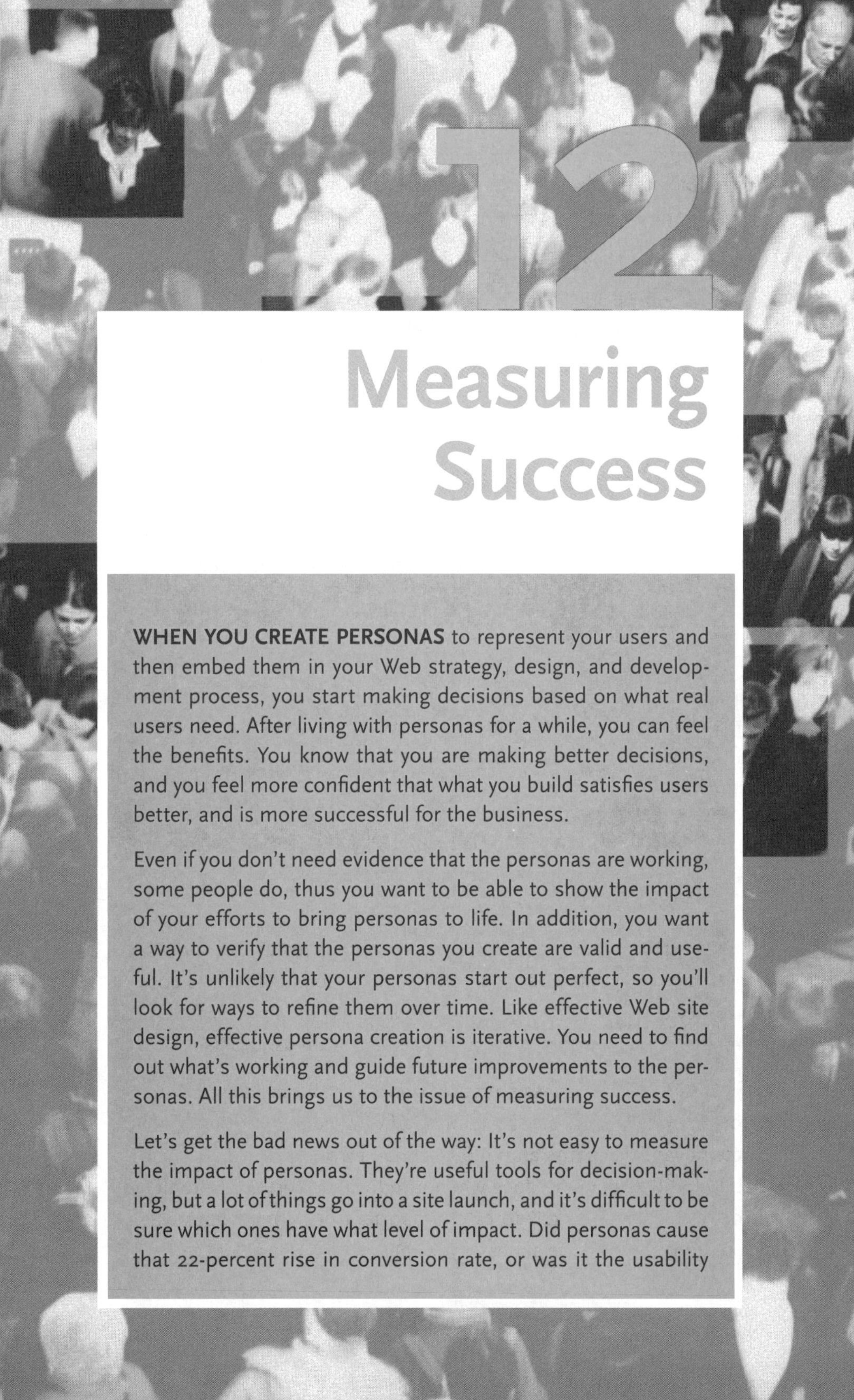

12 Measuring Success

WHEN YOU CREATE PERSONAS to represent your users and then embed them in your Web strategy, design, and development process, you start making decisions based on what real users need. After living with personas for a while, you can feel the benefits. You know that you are making better decisions, and you feel more confident that what you build satisfies users better, and is more successful for the business.

Even if you don't need evidence that the personas are working, some people do, thus you want to be able to show the impact of your efforts to bring personas to life. In addition, you want a way to verify that the personas you create are valid and useful. It's unlikely that your personas start out perfect, so you'll look for ways to refine them over time. Like effective Web site design, effective persona creation is iterative. You need to find out what's working and guide future improvements to the personas. All this brings us to the issue of measuring success.

Let's get the bad news out of the way: It's not easy to measure the impact of personas. They're useful tools for decision-making, but a lot of things go into a site launch, and it's difficult to be sure which ones have what level of impact. Did personas cause that 22-percent rise in conversion rate, or was it the usability test you ran, or the senior designer you hired? It is more likely it was a combination of factors. So how much can you ascribe to using personas? There's no easy answer to this question.

What the industry needs is a controlled experiment. By this, I mean assigning the same project to two teams within the same company, one that uses personas, and one that doesn't. Make sure they have the same access to resources, the same timeline, and so on. Then measure the results of this A/B testing and see what happens.

Anyone want to volunteer?

Fortunately, you can measure success in other ways, and they come in the two flavors represented by these questions:

- Is the site more successful overall because you used personas?
- Are you serving each persona more successfully because of decisions you've made?

This chapter covers both forms of success, and includes a variety of testing methods that you can perform both before and after you launch the site.

Testing Before Launch

Let's start with your normal process. What happens as you approach the end of a Web site's development? You probably have some steps in place for assuring that site's quality. Your quality assurance, or the **QA process**, whether formal or informal, benefits from using personas.

If your QA process is less structured, approach it from the personas' point of view. While playing the role of one of your personas, navigate down likely paths and into common error scenarios. Ask yourself what that persona does when faced with a particular problem. You're much more likely to catch important bugs and issues when you put yourself in the shoes of your personas—one at a time.

If your QA process is more structured, and you create and follow more formalized test scripts, this is another great place to embed personas. Create separate test scripts for each persona, and document all the potential paths each persona might take. Test scripts are valuable for documenting every path that Francis might take on the Web site and how the Web site is supposed to respond to her actions, so that testers can follow these instructions and document any bugs or oddities. A more structured process enables you to take more time to be thorough, covering every aspect of the site that each persona might touch.

Personas help a QA process become more efficient by focusing the testing on what real users do. Even better, personas enable you to prioritize the bugs you uncover during QA. When you find a problem, you can immediately put the problem in the context of which personas might experience it and how critical the problem is to them. My colleagues and I use a Web-based, custom-built bug tracking system that lets us prioritize bugs, based on how much they impact each persona. Personas help us make key site decisions, sometimes last minute, about what issues to fix, based on the needs of real users, not on our own (sometimes biased) opinions.

Personas help us make key site decisions, sometimes last minute, about what issues to fix, based on the needs of real users.

Another way to test your site before launch is with usability testing; here too, personas can help. (You do conduct at least *some* quick usability testing, right?) Whether you're testing early wireframes, page designs, a prototype, or the fully functioning site, personas guide what you test and how you test it. You can plan your test based on what each of your personas wants from the site. There's no need to guess which areas are the most important to test, since the prioritized personas are there to tell you.

In addition, personas make it easier to recruit people for usability tests. Your goal is to find a sampling of users that represent each of your personas. Don't forget that your primary persona deserves special attention, and probably more users for the test.

Do you remember the specialty retailer I've referred to now and then? My team segmented personas for that site based on channel usage, and when the time came to conduct usability testing on a prototype of a new feature, we recruited a cross-section of our personas: Web-only customers, store-only customers, Web and store customers, and so on. We even customized our test sessions based on which persona we were talking to, and, of course, we presented our test findings broken down by persona.

Depending on how you define your personas, recruiting users to match these profiles can be tricky, especially if your key differentiators are amorphous attitudes such as their perception of your company. The solution is to use a quick screener to make sure users match your criteria. It's fast and easy to screen users, whether you do it over the phone or via email.

As with QA, you can prioritize any issues that you discover through usability testing using the personas as your measuring sticks. The issues that are the most problematic for the most important personas are the first to be addressed. Sometimes it's impossible to fix all the usability issues in time for launch; personas help everyone focus on the most important issues to resolve, in the available time.

Beyond usability testing, you can conduct other types of prelaunch qualitative research as well, such as one-on-one **interviews**, or **focus groups** for reactions to new concepts. Here, too, personas help define exactly who you should recruit for this type of research, what types of questions to ask, and which issues to explore.

Testing After Launch

Once your project is live, how do you measure success? Well, for starters, the same way you always did. Think about the metrics your organization cares about. Most likely, you have a variety of them, such as conversion rate, average order size, leads generated, unique visitors, traffic to certain pages or features, and so on. If you see improvements to any and all of the metrics you track, you are free to ascribe as much of them as you wish to personas. (If you don't see improvements, you are equally free to assign blame elsewhere.)

As the person behind the (of course!) successful project, you have people's attention, which means it's a great time to tell more colleagues about personas—what they are, how you create them, how you use them, and how your colleagues should use them. Spread the gospel!

Your quest for metrics can include digging into your **log files** for data specific to the personas. For example, if a specific area of your site is devoted to the needs of a particular persona (for example, an introductory learning center for Francis the First-Time Home Buyer), take a look at metrics within that area. You know that most users visiting that section are Francis personas, so you can feel confident that this section's metrics tell you how well you're satisfying Francis. Are more people viewing more of the content? Francis is probably happier. Better yet, are more people becoming loyal customers after viewing this introductory content? Then you know more Francises are converting.

Of course, you can also ask users directly. A **survey** is a useful way to measure the success of a live site. The beauty of a survey is that the right questions reveal into which persona segment each survey respondent falls. With that information, you can use pivot tables (described in Chapter 6) to slice the survey findings by persona segment. The result is solid data on how well you're satisfying each persona—their satisfaction with the new site, content, and/or features, their prioritization of future improvements, and so on.

A survey is useful for gathering data on what users say, but as you have seen, data on what users actually *do* can be even more powerful and important. Log file analysis might suggest that more Francises are converting (e.g., making a purchase), and a survey tells you what Francises say they are doing, but how can you be sure? How do you know that it is Francis who is really converting? How do you know that Francis is who she says she is in the first place? How do you know that you properly understand her needs and goals?

It would be great if you could look at the actual behavior of all users visiting the Web site in terms of the personas that they most closely resemble. That way, for every clickstream in your log files, you would know which persona was behind the mouse. You would then have a good idea of which ideas and solutions worked and which didn't, and how you could improve or refine your understanding of personas. Taken to the logical extreme, you could then put in place a process where you constantly tested new ideas with personas on your Web site, measured the results, and iterated on both the solutions and your understanding of the personas themselves.

The more you listen to your users, the better you are able to serve them. This is one of the greatest challenges of applying user information. No one gets it 100-percent right the first time, and that's okay. Your goal is to have a process where you are continuously listening, learning, and refining.

One of the most exciting new developments in quantitative personas is a system that does exactly what I've described. This new trend of **categorizing real users into persona segments** revolutionizes the way you work with personas. In order to make this system work, you need to have some version of quantitative personas (either quantitative validation of qualitative segmentation, or quantitative segmentation; see Chapter 6 for more information). You also need some sort of log file analysis system to track user clickstreams on your Web site, and a reasonably good customer database (or a registration database for your Web site) with a lot of information about your existing users. You need to be able to track individual accounts back to their Web site behavior and survey responses (often using cookies or email addresses).

Finally, the user behavior patterns of the personas involve more than just the Web channel (for example, users may browse online and then purchase in the local store), so any downstream purchase or behavior information needs to be available in a manner that you can link back to the online behavior (again using a cookie, customer ID, or email address). In short, to get started, you need to be able to tie your user database to individual visits in your log files.

You can use one of many different measurement systems, but any strong one enables you to do the following:

1. Develop a mechanism to score all your existing users in terms of which persona they most likely belong to.

2. If necessary, develop a mechanism to score new users according to which persona they are most likely to belong to.

3. When developing new features and functions for specific personas, define key metrics that you would want to see improved for each persona.

4. Make sure that, when building those features, these key metrics are stored along with the other user information in the user database.

5. Periodically, run reports against the user database broken out by persona type to see if improvements in those key metrics are apparent for the specific personas you are targeting. If you miss your targets, you might do some further digging into the log file behavior of only those users who fit the targeted personas, or you could follow up with a survey (again targeted at only those users who fit the personas) in order to get a better idea from the personas about how to improve.

6. Periodically rescore your user database to make sure that users haven't changed their persona affinities.

Steps 1 and 2 are perhaps the hardest part of the whole process and typically require a friendly statistical analyst. Developing a mechanism for scoring your existing and new users can sometimes be difficult. If you performed qualitative segmentation of your users, such as by goal of visiting the Web site, you may choose to score everyone by the goal they have for visiting the Web site. One user might identify himself as a new home seeker, and if so, he or she falls into the Francis persona. In this situation, measurement is fairly easy.

If you used quantitative segmentation with multiple variables and statistical segmentation, you have a harder challenge. In this situation, you need to use an analytical tool called predictive modeling. Predictive modeling algorithms (such as CHAID trees) basically work like segmentation algorithms (such as K-means clustering, see Chapter 6), only backwards. Instead of taking all the variables and providing segments for you to turn into personas, predictive modeling takes some or all of the variables you track about your users and tries to find rules that let you predict which persona they will fall into. You then take these rules and apply them to your entire user database. If, however, you find that the information you have in your user database is not enough to score your users, you might need to develop an information acquisition plan, where you decide what information you need from your users to be able to score them, and then you create a plan to collect this information using a variety of means (surveys, user behavior on the Web site, and so on).

Predictive modeling takes some or all of the variables you track about your users and tries to find rules that let you predict which persona they will fall into.

For example, let's return to Patricia the Perfectionist, a persona my team created for VistaPrint. She is a SOHO business owner who uses VistaPrint to create marketing materials for her business. From a financial standpoint, Patricia has an annual two-year spend of $200 on a wide variety of print products—business cards, price tags, invitations, and holiday cards—which places her on the upper end of the types of customers VistaPrint is targeting. Furthermore, just 10 percent of her spending on printing goes to VistaPrint today, and her persona constitutes 20 percent of the VistaPrint customer base, making her an extremely attractive target on which VistaPrint should focus its efforts, because there is a great deal more of her spending that VistaPrint could get. Thus, Patricia became a primary persona, and my team wanted to be sure that we could measure how site improvements impacted Patricia.

First, we built a predictive model against all the data that VistaPrint was currently tracking about its customers to see if we could find some rules that would help us identify the Patricias. Of course, VistaPrint didn't track the same type of information that we asked in the survey, and in this case, it wasn't feasible to ask the entire customer base the same questions that defined the Patricia persona. But a few things that VistaPrint did track, such as the lifetime value of the customer and their most recent purchase, turned out to be highly accurate in predicting if that customer was a Patricia. The statistical analysis leading to the predictive model showed that our final model was 70 percent accurate using this information and a few other tidbits from VistaPrint's customer database.

To adequately test the page designs for the Web site, we used the predictive model to give VistaPrint a way to score its entire customer database. Then VistaPrint could pick out those customers who most closely matched Patricia and recruit them to test the page designs. From this, they could find out whether they would get the desired positive bump in business results. This also became crucial for later phases, when VistaPrint wanted to test changes to the site, products, and channels, as well as to measure improvement across personas.

Through predictive modeling, you can answer the fundamental question: How do you know you're effectively serving the personas, and that the personas are giving you business results? Without this method of measuring success, all users who come to your Web site are lumped together. You have overall metrics such as the conversion rate, but you don't know which users are happy or where the lost opportunities are. With predictive modeling, you can zoom in on Francis and measure the conversion rate for people like her. More specific information about the real behavior of each persona segment translates into better opportunities to test improvements for each persona and measure the results.

There's one final measure of success to discuss: the success of this book. If these chapters have helped you expand the ways you can put users at the center of your decision-making, I'm delighted, and I hope you are too. If you find the practical tips in earlier chapters useful as you conduct user research and segmentation, all the better. And if these ideas and examples help you launch personas within your company and, as a result, you see that they have a real impact on your site and on your business, then kudos for making it happen.

Don't stop here. Personas are an evolving tool. New ideas are percolating everywhere, every day. Join me at www.PracticalPersonas.com as I track new ideas, tell new stories, and rant and rave about the latest happenings revolving around creating and using personas. Join the discussion!

Remember, the user is always watching. The user is ready to have a conversation with you, provided you know what to say and how to say it. The user wants your site to be the one he or she can trust. The user will reward your brilliance and punish your ignorance. The user knows that your business depends on making him or her happy. And the user is always right.

Index

C

D

G

H

I

J

K

L

M

N

O

P

Q

T

U